Oldsmobile V-8 Engines

HOW TO REBUILD 1964–1990

Mike Forsythe

CarTech®

CarTech®

CarTech®, Inc.
838 Lake Street South
Forest Lake, MN 55025
Phone: 651-277-1200 or 800-551-4754
Fax: 651-277-1203
www.cartechbooks.com

Edit by Bob Wilson
Layout by Monica Seiberlich

ISBN 978-1-61325-592-6
Item No. SA502

Library of Congress Cataloging-in-Publication Data

Names: Forsythe, Mike, author.
Title: Oldsmobile V-8 engines 1964-1990 : how to rebuild / Mike Forsythe.
Description: Forest Lake : CarTech Books, 2021. | "Item no. SA502."
Identifiers: LCCN 2021003180 | ISBN 9781613255926 (paperback)
Subjects: LCSH: Oldsmobile automobile–Motors–Maintenance and repair.
Classification: LCC TL215.O4 F67 2021 | DDC 629.25/040288–dc23
LC record available at https://lccn.loc.gov/2021003180

Written, edited, and designed in the U.S.A.
Printed in China
10 9 8 7 6 5 4 3 2 1

Title Page: Photo Courtesy David Newhardt.

DISTRIBUTION BY:

Europe
PGUK
63 Hatton Garden
London EC1N 8LE, England
Phone: 020 7061 1980 • Fax: 020 7242 3725
www.pguk.co.uk

Australia
Renniks Publications Ltd.
3/37-39 Green Street
Banksmeadow, NSW 2109, Australia
Phone: 2 9695 7055 • Fax: 2 9695 7355
www.renniks.com

Canada
Login Canada
300 Saulteaux Crescent
Winnipeg, MB, R3J 3T2 Canada
Phone: 800 665 1148 • Fax: 800 665 0103
www.lb.ca

CONTENTS

Introduction **4**

Chapter 1: Generation II Oldsmobile V-8 Engines **5**
- Engine Identification 5
- GM Corporate Use 6
- VIN Identification 7
- Engine Family Identification 8
- Parts Interchangeability 8
- What Is an Overhaul? 8
- When Is an Overhaul Necessary? 8
- Alternatives to a Full Overhaul 9

Chapter 2: Tools, Equipment, and Supplies **10**
- Work Area 10
- Storage 10
- Workbench 10
- Safety Equipment 10
- Tools 11
- Fastener Sizes 20
- Torque 21
- Cleaning Chemicals 21
- Penetrating Oil 22
- Locking Compound 22
- Lubricants 22
- Sealants 22

Chapter 3: Diagnosis **23**
- Visual Clues 24
- Noise Diagnosis 25
- Spark Plug Condition 26
- Vacuum Gauge Usage 28
- Compression Check 29
- Oil Pressure Check 30
- Camshaft Lobe Lift Check 31
- Timing Chain Slack Check 31
- Power Balance Test 31
- Cylinder Leakdown Test 32
- Cooling System Tests 33

Chapter 4: Engine Removal and Disassembly **34**
- Remove the Hood and Disconnect Components 34
- Drain Coolant and Disconnect Hoses 36
- Remove Radiator and Transmission Lines 38
- Remove Accessories and Distributor 39
- Drain Remaining Fluids 41
- Disconnect the Engine 41
- Remove the Engine 43
- Remove External Components 44
- Remove Intake Manifold and Valve Covers 46
- Disassemble the Valvetrain 48
- Remove the Water Pump, Timing Cover, and Fuel Pump 50
- Strip the Block 52

Chapter 5: Cylinder Head and Valvetrain Overhaul **53**
- Disassembly 53
- Cleaning 55
- Inspection 56
- Assembly 60

Chapter 6: Engine Block Overhaul **62**
- Disassembly 62
- Cleaning 68
- Inspection 73
- Machine Shop Inspections 79
- Reassembly 82

Chapter 7: Final Assembly **89**
- Oil Filter Adapter 89
- Oil Gallery Plugs 89
- Oil Pressure Sending Unit 91
- Oil Filler Tube 91
- Engine Front Cover 91
- Water Pump 93
- Oil Pan 94
- Vibration Damper and Hub 94
- Fuel Pump 95
- Cylinder Heads 95
- Valvetrain 96
- Intake Manifold 98
- Thermostat and Housing 99
- Pre-Oiling the Engine 100
- Distributor 101
- Valve Covers 101
- Engine Mounts 101
- Exhaust Manifolds 101

Chapter 8: Engine Installation and Start-Up **102**
- Preparing the Engine 102
- Preparing the Engine Compartment 103
- Installing the Engine 103
- Choosing Oil 106
- Starting the Engine 107
- Breaking in the Engine 108
- Oil Consumption 108
- Maintenance 108

Chapter 9: Performance and Economy Modifications **109**
- Cylinder Heads 110
- Displacement 111
- Camshaft Selection 111
- Camshaft Specifications 112
- Valve Lifter Types 113
- Valve Springs 114
- Pushrods 114
- Rocker Arms 114
- Critical Valvetrain Safety Checks 115
- Exhaust Manifolds 115
- Headers 116
- Exhaust Systems 117
- Ignition Systems 118
- Intake Manifolds 120
- Carburetors 122
- Electronic Fuel Injection 125
- How Does It Run? 125

Appendix: Specifications **128**

Source Guide **143**

INTRODUCTION

It's a common misconception that an engine overhaul is beyond the capability of the average do-it-yourself (DIY) mechanic. Sure, it's an exacting process. Sure, it's time-consuming. But you can do it if you take your time and thoroughly study each step of the process. It helps if you're a detail-oriented person. If you're not detail oriented, this is your chance to learn!

It is important to be meticulous when cleaning, measuring, and reassembling the engine. Don't rush any part of the overhaul. Leave yourself plenty of time. Hurrying the process can lead to forgetting to tighten a bolt or to installing a piston ring upside down. Seemingly small mistakes like this can have serious consequences.

My approach in writing this book considers that decades have passed since the last Oldsmobile V-8 engine was built. Many readers, I assume, are Oldsmobile enthusiasts who are intent on restoring their collector cars. Then, there are some who just want to breathe new life into their tired old friend. In either case, engine inspections are likely to reveal extensive wear on many components. The information in this book will help to identify the extent of the wear and present overhaul options for the cost-conscious rebuilder as well as the spare-no-expense restorer.

Many tasks in this book can be carried out in more than one way. I always present the best method. In some cases, alternative methods can be used that have advantages, such as being quicker or not requiring a special tool. In these cases, I document the alternative method(s) as well. All methods that I discuss are safe and follow accepted shop practices.

CHAPTER 1

Generation II Oldsmobile V-8 Engines

The second-generation Oldsmobile V-8 engine began production in 1964, and it represented a significant upgrade over the original "Rocket" design. Offering reduced weight, greater efficiency, and improved power potential, the updated engine helped improve car sales. Oldsmobile's popularity rocketed through the 1970s, and the brand regularly achieved sales of 1 million cars per year through the 1980s. The legendary durability of the venerable Oldsmobile V-8 was undoubtedly a big part of this success.

This book covers second-generation Oldsmobile V-8 engines installed in vehicles from 1964 through 1990. These engines were available in displacements of 260, 307, 330, 350, 400, 403, 425, and 455 ci. They were used in nearly all V-8-engined Oldsmobiles through the 1970s.

The Oldsmobile V-8 was also used by other General Motors (GM) automotive divisions and even in GMC motorhomes of the 1970s. If you go waterskiing, you might even see an Oldsmobile engine in a jet boat, as Oldsmobile engines became popular in certain marine applications.

Engine Identification

When installed in a vehicle, an Oldsmobile V-8 engine can be immediately distinguished from engines of other manufacturers. Look for the bypass tube and hose attached to the thermostat housing at the front of

Enthusiasm for Oldsmobile V-8 engines remains strong, even decades after the last example was manufactured. With millions having been produced, these durable powerplants are destined to be popular for decades yet to come.

Regardless of the year of manufacture, all Oldsmobile V-8 engines have this unique bypass tube/hose attached to the thermostat housing. If the engine does not have this bypass tube, it is not an Oldsmobile engine.

The 1976-and-earlier engines have 10 nuts securing the valve covers (bottom). Later models have only 5 nuts/bolts (top), although you can still see the ears where the other 5 bolts would have gone.

the engine, just below the upper radiator hose. Only Oldsmobile engines have this hose/tube.

Another quick identification trick is to look at how many nuts or bolts secure the valve covers. On 1976-and-earlier models, 10 fasteners secure each valve cover. On later engines, there are only 5.

Although Oldsmobile engines tend to look similar, there are many subtle differences that are critical in terms of finding the correct internal parts. Fortunately, Oldsmobile provided an easy way to identify the specifics of its engines. On every Oldsmobile-manufactured engine, there is a number cast into the block at the top front, just below the bypass tube. This number identifies the engine displacement and the year of manufacture.

Just forward of the thermostat housing is a number cast into the engine that can be used to identify the displacement.

GM Corporate Use

Oldsmobile engines were used in more than just Oldsmobiles. In addition to their primary use in Oldsmobile cars, Oldsmobile engines were used by every GM division at some point or another. With the exception

Engine Block Casting Numbers		
Year	**Casting Number**	**Displacement (Cubic Inches)**
1964–1967	381917	330
1964–1967	394417	330
1965	389298	400
1965	386525	425
1966–1967	381917	330
1966–1967	390925	400
1966–1967	389244	425
1966	389244	425
1967	394417	330
1967	390925	400
1967	389244	425
1967	389244	425
1968–1976	395558	350
1968–1969	396026	400
1968–1969	393605	400
1968–1976	396021	455
1972–1976	396021	455
1975–1982	554965	260
1975–1976	550355	260
1976–1977	395558	350

Engine Block Casting Numbers		
Year	**Casting Number**	**Displacement (Cubic Inches)**
1968–1976	396021	455
1975–1976	231788	455
1977–1982	557751	260
1977–1980	557752	350
1977–1980	554964	350
1977–1979	554990	403
1977	557265	403
1978–1979	557265	403
1978–1980	557791	260
1978–1980	557795	260
1978–1980	557838	350
1978–1979	557893	403
1980–1984	3161	307
1987	6509	307
1985–1990	4790-5-0	307
1978–1980	560382	350 Diesel
1978–1980	558306	350 Diesel
1978–1980	554964	350 Diesel
1978–1980	4468-D3	350 Diesel
1980–1985	7582	350 Diesel

of Chevrolet, the Oldsmobile engine endured longer than engines from other GM divisions.

Not only were Oldsmobile engines installed in cars from other GM divisions but also engines from other GM divisions were sometimes installed in Oldsmobiles at the factory. In particular, the Chevrolet small-block (305) and Pontiac 301 were commonly installed in Oldsmobile cars in the 1980s.

During this time, GM commonly (and confusingly) referred to the Chevrolet 305, Pontiac 301, and Oldsmobile 307 generically as "5.0 liter" engines. There is very little that these three separate engine designs have in common other than their approximate metric displacement. If in doubt, look for the bypass hose/tube shown earlier to be sure that you have an Oldsmobile engine in your Oldsmobile!

VIN Identification

The engine can sometimes be identified by referencing the vehicle identification number (VIN). The VIN is found in one of two places, depending on the year of manufacture. If you have a 1967-or-earlier vehicle, a VIN plate is in the front doorjamb and is visible when the driver's door is open. For 1968-and-later vehicles, a VIN plate is visible through the windshield at the base of the dash on the driver's side.

GM VIN numbers were in different formats over the years. All 1981-and-later models use a standardized 17-digit VIN. The eighth digit identifies the engine and the tenth digit identifies the model year. Prior to 1981, GM VINs were not as standardized and took multiple formats over time.

On 1971-and-earlier models, the VIN does not include information related to engine identification. On these models, there is a data plate riveted on the firewall on the driver's side of the engine compartment. The information on this plate only identifies whether a V-8 or a 6-cylinder engine was installed at the factory. No specifics about the engine are provided.

On 1972–1980 models, a 13-digit VIN code was provided. On these models, the fifth digit identifies the engine type and the sixth digit identifies the model year.

Oldsmobile 1972-and-Later Engine VIN Codes

VIN Letter	Engine Displacement
9	307*
F	260
G	305
H	350 (1977 and earlier)
H	305 (1979 and later)
J	350
K	350 (1976 and earlier)
K	403 (1977 and later)
L	350
M	350
R	400 (1975 and earlier)
R	350 (1976 and later)
S	400 (1975 only)
S	455 (1976 only)
T	455
U	455 (1976 and earlier)
U	305 (1977 and later)
V	455
W	455
X	455
Y	307*

* VIN 9 and VIN Y 307 engines were produced during the same model years in the 1980s and 1990. The engines appear similar, and both were equipped with 4-barrel carburetors.

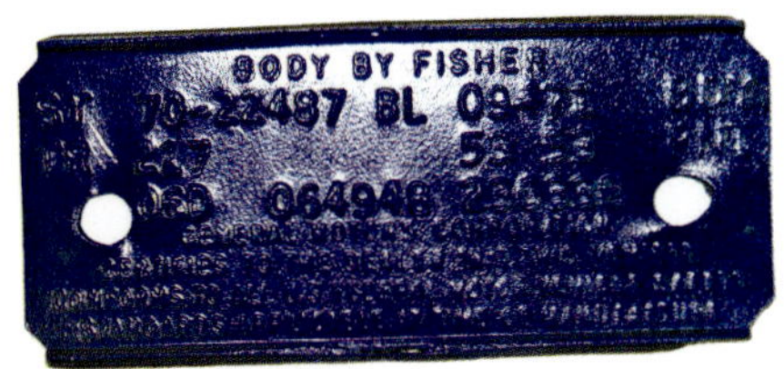

On 1971-and-earlier GM cars, the VIN does not indicate the type of engine installed in the vehicle. A body code plate like this is attached to the firewall. The plate does not provide much detail as to the engine installed but can identify whether the car was originally equipped with a V-8 or a 6-cylinder engine.

VIN Derivative on the Engine Block

The 1968-and-later Oldsmobile engines also have a small-font number stamped into a machined pad near the front of the engine, just below the cylinder head on the driver's side of the engine. This number begins with a three-digit code. The first digit is the division code:

1 = Chevrolet
2 = Pontiac
3 = Oldsmobile
4 = Buick
6 = Cadillac

Note that the division code identifies the car line in which the engine was installed, not the engine type. As we know, Oldsmobile engines were installed in vehicles from all GM divisions, so any of these numbers is possible.

The second digit identifies the year of manufacture. On 1979-and-earlier models, this is the last digit of the year of manufacture (9 = 1969, 0 = 1970, 1 = 1971, etc.). On 1980-and-later models, a letter is used instead of a number (A = 1980,

The VIN derivative number uniquely identifies a particular engine to its chassis. It is stamped into a machined pad just below the cylinder head on the driver's side of the engine. The last six digits of this number should match the last six digits of the VIN.

B = 1981, etc.). The third digit is a letter code that identifies where the engine was manufactured.

The six numbers that follow the three-digit code should match the last six numbers of the VIN (known as the "sequence number"). If the last six numbers of the VIN match these six numbers, it means the engine is the same one that was originally installed at the factory. In other words, it's the numbers-matching engine for the car.

Engine Family Identification

Second-generation Oldsmobile engines can be divided into two major categories: small-block and big-block. Small-block and big-block engines share a fundamentally similar design where some parts will interchange between small-blocks and big-blocks. Here's how it breaks down in terms of engine displacement:

Small-block: 260, 307, 330, 350, 403
Big-block: 400, 425, 455

Keep in mind that these categories are about the design of the engines, not necessarily the engine displacement. This explains the odd phenomenon whereby a 400 is a big-block, but a 403 is a small-block.

Parts Interchangeability

Generally speaking, there is wide parts interchangeability within the engine families (i.e., parts from small-block engines interchange with other small-block engines and parts from big-block engines interchange with other big-blocks). However, parts interchange between engine families is more limited. For example, crankshafts, connecting rods, and intake manifolds will generally not interchange between small-block and big-block engines.

That being said, many parts do interchange between engine families, such as camshafts, rocker arms, exhaust manifolds, distributors, water pumps, and fuel pumps. Small-block owners are often happy to discover that cylinder heads from big-block engines will swap onto small-block engines without much effort and will generally result in a performance gain.

One very special note is that many 1965–1967 camshafts and lifters do not interchange with 1968-and-later camshafts and lifters. The earlier and later engine blocks have a different lifter bore angle. This has confounded many an unaware Oldsmobile engine builder!

The internet is awash with information regarding parts swapping among engines to achieve greater strength and performance. If you're building a budget performance engine, do some further research. However, most Oldsmobile engines are gone from the junkyards, and people selling used high-performance parts are usually aware of their value.

If you're thinking about purchasing used parts, consult with an automotive machine shop to make sure the parts will be worth using, especially after the necessary machine work is carried out. There is a huge variety of new parts now available for Oldsmobile engines at reasonable prices. It's usually best to go with new, high-quality parts versus taking chances on parts that are now decades old.

What Is an Overhaul?

Overhauling an engine means restoring the internal parts to new-engine specifications. At minimum, an overhaul involves replacing the piston rings and reconditioning the cylinder bores (honing or reboring). If the cylinders are rebored, new pistons need to be installed. The main and connecting rod bearings also need to be replaced. If there is any damage to the crankshaft bearing journals, the crankshaft will be reground, requiring oversize bearings to be installed.

The cylinder heads will also receive close attention. The sealing surfaces of the valves and seats will be resurfaced and valve oil seals replaced. The valve guides, springs, retainers, and seals are inspected and replaced as needed. The camshaft and valvetrain components—rocker arms, pushrods, and lifters—are carefully inspected.

At the time of overhaul, it's also wise to replace the water pump, distributor, alternator, and starter. The goal is to have everything under the hood fresh and ready to deliver many years of trouble-free service.

When Is an Overhaul Necessary?

There are no hard-and-fast rules as to mileage before an overhaul is needed. An Oldsmobile engine that has been driven normally, had regular oil changes, and not overheated can achieve 200,000 miles before an overhaul is needed. Conversely, a car that has been neglected or seriously overheated can fail very early in its life. Diagnosis is needed to determine the condition of the engine. Diagnosis is covered in Chapter 3.

Overheating is the most common cause of early engine failure. For this reason, it's essential to replace cooling system components at the time of overhaul to be sure that the new engine will last. Always replace the cooling system hoses, water pump, and thermostat. Have the radiator serviced or simply replace it with a new one.

Before starting the overhaul, read through this book and become familiar with the requirements and scope of the process. An engine overhaul is relatively straightforward with the correct tools and equipment; however, the job is time consuming. Even if you think the overhaul will be a simple one, plan on the vehicle being down for several weeks. Overhauls almost always take longer than planned, as there will be unforeseen delays involved with scheduling machine work and obtaining parts.

Alternatives to a Full Overhaul

Sometimes the inspection and reconditioning of original parts is not the best way to go due to the cost of parts, machine work, and time. If the engine block, heads, and crankshaft are in reasonably good shape, an overhaul can be done at low cost. However, if a major component is badly worn or damaged, the job can be much more costly and time consuming. In such cases, consider other options.

Rotating Assembly

Engine parts suppliers frequently sell reconditioned kits that include a reground crankshaft, connecting rods, pistons, bearings, and rings. The kit will be ready to install and may also include the gaskets and seals needed to reassemble the engine block. Some machine work on the block will still be necessary, such as a cylinder rebore, align-honing the main bearing journals, and resurfacing the cylinder head gasket surface (commonly known as "decking").

Short-Block

A short-block is a complete engine block assembly, including the crankshaft, pistons, connecting rods, bearings, rings, camshaft, oil pump, timing chain, and seals. Your existing cylinder heads and valvetrain can be bolted into place, assuming that those parts are in good condition.

Long-Block

Long-blocks are basically short-blocks with new or rebuilt cylinder heads installed. Long-blocks will have the valvetrain components installed and correctly adjusted. If you purchase a long-block, all you will need to do is install the engine covers and external components. Long-blocks also frequently have warranties, which is another good reason to go this route.

Used Engine

Salvage yards frequently have used engines available and will sometimes provide a brief warranty so that you can verify whether the engine runs normally after installation in your vehicle. A significant amount of time and money can be saved by choosing a used engine, but there is a risk of major engine problems arising in a short time.

If possible, try to find an engine that can be inspected before removal from the vehicle. That way, you can verify the mileage and the condition of fluids and possibly hear and see how it runs before it's pulled from the vehicle. Also, if the vehicle has been wrecked, it's a clue that the engine was running prior to the wreck and is more likely to be in good condition.

Used Oldsmobile engines are still available at some wrecking yards. While they offer a quick and inexpensive solution, you're usually guessing as to the condition of internal components. Also, there are many small variations among engines of different years and models, providing potential headaches that are hard to foresee.

CHAPTER 2

Tools, Equipment, and Supplies

An engine overhaul requires a significant investment in tools and equipment. Some items can be rented or borrowed, but hundreds of dollars can be spent on renting by the time the job is complete. This chapter will help you understand the tools of the trade, as access to these tools will be part of what determines the level of work that can be done on your own.

The tools and equipment that are purchased should reflect your future plans and interest in an engine overhaul. If this will be your only engine overhaul and/or you are on a budget, just get the basics and borrow or rent the rest. If you're interested in learning more about engine overhaul and possibly doing another in the future, you might want to buy some items that aren't essential but that you might reuse.

When it comes to hand tools that will receive heavy use, make sure that they are good quality, made of forged steel, and come from a reputable manufacturer. It isn't necessary to buy the best of the best, but also don't get bargain-basement quality. You will be sorry.

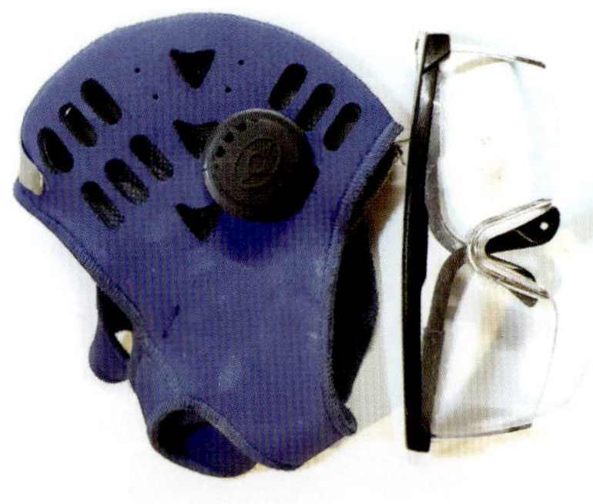

Get a pair of safety glasses and leave them on whenever you're at work. Most eye injuries happen when they are least expected. A dust mask should be used whenever there's debris in the air, such as when cleaning parts.

Work Area

You don't need a full workshop or even a garage to carry out an overhaul, but a workspace is essential. This area must be organized, safe, and clean. It is best if the work area is indoors, but a sheltered outdoor area can work if there is an indoor area available to store parts.

Storage

A disassembled engine takes up more space than you might expect. Be sure to have plenty of shelf space to store the parts—preferably not the closet! Parts taken out of an old engine are very dirty, and they shouldn't be stored in a living space. Cabinets with plastic drawers are available inexpensively, but cardboard boxes work well too. Label all parts and store related items together wherever possible.

Workbench

It's almost impossible to carry out an engine overhaul without a workbench. The bench should be capable of handling about 100 pounds, since it will need to support heavy components, such as the crankshaft and cylinder heads. Benches are available inexpensively and can also be easily built with 2x4 lumber and 1/2-inch plywood. A good bench vise is a great accessory that will be used frequently.

Safety Equipment

Work should be performed with the appropriate safety equipment. First, think about what protection is needed. Safety glasses and gloves will be used frequently. A fire extinguisher and respirator should be available whenever you're working with hazardous or flammable liquids.

Heavy gloves should be worn when doing heavy work, such as engine removal. Mechanic's gloves are lightweight but offer protection from grease and scratches. Vinyl gloves provide protection from grease and harsh chemicals.

Whenever you work with flammable materials, especially gasoline and solvents, have a fire extinguisher close by. When you start an engine for the first time, small fires can get started from fuel leaks and backfiring. Be prepared.

Tools

A basic set of general-purpose tools is required to do any level of work involved with an overhaul. Many tools in the set are essential, while others are nice to have but not essential. Depending on the issues that are encountered, additional tools are likely to be needed.

General-Purpose Tools

- SAE combination wrench set, 3/8-inch through 1-inch sizes
- Adjustable wrench (10-inch)
- Flare-nut wrench set
- 3/8-inch drive SAE socket set, 3/8-inch through 1-inch sizes
- 1/2-inch breaker bar
- 1/2-inch-drive-to-3/8-inch drive reducing adapter
- Torque wrench (1/2-inch drive with range of 20 to 120 ft-lbs)
- Screwdrivers (various sizes, lengths, and tip types)
- Allen wrenches
- Slip-joint pliers
- Locking pliers
- Long-nose pliers
- Ball-peen hammer
- Rubber mallet
- Feeler gauge set (flat and wire type)
- Gasket scraper
- Small wire and plastic-bristle brushes (for cleaning oil passages)
- Small machinist's ruler that measures in 64ths of an inch
- SAE tap-and-die set
- Bolt-grip puller (for removing the harmonic balancer)
- Floor jack (can sometimes be rented)

Here are the business ends of the two most useful wrench types. The box-end wrench (right) engages a hex head on all six flats. Use it whenever there is sufficient access around the head. The open-end wrench engages only two flats and is therefore more prone to slipping and damaging fasteners. Use it only when access is limited or on square-head fasteners.

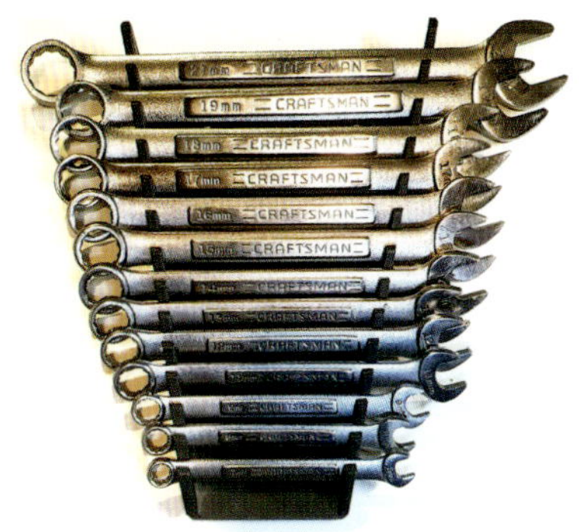

Start with a quality set of combination wrenches. Later Oldsmobile engines use both standard and metric fasteners, so it's best to buy both.

Wrenches and sockets are available in 6-point or 12-point. Six-point wrenches provide a stronger grip on the fastener but have fewer engagement angles than 12-point designs. Use 6-point wrenches and sockets whenever possible. A notable exception is later-model Oldsmobile connecting rod nuts that have a 12-point head. Use a 12-point 9/16-inch socket.

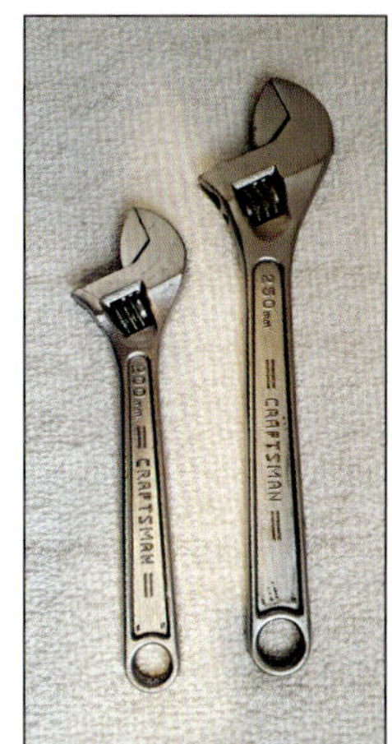

Adjustable wrenches are handy but do not grip fasteners very tightly. They can be used as backup wrenches when tightening bolts that have nuts on the other end or when bolts don't need to be very tight. During use, the movable jaw should point in the direction the wrench is being turned.

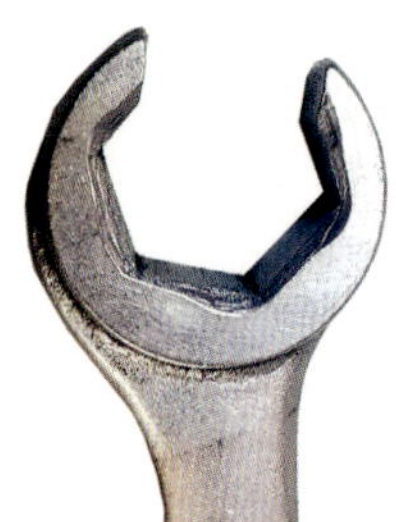

This type of wrench is called a flare-nut wrench, a tubing wrench, or a line wrench. It's used for threaded fittings on fuel lines, transmission fluid lines, and power steering lines. Don't try to loosen line fittings with an open-end wrench. You will damage the fitting.

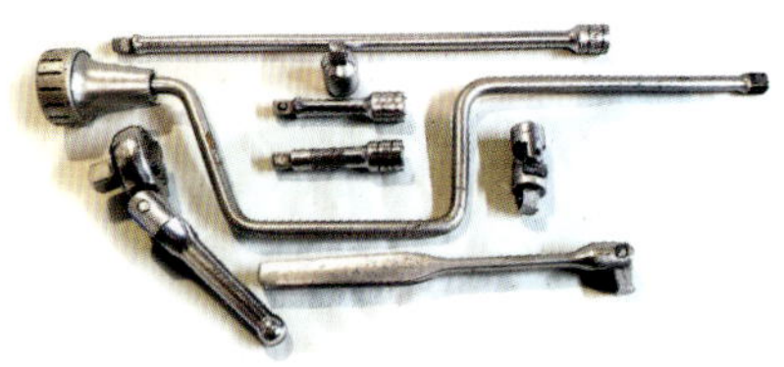

A large variety of socket drive accessories are available to extend reach, change angle, or speed the removal process. The cranked "speed handle" (center) shaves some time when a job requires removing a lot of bolts, such as oil pan removal.

Pliers and other gripping tools should be used only when wrenches or sockets are not appropriate. Do not use these tools to tighten or loosen bolts or nuts except as a last resort on a damaged fastener.

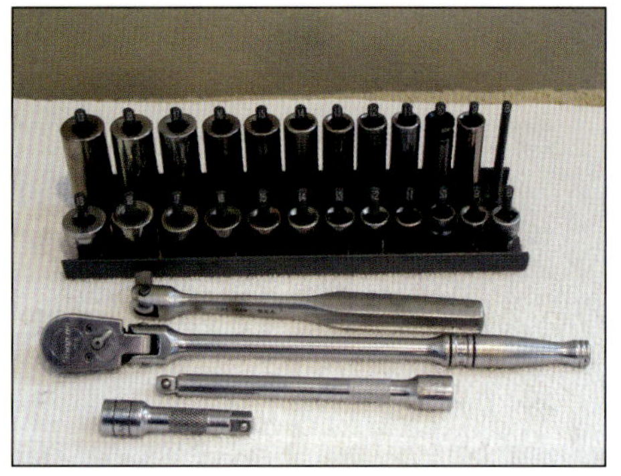

The majority of the fasteners involved with an Oldsmobile engine overhaul can be removed with 3/8-inch-drive standard sockets. Most of the bolts on Oldsmobiles are SAE sizes, but starting in about 1973, there was a slow integration of metric fasteners. Metric sockets may be needed for later-model vehicles.

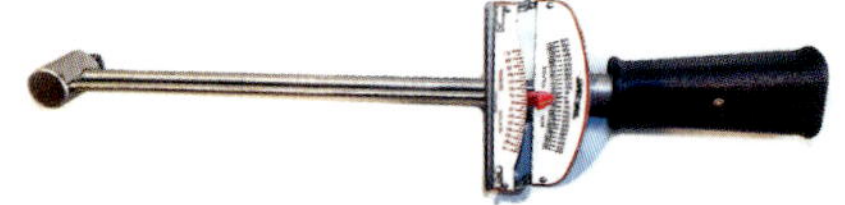

A beam-type torque wrench is the cheapest option. If you purchase one from a quality brand, it will usually do the job well enough. However, the "click type" torque wrench is more accurate and highly recommended. It will likely be used for other jobs long after the overhaul is complete.

Phillips screwdrivers are not all the same. It's important to select the right tip size for the screw being removed. From left to right are size numbers 1, 2, and 3. This range of sizes should cover automotive work. Insert different sizes until the best fit is found and make sure that the tip is not worn. Phillips screw heads are easily stripped.

Three socket drive sizes are commonly used: 1/4, 3/8, and 1/2 inch. The 3/8 drive (in the center) is by far the most common. For a starter set, get a 3/8-inch drive and build onto it when you have budget for more tools. It's also good to have a 1/2-inch-drive breaker bar and an adapter to 3/8 inch. This can be used to remove extra-tight bolts.

A torque wrench is absolutely essential when reassembling your engine. It must be used when tightening the critical fasteners, which are the main-bearing cap bolts, connecting-rod cap nuts, cylinder-head bolts, and intake-manifold bolts. If they are not torqued properly, there may be leaks or worse.

Screwdrivers are relatively cheap, so get a set with a wide variety of lengths and sizes. Spend a little extra for a quality brand.

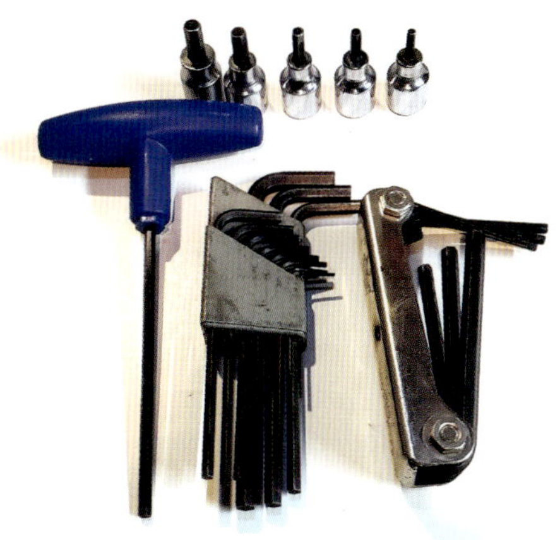

Allen wrenches are needed for removing threaded pipe plugs in the engine. Get a good set because Allen-head plugs and setscrews are commonly found on all types of machinery. The bit type (top) attach to a ratchet or an extension, making them the most versatile design.

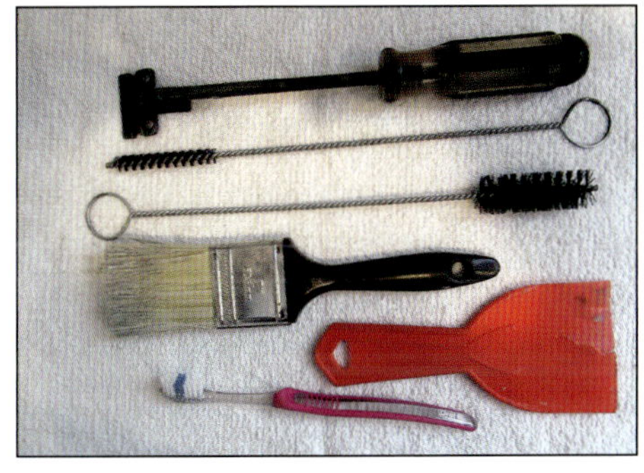

A variety of brushes and scrapers are needed to do a good job cleaning the engine.

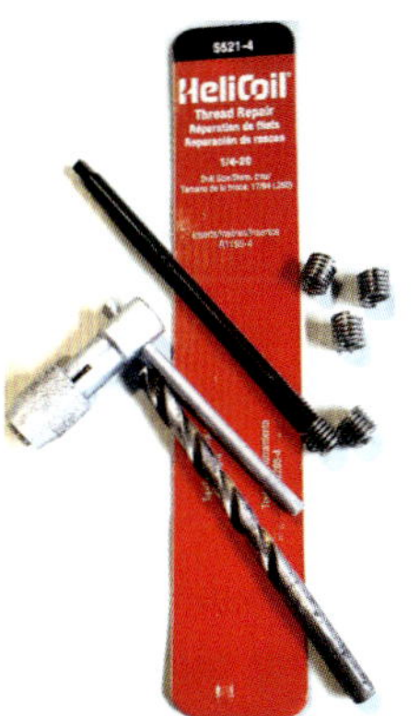

If the bolt holes are stripped out or otherwise damaged, repair them with thread inserts. The most popular brand is Heli-Coil. To use a Heli-Coil, drill the bolt hole oversize, tap it as specified, then thread the Heli-Coil into place. You'll have a permanent repair that uses the same bolt size.

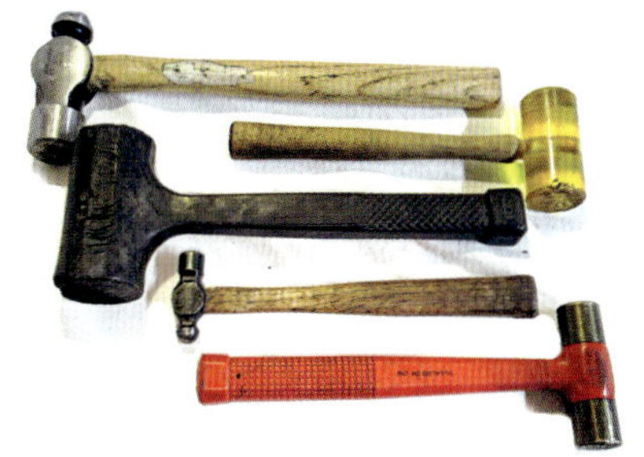

A wide variety of hammer sizes and types are available. At minimum, get a medium-sized steel hammer, preferably a ball-peen type, and a soft-face hammer.

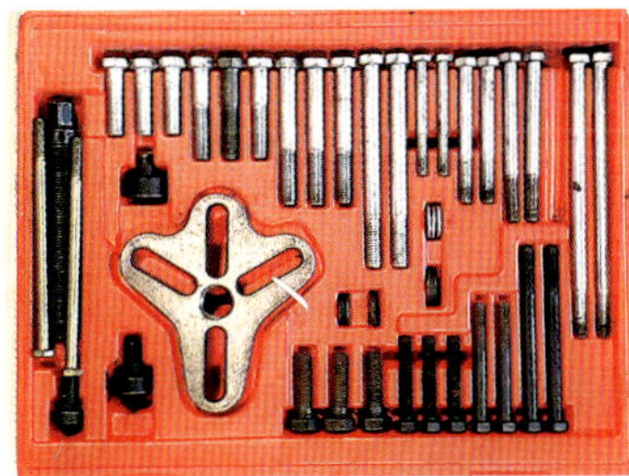

A bolt-grip puller is needed when removing the harmonic balancer. It's best to get a full puller set with a variety of bolt sizes and lengths.

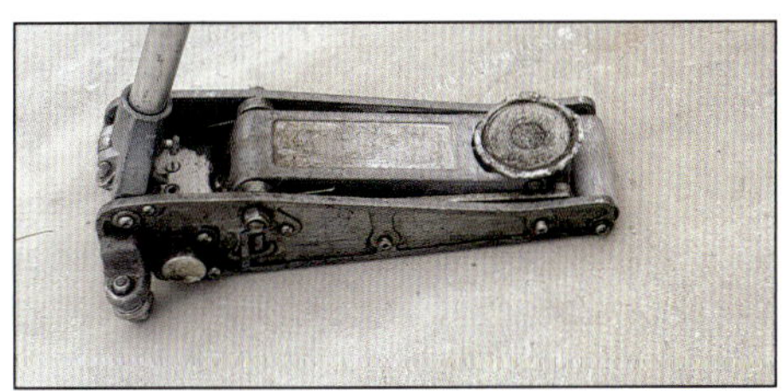

A quality floor jack is a great tool to have whenever you need to access the underside of the vehicle. For overhaul, it will support the transmission as it is removed from the engine. Use jack stands whenever you're under the vehicle. Don't rely on only the jack.

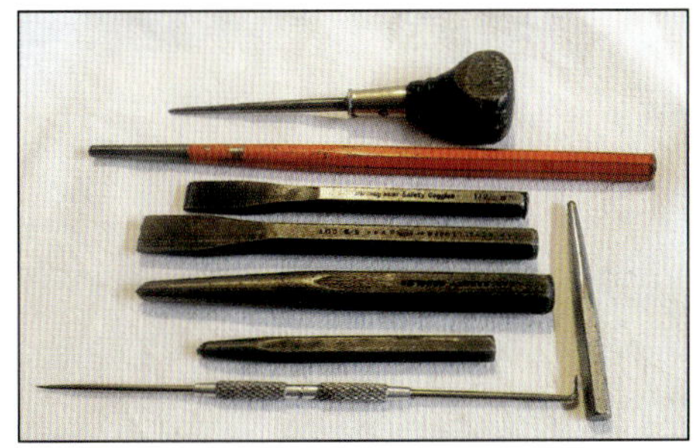

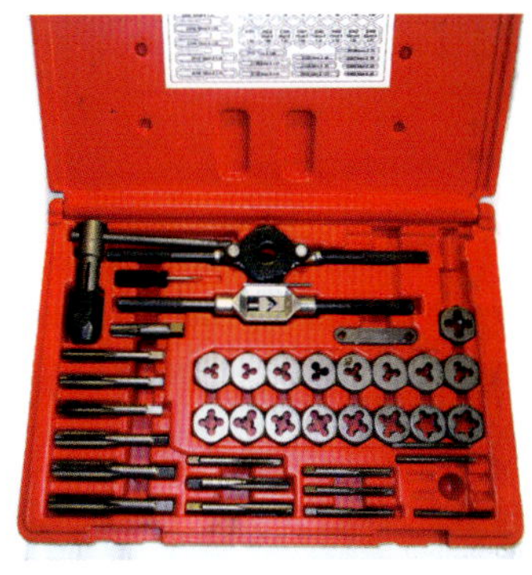

A tap-and-die set is needed to clean the threads on critical engine fasteners. It will likely be needed to repair damaged threads, which will often be encountered on older engines.

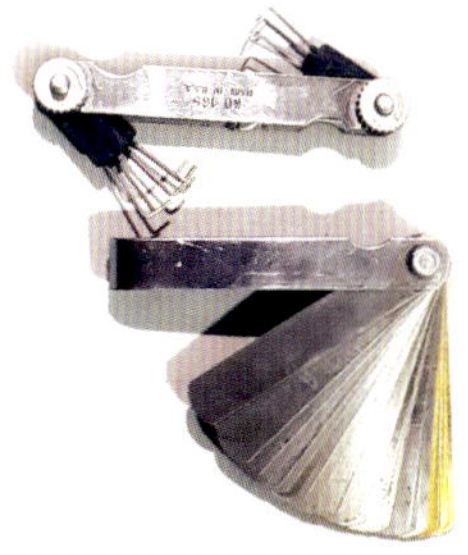

Feeler gauges are manufactured to precise thicknesses and are used to measure clearances between surfaces. To use them, slide different thicknesses into the gap being measured. One should slide through with a bit of resistance. The number on the gauge is the clearance. Wire-type feeler gauges are used to measure spark plug gaps, but we'll use them to measure hydraulic lifter preload.

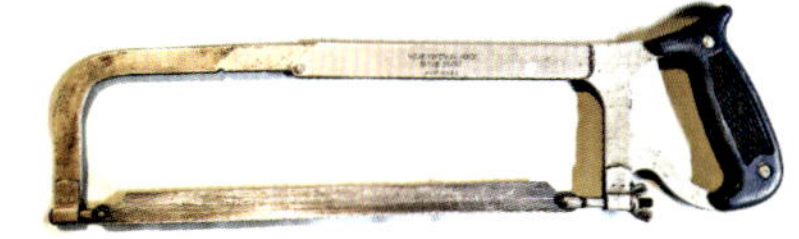

Although it may not be needed for an engine overhaul, a hacksaw is great to have for tasks like cutting oversize bolts to length.

Punches and chisels will probably be necessary during the overhaul, and it's most economical to buy them in a set. Make sure they are designed for metal work. Wood chisels won't do the job and will get dull very quickly.

While not always necessary during an engine overhaul, files are useful for cleaning up burrs remaining after cutting and machining operations.

Broken bolts present problems. Here are some solutions: At the top is a nut splitter for those situations where a nut is stuck. Next are external extractors that grab the outside of a broken bolt's shank. The round tool also grabs the bolt shank externally. EZ-outs are below. They can unscrew a broken bolt after a hole is drilled in the bolt.

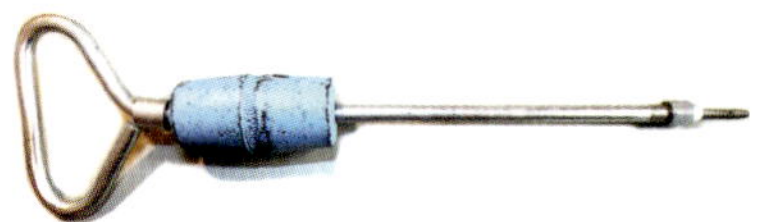

A slide hammer can be used to remove a stuck component when it can't be driven out because access at the rear is restricted. Slide hammers are commonly used to pull out dents in bodywork, but they definitely have their place in mechanical work as well. Sets usually include interchangeable hook and screw ends to handle a variety of tasks.

Pickup tools on long, telescopic handles are inexpensive and can be invaluable when a fastener or a tool is dropped into an inaccessible area. The magnetic tool shown in the center is the easiest to use. A mirror on a telescoping handle (right) will save you from much grief if a fastener falls into an area where you can't see.

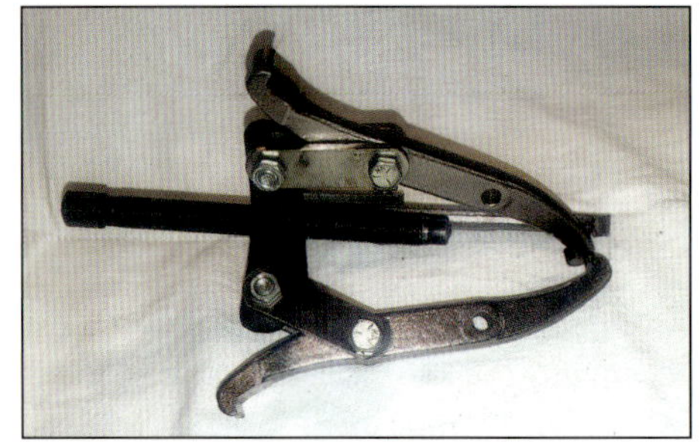

You might need a jaw-type puller to remove the crankshaft timing gear. There are a variety of pullers available, but we recommend getting a three-jaw type. They are the most commonly available and are strong and versatile. Two-jaw pullers can get into tighter places but are not as strong.

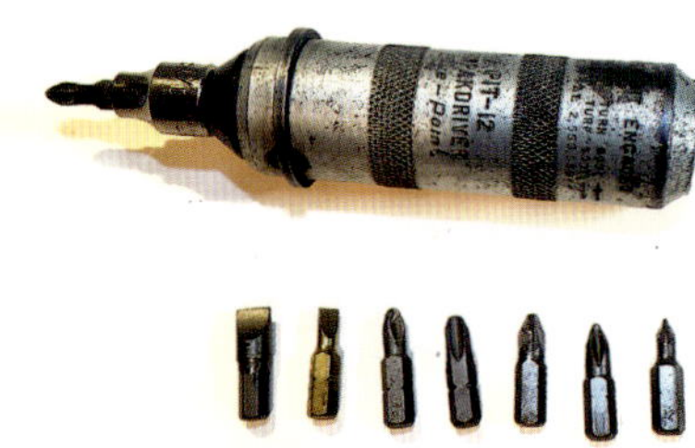

A hand impact driver is placed over a screw and hit with a hammer. Under impact, the tool rotates the drive end of the tool slightly. Because the tool is being driven down while being rotated, the drive tip cannot jump out of the screw head. Impact drivers are particularly useful on tight Phillips screws.

Solid-frame pullers are sometimes called "Pitman-arm pullers" because they are most commonly used for steering and suspension work. They are available in a variety of sizes and are extremely strong. If a crankshaft gear is really stuck, a puller like this might work.

If you replace the power steering pump, this type of special puller is needed to remove the pulley and transfer it to the new pump.

Power Tools

Power tools will make the job go faster, but they also might be required for the situations that develop during an overhaul. If a fastener is broken, it will likely need to be drilled out. An impact gun can be used to deal with stubborn bolts in rotating components much more easily. If you're on a budget, wait until the need arises for these tools.

For removing small components from blind holes, a slide-hammer puller set is invaluable. In an engine overhaul, it's commonly used for removing lifters stuck in their bores and pilot bearings from the rear of crankshafts.

You likely already have a drill and drill bits. They might be needed to deal with broken fasteners, but the type of bits used will matter. They need to be high-speed steel (HSS), black oxide coated, titanium coated, or cobalt coated. The better bits are pricier but will do the job better and last longer. Never use bits designed for woodworking.

An air compressor allows you to use pneumatic tools. Also, high-pressure air is great for cleaning and drying parts. Put a nozzle on the end of an air hose and you have the perfect tool for blowing out the various passages in the cylinder block and heads. Use safety glasses.

Electric or air-powered impact tools can speed along the process of disassembly and are great for removing fasteners at the center of rotating components, such as the camshaft and crankshaft bolts. Since they deliver a rapid pulse of impacts, the bolt will break loose before the shaft can turn. It's best not to use impact tools during reassembly.

Rotary tools are commonly used by hobbyists, but they are also found in the toolboxes of mechanics. They are handy for cleaning small parts and also for cutting off stuck fasteners in restricted areas.

A die grinder is a great tool to have. When used with abrasive pads, this tool can make the job of cleaning gasket surfaces easy.

A bench grinder is an essential tool for any well-equipped shop. In addition to grinding metal parts, wire wheel attachments are available that can be a huge help when cleaning small parts. Get a wire wheel with very fine bristles for engine cleaning work.

Grinding wheels are designed for use on steel and iron, which shed molten bits during grinding, seen as sparks. Don't grind aluminum on a grinding wheel, as it does not shed the ground metal like steel. Instead, it adheres to the wheel like this, which pretty much ruins the wheel.

Special Tools and Equipment for an Overhaul

There are a number of specialty items that are specific to overhauling engines. Depending on how much of the disassembly and reassembly is planned, not all of them may be needed. An engine hoist and a stand are required, both of which can be rented.

An engine hoist is required for removing and installing the engine. This tool is commonly available from equipment rental companies. Do not attempt to remove the engine using an A-frame or by attaching a chain to a roof rafter.

An engine tilter is a great aid when removing and installing an engine. Attached between the hoist and the engine, the tilter allows the engine to move to the exact angle needed. Often it is needed to re-angle the engine during the removal/installation process, which is difficult to do without this tool.

An engine stand is also required. It will need to be rated for at least 500 pounds. Engine stands are available for rent, but it often makes more financial sense to buy one. You won't know for sure how long you'll need the stand (it's always longer than you think), and if you buy your own stand you can always sell it after your overhaul is complete.

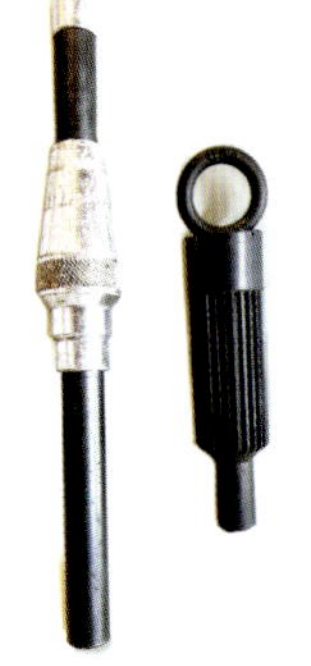

For a manual transmission, align the clutch pressure plate and disc before installation. On the left is a universal tool. On the right is a plastic tool that's designed for a specific application. Often clutch manufacturers will include the correct plastic tool with their clutch kit.

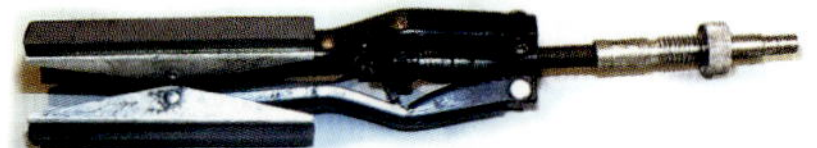

If you'll be assembling cylinder heads, get a valve lapping tool to confirm that the valve work was done correctly.

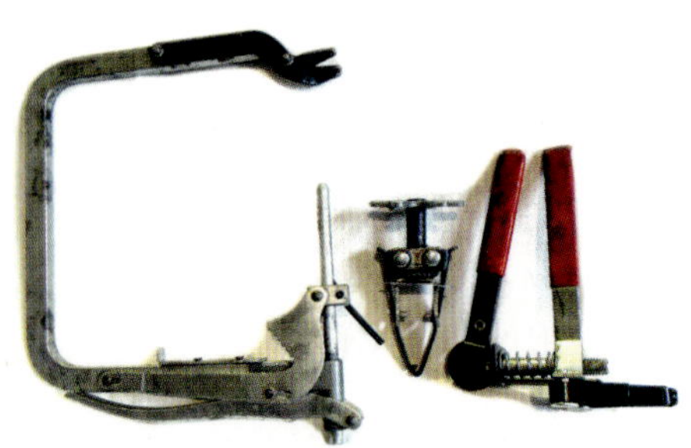

If you're planning to do cylinder head disassembly, a valve spring compressor is needed. The C-clamp type is fastest and easiest to use, but it's also the most expensive.

This tool is for measuring valve spring installed height. You can measure the installed height with calipers, but there's some trial and error involved, and the readings may not be completely accurate. This tool is accurate and gets the job done quickly.

Cylinder honing is best left to a professional. Machine shops will have special equipment that can do the job perfectly. Don't take any chances, as the incorrect finish on cylinder walls will result in piston rings not breaking in properly.

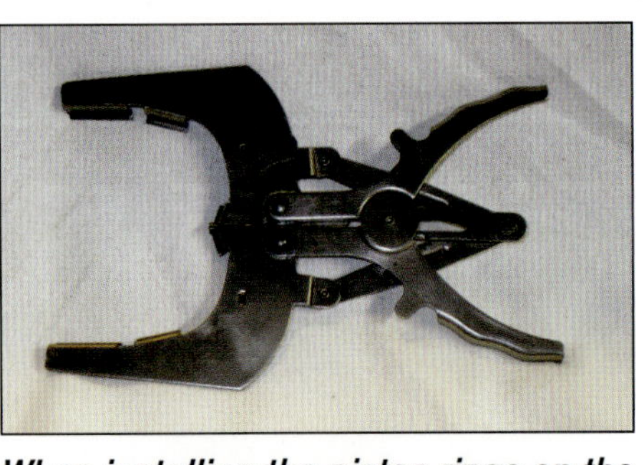

When installing the piston rings on the pistons, they will need to be expanded to fit over the piston head. If you try to do this by hand, some rings will almost certainly break because they're brittle cast iron. A piston-ring expander allows ring installation without breakage.

The piston rings need to be compressed when they are installed in the cylinders. This is another job you won't be able to do effectively by hand. A ring compressor will be needed for this job.

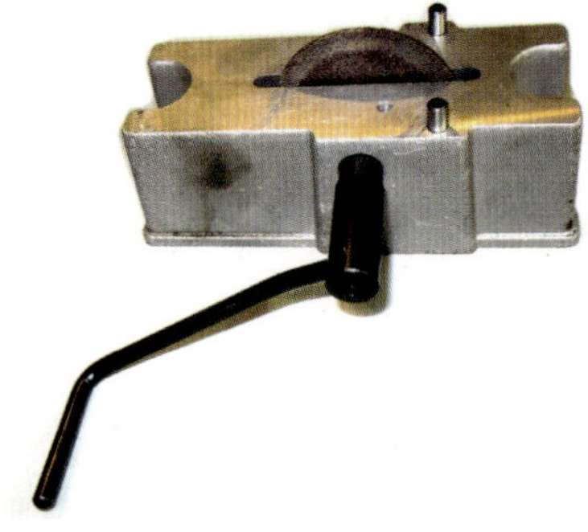

A piston ring filer is needed when ring end gap is below specification. It is essential if you're using "file-to-fit" rings, which are commonly used for high performance and racing. Assuming the machine work is spot on, standard rings shouldn't require any filing.

Precision Measuring Tools

The differences between serviceable and worn-out engine parts are measured in thousandths of an inch. If you've never overhauled an engine before, have an expert help you take the critical measurements to be sure that you don't make any mistakes. If you take the measurements yourself, purchase or borrow precision tools. The following are tools that are typically used when inspecting and reassembling an engine.

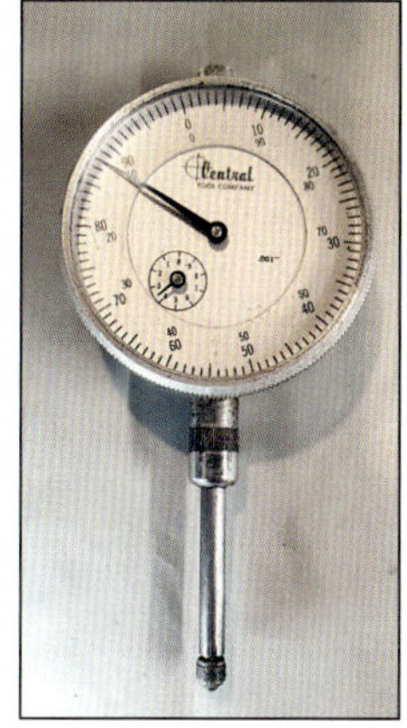

If you perform inspections yourself, you will need a dial or digital indicator that precisely measures up-and-down movement. Inexpensive indicators are available, but we recommend getting a quality indicator to ensure good accuracy. Many of the latest designs have digital readouts and are easier to use.

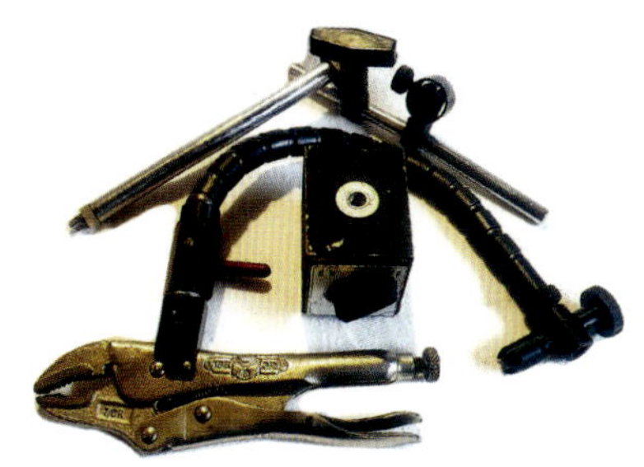

A dial or digital indicator can only be as accurate as the stability of its mounting base. Bases have different methods of attaching the gauge to the base and the base to the mounting surface. Here we see a magnetic base and a clamp-on base. Shown at the top are solid rods with pivots that are pretty much obsolete. Most mechanics prefer a flexible connector between the gauge and the base.

Reading a Micrometer

For most people, the markings on a traditional micrometer are confusing and intimidating. These days, people learning the basics of precision measuring are likely to purchase a digital micrometer and avoid the process of learning to read a traditional micrometer. However, once you know how to read an old-school micrometer, you'll be glad you learned. They are less expensive than digital and more reliable in that you don't have to worry about battery failure or damage to the digital display.

For some, the confusing part is that there are markings on both the thimble (the part that rotates) and the sleeve (the part that does not rotate). Both of these sets of markings are used in conjunction with each other to obtain a measurement.

One full rotation of the thimble (360 degrees) will move the spindle (the moving part that contacts the item being measured) by 0.025 inch. There are 25 marks around the thimble, each representing 0.001 inch.

The marks on the sleeve each indicate 0.025 inch of rotation. So, rotating the thimble one full revolution will move the thimble from one mark on the sleeve to the next mark on the sleeve. After each four marks on the sleeve is a number. The number represents 0.1 inch of movement. So, four turns of the thimble equals four marks uncovered on the sleeve, which is 0.1 (one tenth or 100 thousandths) of an inch. So, what do you get if you rotate the thimble 40 times? That's right: 1 inch.

Okay, students, what's the reading? Let's see . . . Starting from zero on the sleeve, we see five lines. That's $1.25 (five quarters). The thimble is rotated past the zero, to the number three on the thimble. So, add three cents to the total, and we have $1.28. Now, take away the dollar sign and move the decimal point one to the left. The measurement is 0.128 inch. Got it?

Remembering that one full rotation of the spindle is 0.025 inch, there are 25 graduations on the thimble. What does each of these marks represent? That's right, one thousandth of an inch. A trick for reading a micrometer is to think of the marks as money. Each mark on the sleeve represents a quarter and the numbers represent dollars. On the thimble, each mark represents a penny. So, all you have to do is add it up the way you would with the money in your pocket! ■

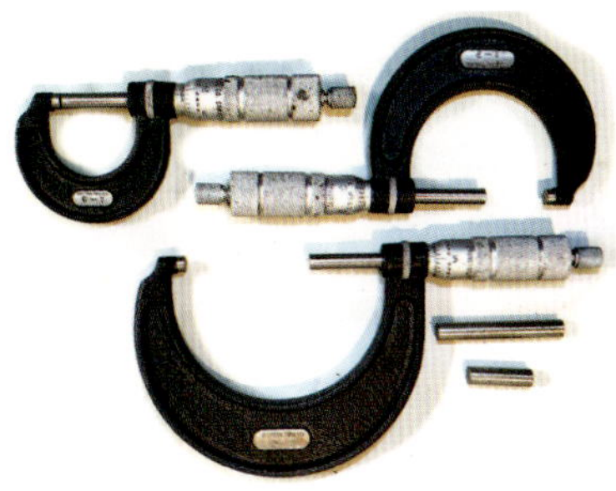

Micrometers are the ultimate in precision for dimensional measurements. When it comes to micrometers, quality is everything. Don't buy cheap micrometers. Shown here are the common sizes needed for engine work, allowing you to measure up to 3 inches. Many modern micrometers have digital readouts, which are easy to read.

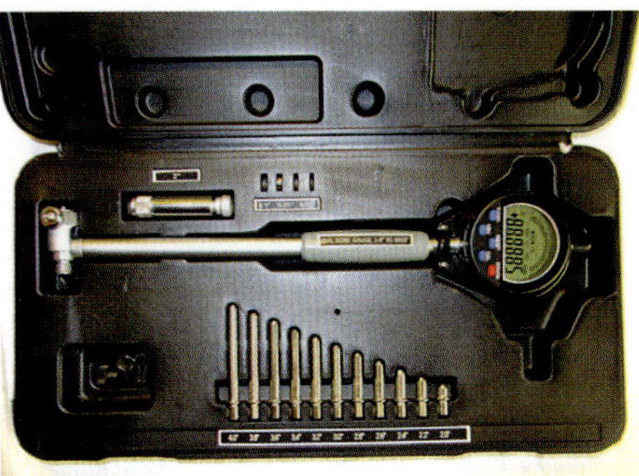

A cylinder bore gauge is necessary to obtain accurate readings on a worn engine. Cylinders do not wear evenly. Normal wear causes the cylinders to become tapered and out of round. Bore gauges are expensive, and a machine shop will almost certainly have one.

A degree wheel is needed if you plan on "degreeing" the camshaft. This is normally done when installing aftermarket performance camshafts.

Testing Equipment

Before beginning the overhaul, it's a good idea to thoroughly understand the engine's problems. Knowledge of these problems will help guide you during the inspections. Be sure that you've found the problems that were causing the symptoms that led to the overhaul.

After the overhaul is complete, confirm that the engine is in top running condition. A compression test after the first few thousand miles of driving is a good idea. Compare the readings to what was recorded before the overhaul.

Chapter 3 deals with the diagnostic methods to employ during use of the following diagnostic tools. Depending on the symptoms, some of these diagnostic tools might be required to confirm that an overhaul is required.

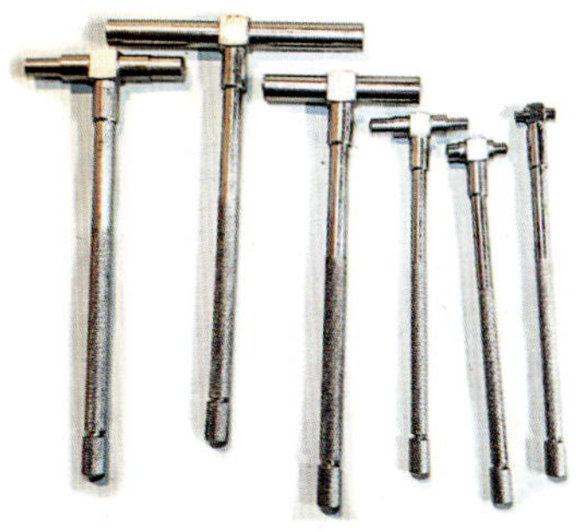

Telescoping gauges make it possible to measure bores without internal measuring tools. The gauge is expanded to the size of the bore and locked. A micrometer is then used to measure the gauge. It takes some practice to do this precisely.

Whether or not you purchase a set of micrometers, purchase a set of calipers. They can measure up to 6 inches and can be found at reasonable prices. They allow for quick measurements, but don't make major machining decisions based on these readings. Calipers are not as accurate as micrometers.

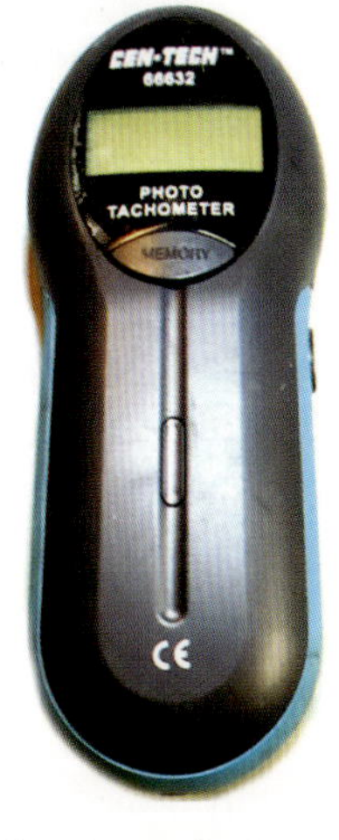

Even if the vehicle has a tachometer on the dash, it's unlikely to be accurate at low RPM. When adjusting idle speed or looking for small variations in engine speed (such as during a power balance test), a diagnostic tachometer should be used. Most tachometers read the ignition signal. This type reads directly off the harmonic balancer.

A timing light is essential for checking ignition timing and can also be used to identify certain problems related to the ignition system. When performance tuning, a great feature to have is "dial-back," which allows you to check the distributor's advance curve.

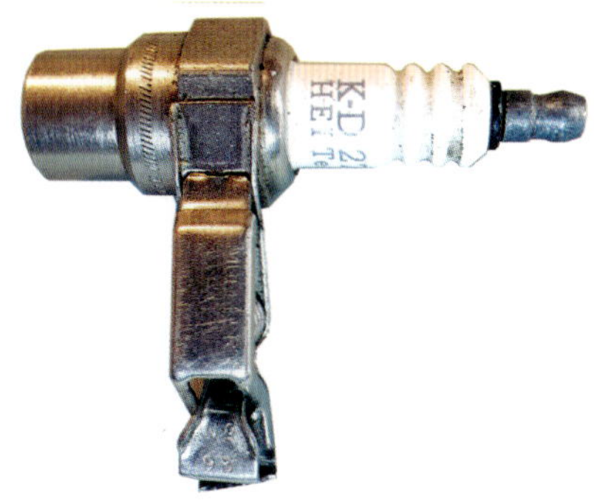

This little tool is used to confirm that an adequate spark is being delivered to the spark plug. It is useful when diagnosing rough-running or no-start problems.

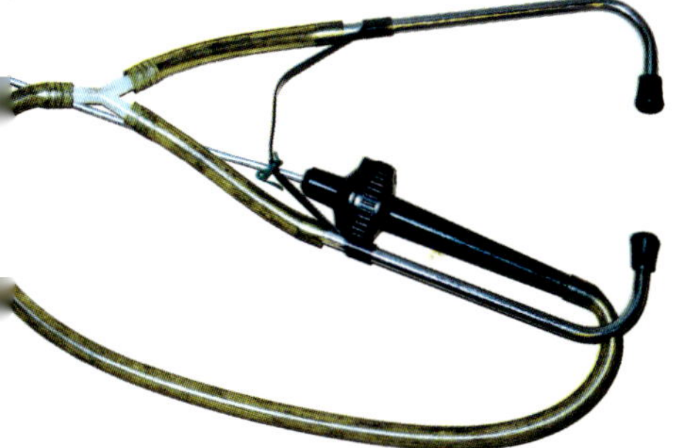

A stethoscope is very handy for pinpointing noises in an engine compartment.

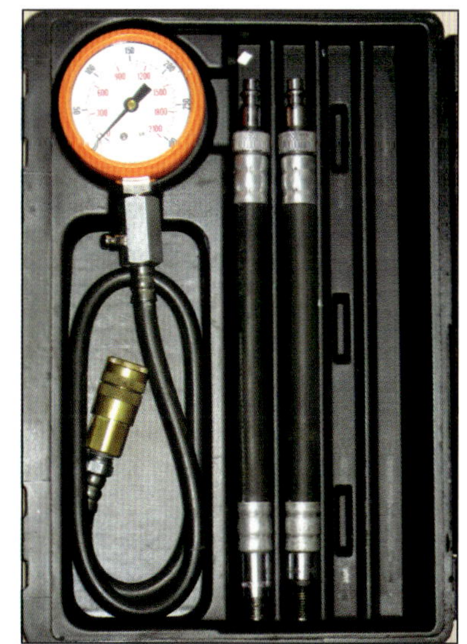

A compression tester is an essential diagnostic tool. It is relatively inexpensive and can reveal many problems within an engine.

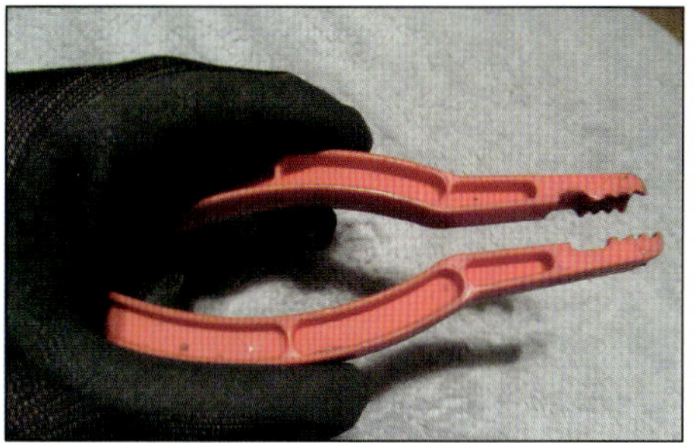

Here's a very inexpensive tool that will keep you from getting shocked during a power balance test. It grips the spark plug wire terminal securely for removal, but it is made of plastic and therefore prevents you from getting shocked. It also helps keep your hand a safe distance away from hot exhaust manifolds.

A remote starter switch is not required but is very handy when performing a compression test or aligning timing marks. It is connected between the positive terminal on the battery and the "S" terminal on the starter. Squeezing the trigger cranks the engine.

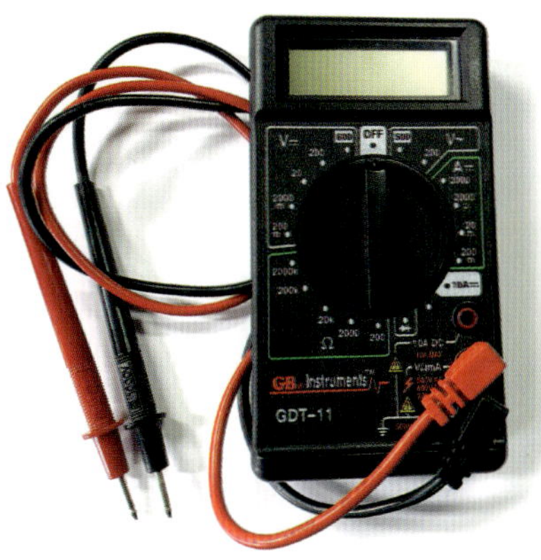

After installing the engine, it's common to find new electrical problems caused by pinched wires or incorrectly installed electrical connectors. An inexpensive multimeter is helpful in diagnosing these problems.

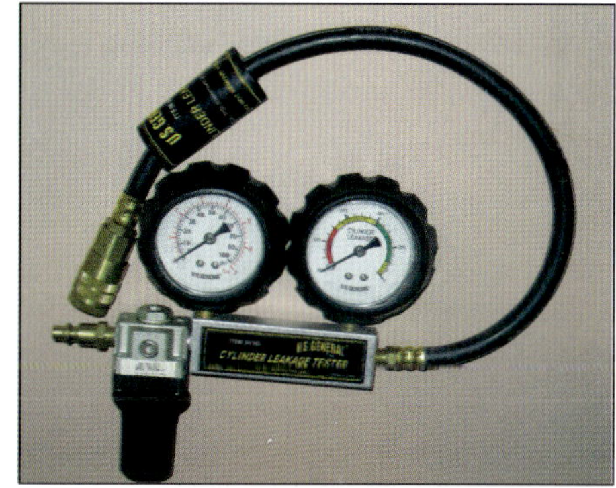

A leakdown tester is needed to perform a leakdown test on an engine with low compression. It will help find the source of the compression leak and indicate the percentage of leakdown occurring in the cylinder. An air compressor is needed to use one.

A combustion leak detector will identify if there's any combustion gases finding their way into the cooling system. Combustion gasses in the coolant usually indicate a blown head gasket but can also be caused by a cracked cylinder head or engine block.

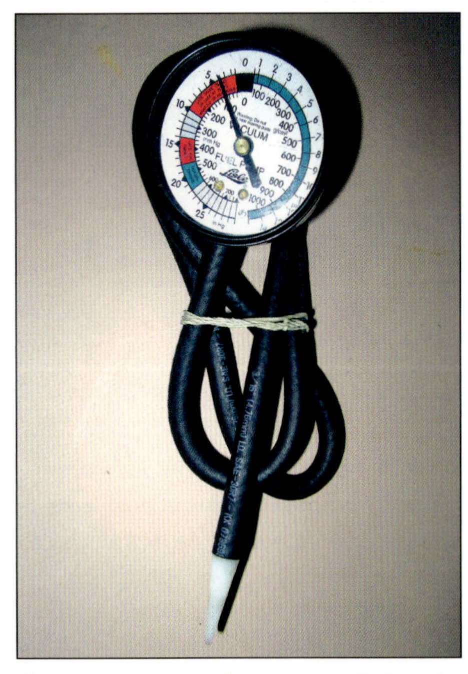

A vacuum gauge is an essential and inexpensive diagnostic tool. Chapter 3 provides instructions as to its proper use.

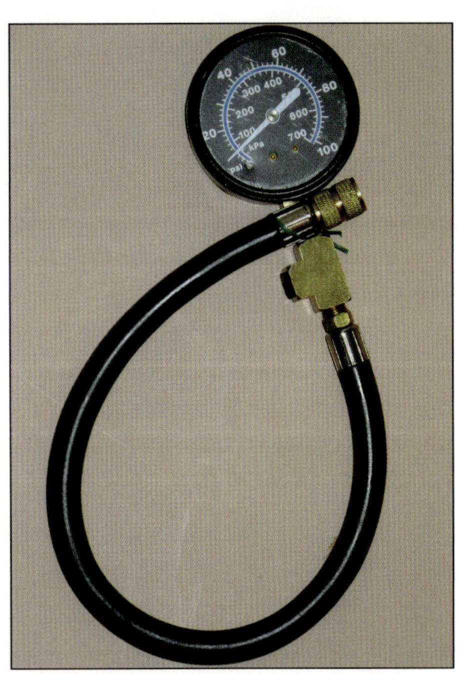

Oil pressure gauges are commonly available from auto parts suppliers. They can also be fabricated if you have a mechanical pressure gauge with a range of 0 to 100 psi. Just make sure the connections and hoses are capable of handling the pressure.

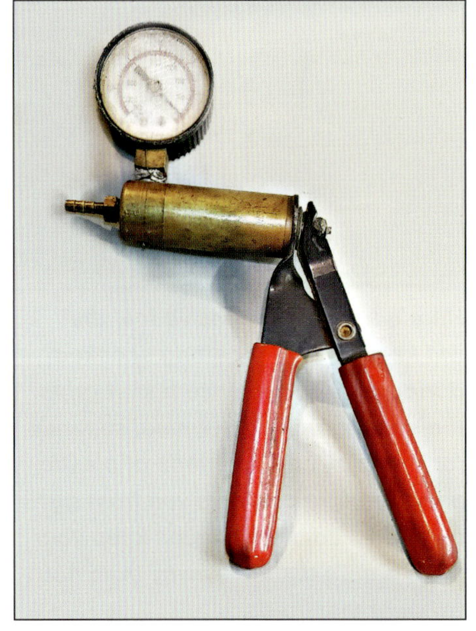

A vacuum pump is used to test for proper functioning of vacuum-controlled devices, such as the exhaust gas recirculation (EGR) valve.

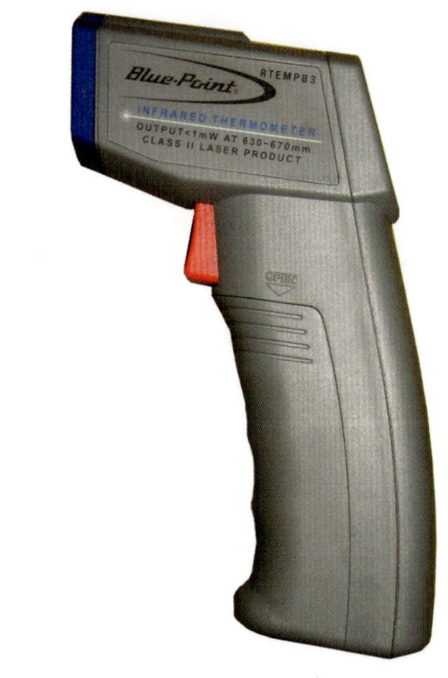

An infrared thermometer "shoots" the temperature of a component from a distance. It is great for checking the relative temperature of the cylinders. Check each exhaust manifold runner or header tube where it exits the head. The temperatures should be very similar. A cylinder that is not firing will have a lower temperature.

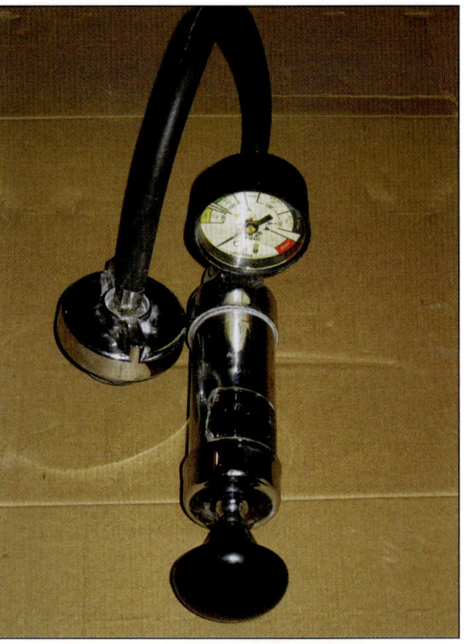

A cooling system pressure tester can help to diagnose internal cracks and head gasket failure. It is also very helpful after engine reassembly and installation to ensure that there are no leaks prior to starting the engine.

Fastener Sizes

Later-model Oldsmobiles employ a mixture of standard (inch-size) fasteners and metric fasteners. You need to be able to identify the differences so that you can use the appropriate tool.

Bolts are identified by their diameter, thread pitch, and strength rating. A 3/8-16 Grade 5 bolt is 3/8 inch in diameter, has 16 threads per inch, and has a Grade 5 strength rating. This is a common bolt found on an Oldsmobile engine.

Looking at the head of the bolt, there are three radial lines. Radial lines on the head are the easiest way to identify a standard bolt. However, low-grade standard bolts (Grade 1 or 2) do not have any marks on the head. This makes them easier to confuse with metric bolts, as some metric bolts do not have markings on their heads either.

On the left is an SAE bolt. The six radial lines indicate its strength grade, which is Grade 8. Why six lines for Grade 8? That's a long discussion we don't need to have here. Just know that you have to add two to the number of lines you see in order to determine the rating. On the right is a metric bolt head. The strength rating is indicated by the number (8.8).

Metric bolts are also identified by diameter, thread pitch, and strength rating. A common metric bolt size is M10-1.5, 8.8. This is a bolt with a diameter of 10 mm, 1.5 mm between threads (thread pitch), and a strength rating of 8.8. There are three common strength ratings on metric bolts: 8.8, 9.8, and 10.9. The higher the number, the higher the strength rating. For purposes of identification, the metric strength marking is a dead giveaway. If you see 8.8, 9.8, or 10.9 on a bolt head, it's metric.

Sometimes it is difficult to determine which wrench or socket to use. On late-model Oldsmobiles, there's always a chance of encountering metric fasteners. Don't use a tool that fits too loosely on the bolt/nut head; otherwise, the corners of the fastener will round off. If you're having a hard time picking the correct tool and/or aren't sure if it's standard or metric, the following information may help:

- 3/8 inch is slightly smaller than 10 mm. This is usually a close-but-no-cigar fit. If your 3/8-inch tool is a tad too small, it's probably a 10 mm.
- 7/16 inch is almost exactly 11 mm. Either size of wrench/socket will work interchangeably.
- 1/2 inch is slightly smaller than 13 mm, and 13 mm fits too loosely on a 1/2-inch fastener head to be used safely.
- 9/16 inch is almost exactly 14 mm. Either size wrench/socket will work interchangeably.
- 5/8 inch is slightly smaller than 16 mm. A 5/8 will work on a 16-mm bolt, but usually a 16-mm wrench is too loose on a 5/8-inch bolt head.
- 11/16 inch is bigger than 17 mm but smaller than 18 mm. They are not close. Use the correct tool.
- 3/4 inch is almost exactly 19 mm. The tools can be used interchangeably.

Torque

Critical fasteners have torque specifications that must be followed. These specifications are listed in the Appendix. Sometimes there are no listed torque specifications. In those cases, the following information may help.

Fastener strength rating and material should be considered when applying a torque value, which is why there is a range given. For example, a short, low-strength bolt threading into aluminum should be torqued to the low end of the torque range. A long, high-strength bolt going into cast iron can handle torque toward the top of the torque range.

Torque Specifications

US Sizes	Approximate Torque Range
1/4-20	5 to 10 ft-lbs
5/16-18	12 to 18 ft-lbs
3/8-16	20 to 30 ft-lbs
3/8-24	25 to 40 ft-lbs
7/16-14	40 to 50 ft-lbs
7/16-20	40 to 60 ft-lbs
1/2-13	55 to 80 ft-lbs
Metric Sizes	**Approximate Torque Range**
M6	5 to 10 ft-lbs
M8	15 to 20 ft-lbs
M10	30 to 40 ft-lbs
M12	50 to 70 ft-lbs
M14	80 to 140 lbs

Cleaning Chemicals

Engine degreaser is commonly available from auto parts sources. It is a heavy duty solvent designed to break down thick accumulations of gunk on an engine and is best used before the engine is removed from the vehicle. Use plenty (get two large cans), let it soak in, brush the gunk as much as possible, then use high-pressure water to wash it off. Engine degreaser works best if the engine is warm.

There are two common varieties of spray solvents that are available from any auto parts store: brake system cleaner and carburetor cleaner.

Brake system cleaner is best for light cleaning, especially on gasket surfaces. Originally designed to protect the rubber seals in brake systems, it is the preferred cleaner when rubber and plastic may be involved. Brake system cleaner leaves behind a perfectly clean surface, making it ideal for final assembly when gasket

On the left is engine degreaser, which is the harshest of the generally available cleaners. In the center is carburetor cleaner, which is not as harsh but leaves behind a slight residue. Brake system cleaner is the safest of the three. It does not leave a residue and won't damage most plastic or rubber.

mating surfaces have to be perfectly clean.

Carburetor cleaner is another aerosol cleaner solvent that is somewhat more aggressive than brake cleaner. It is ideal for removing gum, varnish, and carbon. It also contains a tiny bit of lubricant that dries and remains on surfaces, even though it's almost impossible to detect. This residue generally doesn't matter for engine cleaning purposes, but carburetor cleaner should not be used for final cleaning of gasket surfaces.

Penetrating Oil

Penetrating oil is a must-have for rusted fasteners, particularly on exhaust components that are often frozen in place by heat cycling over the years.

Locking Compound

Locking compounds, commonly known by the brand name Loctite, can be used on external bolts that might vibrate loose during operation. Locking compounds are commonly used on flywheel/flexplate bolts and harmonic balancer bolts. For these purposes, use the blue variety that is designed to allow the bolts to be removed later. The red variety is for permanent installations that will never be disassembled.

Lubricants

When assembling an engine, it's essential that all moving parts are protected against wear. When you first start the engine, you will be bringing it quickly to a raised RPM level. Without adequate protection, an initial dry start could ruin the engine.

For main and connecting rod bearings, a thick assembly lube is required to protect the bearings until an adequate oil film builds up. For camshafts and lifters, especially conventional flat lifters, a special camshaft lubricant is available that provides enhanced lubrication for camshaft lobes and lifter faces, which are under extreme pressure during break-in.

Standard engine oil should be used in cylinder bores and on piston rings. Don't use a thick lubricant in the cylinders, since you want some friction between the rings and cylinder walls to be sure that break-in occurs quickly. If break-in is delayed, a glaze can form on the cylinder walls, which could prevent ring break-in from ever happening.

Sealants

When assembling the engine, great care must be taken to ensure there will be no leaks. Over the years, new sealants and sealing techniques have been developed that are far superior to factory methods. For a preview of what goes into sealing the engine, take a look ahead to Chapter 7.

Every moving part in the engine requires lubrication during assembly. Put thick assembly lube (left) on the bearings, high-pressure lubricant (center) on the camshaft and lifters, and engine oil on the piston rings and cylinder walls.

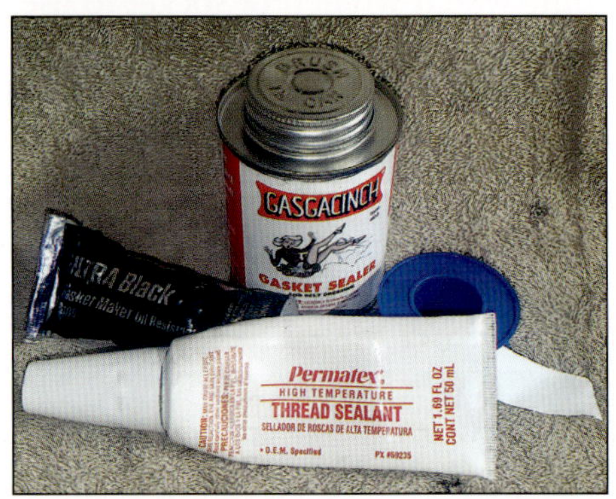

Here are sealants used in engine assembly. Gasgacinch holds gaskets tightly in place, keeping them from moving or deforming during installation. Teflon thread sealant (either in tape form or liquid type) seals threaded fittings. At the front is RTV sealant (sometimes called silicone), which is great for surfaces that are scratched or uneven.

Diagnosis

This chapter covers diagnostic checks that should precede engine mechanical work. Engine diagnosis requires a careful, systematic approach to avoid unnecessary work and to be certain there are serious problems with an engine before taking it out of the vehicle. Misdiagnosis is common, even by professionals.

Always confirm your assumptions with thorough testing. It's also a good idea to consult with an Oldsmobile engine expert. Second opinions are always a good idea.

Most Oldsmobile engines were manufactured during a time before electronic control systems. Routine adjustments and other maintenance is required to keep these engines running well. Some attention to the spark plugs, plug wires, distributor cap/rotor, ignition timing, and carburetor adjustments can greatly improve an engine's performance and fuel economy.

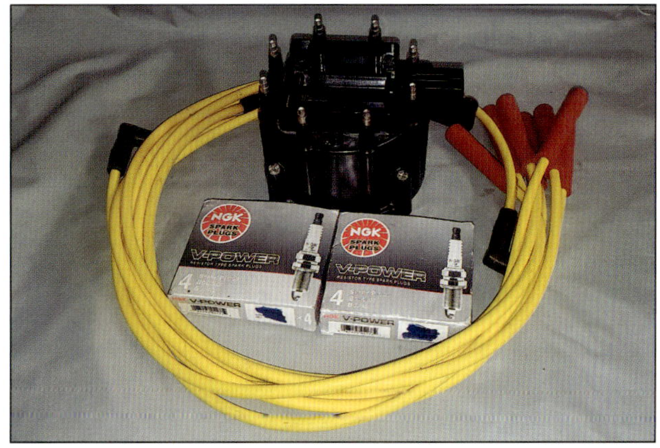

Tune-up parts are inexpensive and relatively easy to install. A basic tune-up is a smart first step in diagnostics, as it eliminates potential problems that can be difficult to find. After an overhaul is complete, these new parts will be needed anyhow. It's best to buy them now.

Oil additives with detergents, such as Sea Foam and Marvel Mystery Oil, can sometimes solve issues related to combustion deposits and sludge that have accumulated within the engine over its years of service. Some oil additives include agents that can swell rubber seals and sometimes reduce or eliminate small leaks. If you're on a budget and just want to nurse the engine along until you can afford an overhaul, such additives may be worth considering.

Unless the engine has obvious serious problems, we recommend an oil change and thorough tune-up before going deeply into diagnosis. If nothing else, this will eliminate potential

When you disassemble an engine, the wear and damage can be obvious or subtle. Seldom will you see parts as mangled as those shown here. It's important to perform thorough diagnostics before disassembly so that you can properly focus your inspections during the overhaul.

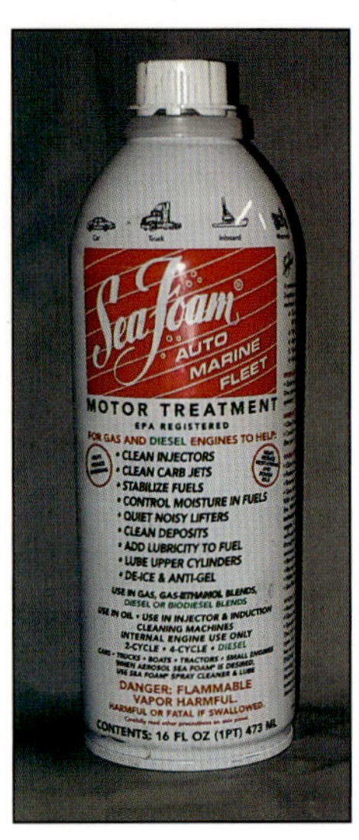

Don't expect to fix serious engine problems with the contents of a bottle, but oil additives can be helpful with certain problems. Additives, such as Sea Foam, can dissolve deposits and potentially free a stuck hydraulic lifter.

small problems and help focus your diagnostic strategy. The information in this chapter will help you decide if the engine needs an overhaul and also what you might expect to see after the engine is disassembled.

If the condition of the engine is a concern because of decreased performance or fuel economy, perform a vacuum test, a power balance test, and a compression test. If the problem is not obvious after these tests, also check camshaft lobe lift and timing chain slack. If the engine is making unusual noises, check the oil pressure and make use of the information in this chapter dealing with noise diagnosis.

Visual Clues

Your eyes (and ears) are your best diagnostic tools. Take some time to thoroughly survey the engine compartment, looking for anything suspicious. A large percentage of problems thought to be internal to the engine end up being simple and obvious.

Smoke

Smoke emitting from the vehicle's tailpipe can provide an indication of internal engine condition. Smoke caused by excessive oil consumption is bluish-gray in color. If there is smoke of this color at the tailpipe, oil is entering the combustion chambers and being burned. This generally indicates internal engine problems, although oil can be drawn into the engine through a malfunctioning positive crankcase ventilation (PCV) system.

Oil burning is often most pronounced during closed-throttle deceleration, when vacuum is high. A good test is to drive the vehicle in a low gear at elevated RPM, then take your foot off the accelerator. You should feel strong engine braking. Watch for blue smoke.

It's often helpful to have someone in another vehicle follow you during this test. Blue smoke during this test generally points to worn valve guides and/or piston rings. Perform a compression test to identify the issue. Blue smoke only at start-up frequently indicates failure of the valve seals.

Loose Components

Sometimes loose external components can cause noises that mimic internal engine noises. Check the belts and pulleys on the front of the engine, as well as the vibration damper. Also check brackets and engine mounts.

Leaks

Engines are often overhauled because of oil consumption. Before deciding that the engine needs an overhaul due to oil consumption, make sure that oil leaks aren't the culprit. Park the vehicle in the same place every day on pavement, then look for oil stains or puddles of oil. Even a few drops can indicate the source of a significant oil loss.

It's not enough to know that your car is leaking oil. You must know how much it's leaking if you're to figure out how much of the oil is disappearing out the tailpipe. Parking over a fresh piece of cardboard every night will help you determine the severity of the oil leak.

When observing drips from underneath the vehicle, keep in mind that engine oil is just one potential source. Transmission and power steering fluids can be mistaken for engine oil. These fluids are less viscous (thinner in consistency) than oil. Also, transmission fluid has a red tinge.

Look carefully under the vehicle to see which component is wet with the fluid. Keep in mind that fluid can be blown rearward during driving, which can make the origin point of the leak more difficult to identify.

If any drips are evident, raise the vehicle and inspect the underside. Sometimes leaks will show up only when the engine is hot, under load, or on a hill. Look for signs of leakage as well as active drips. If a significant oil leak is found, correct it before taking oil consumption measurements.

Oil Consumption

If the engine is consuming oil, this can be a sign that cylinders,

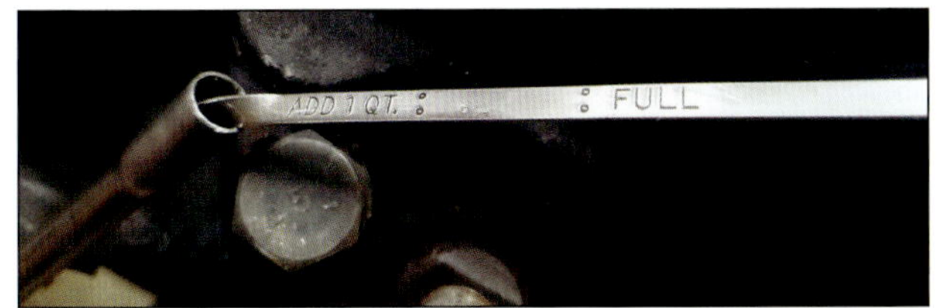

When measuring oil consumption, precision is critical. Check the oil frequently on level ground. Ideally, do it at the same place every time.

pistons, rings, valve seals, and/or valve guides may be worn. A clogged PCV system can also increase oil consumption.

Modern engines in good condition use very little oil. Oil loss between oil changes is frequently undetectable. This is largely attributable to improvements in design and materials used in pistons, piston rings, and valve seals. It's important to understand that Oldsmobile engines were manufactured during a period when most engines had noticeable oil consumption between oil changes.

Do not judge your Oldsmobile engine by comparing it to a new, modern engine. Even for engines built during the same era, normal oil consumption rates vary greatly for a number of reasons. For example, high-performance engines often employ forged pistons that have more clearance between the piston and cylinder wall. It's normal for an engine with forged pistons to consume more oil than an engine with conventional cast pistons.

To measure oil consumption accurately, park the vehicle on a level surface and turn off the engine. Wait several minutes to allow the oil to drain into the oil pan, then remove the dipstick. Wipe the dipstick off and reinsert it fully. Pull it out carefully and read the level. Fill the pan to the "Full" mark with the correct grade and viscosity of oil and note the mileage.

Continue checking the oil level, using this same checking procedure, until 1 quart of oil has been consumed. Again, note the mileage. While engines tend to use oil at different rates, if there is blue exhaust smoke and/or oil consumption higher than about a quart in 700 miles, there's certainly a problem.

Noise Diagnosis

Caution: Keep clear of moving components when performing these checks.

All moving parts can create sounds for various reasons. Often the engine is blamed when the actual problem is in the transmission or driveline. Be sure to isolate the noise. A knocking sound from under the hood could be loose torque converter bolts or a damaged vibration damper.

To isolate a noise, first apply the parking brake and place the transmission in neutral (manual) or park (automatic). Start the engine with the hood open and determine if the noise is actually coming from the engine. Rev the engine slightly and see if the noise increases along with engine speed.

If the noise seems to be coming from the engine and varies with engine speed, it is probably an engine issue, although knocking noises that vary with engine speed are sometimes associated with the flywheel, drive plate, or torque converter.

Identify the type of noise. If it's a squealing sound, check accessory belt tension. Spray some belt dressing on the belts. If the noise goes away, the belts need adjustment or replacement. Another trick is to remove the drive belts and run the engine for a short time to be sure the noise is not coming from the accessories (power steering, water pump, alternator, air-conditioner compressor pulley).

Sounds tend to echo in the engine compartment, which can create diagnosis errors. A small investment in a mechanic's stethoscope will pay off by helping to precisely locate engine noises.

Does the sound occur at crankshaft speed or half of crankshaft speed? Determine this by connecting a timing light to any spark plug wire. Listen and watch the flashing of the light. If the sound occurs every time the light flashes, this is half of crankshaft speed. If the noise occurs twice for every flash, this is crankshaft speed.

Tapping and knocking noises are the most common noise types that are heard when diagnosing engine problems. Knocking sounds that occur at crankshaft speed are usually caused by crankshaft or connecting rod and bearing problems. If the noise occurs at half of crankshaft speed, the source of the noise is likely the lifters, rocker arms, valves, valve springs, or fuel pump. Listen for these sounds near the top of the engine.

A helpful tool for pinpointing the source of a noise is a mechanic's stethoscope. If you don't have one, you can also use a long piece of hose or a long screwdriver. Hold the handle of the screwdriver or end of the hose against your ear and place the tip of the screwdriver or other end of the hose on areas where you suspect problems.

The listening device can be moved around until the sound is most pronounced. Note which cylinder is closest to the noise, then, with the engine off, pull the spark plug wire from the associated cylinder from the distributor cap. Start the engine and see if the noise changes. If the noise goes away or reduces significantly, you may have identified a cylinder that has a bad connecting rod bearing or other problem.

Noises in the upper part of the engine are usually associated with the valvetrain (lifters, pushrods, rocker arms) and are heard as tapping sounds at half of crankshaft speed. With the valve cover removed from the associated cylinder bank, briefly start the engine and allow it to idle slowly. Oil will spray from each rocker arm, so use care to avoid a mess. Special tools are available to deflect the spray, but standing a piece of cardboard up at the lower edge of the cylinder head can help catch and direct the oil back into the cylinder head.

While the engine is running, check that the valves are opening the same amount and that the pushrods are rotating slowly. Press your thumb against the top of each rocker arm, directly above the valve. If the noise stops or lessens, the source of the noise has been found.

First check the valve adjustment (see Chapter 7). If that's okay, remove the rocker arm and pushrod, inspecting them carefully for excessive wear and damage. If there's no problems with the rocker arm or pushrod, the lifter is most likely the problem.

Knocking is the most common noise heard from the lower end of the engine. The source of knocking is usually excessive clearance in the main or connecting rod bearings or low oil pressure.

Connecting rod knock is most pronounced when the throttle is opened briefly and then quickly released. The noise is usually caused by excessive bearing wear or insufficient oil pressure.

A main bearing knock is a low-pitched knock deep within the engine. It is loudest when the engine is first started. It might also be noticed under heavy load. Disconnecting the spark plugs from the adjacent cylinders can sometimes help identify the location of the knock.

Piston slap is most pronounced when the engine is cold, then gets quieter as the engine warms up. Listen at the side of the engine, at each cylinder, just below the cylinder head. A light piston slap may sound dull or hollow, while a heavy piston slap will sound more like a knock or a rattle.

Piston slap will often lessen or go away when the associated cylinder's spark plug is disconnected. Another trick is to slowly retard the ignition timing while listening. If the slap lessens or goes away, the most likely problem is piston slap. Note: High-performance engines equipped with forged pistons run greater piston-to-bore clearance than engines with standard cast pistons. Engines with forged pistons often exhibit some piston slap on cold start, but that should go away when the engine is fully warmed up.

Piston pin problems are heard as a double click at idle and low speeds. Disconnecting the associated spark plug will often cause the noise to go away.

Piston rings can become loose in their grooves due to wear or breakage. This results in a chattering noise that is loudest when accelerating. A leakdown test will help identify this problem.

Spark Plug Condition

Note: If the spark plugs have been in service for some time, the deposits shown will be cumulative and may not accurately represent the engine's current running condition. If there is anything concerning on the plugs, replace them with a new set, operate the vehicle for a week or so, then check them again.

The condition of the spark plug firing end can provide a great deal of information about what is happening in the combustion chamber of the engine. Learning to read spark plugs is a great skill to develop, as it helps both in tuning and engine diagnostics.

Mark each spark plug wire to avoid getting them mixed up. Special markers are commonly available, but using masking tape and a marker also work.

Use compressed air to blow away dirt from around the spark plug holes, which will prevent it from entering the cylinder when the spark plugs are removed. If you don't have an air compressor, a can of compressed air from an office-supply store will work just as well.

Keep the spark plugs organized because each provides a window into the condition of its associated cylinder. When plugs vary in condition from cylinder to cylinder, it's important to understand why. Take note of the brand and number on each spark plug. Compare this to the factory recommendations to be sure that the spark plug is the correct type and heat range.

Carefully examine each plug tip. The ideal condition of the spark plug tip has only a light accumulation of deposits on the insulator, which should have a tan or light gray appearance (as shown here). The side electrode should be shaded between light and dark gray.

The spark plug on the left has shiny black deposits, which indicate oil consumption in the associated cylinder. The spark plug on the right shows sooty black deposits, which indicate that the engine is running rich or the heat range is too cold.

A bright white insulator indicates that the mixture is lean, and the combustion chamber is excessively hot. If this is accompanied by melting of the electrodes or insulator, high temperatures have led to detonation. Detonation may have also damaged the pistons.

Mechanical damage to a spark plug usually means that its "reach" into the combustion chamber is too deep, causing contact with the piston. Another possible cause is that a foreign object has found its way into the cylinder and has been bouncing around, causing damage.

Before beginning, drive at highway speed and allow the engine to warm up thoroughly. Do not allow the engine to idle excessively. Turn off the engine and wait until it cools to avoid getting burned by touching hot components. Label the spark plug wires so that you can reinstall them on the correct spark plugs.

Plugs that are wet with oil indicate the engine is consuming a large amount of oil in the combustion chamber. This is also associated with bluish smoke emitting from the tailpipe. This level of oil consumption indicates an engine overhaul is needed.

If the plugs have shiny black deposits, some oil is seeping into the cylinders. The engine is worn. If you're not ready to overhaul the engine yet, try installing a spark plug with a hotter heat range (to help burn off deposits) and delay repair/overhaul.

Sooty black deposits on all of the plugs usually indicate the engine is running rich. If only some (or one) plugs have sooty deposits, it usually indicates a misfire due to an ignition problem or low compression. Sooty carbon deposits are *not* an indication of oil consumption (oil deposits are wet and/or shiny).

If all of thc plugs are the same heat range but there is a large variance in rich/lean indications among the cylinders, it's likely that there is a vacuum leak at the intake manifold. It is most likely at the mating surface between the cylinder head and intake manifold.

Vacuum Gauge Usage

An inexpensive vacuum gauge is a great investment that will help diagnose a myriad of engine problems. Careful interpretation of the readings is important, though, as they can be misleading and easily confused. Be sure to confirm your findings with other tests.

When interpreting readings, note the reading as well as the amount and rate of needle movement. All are important. Gauges are usually graduated in inches of mercury (in-Hg).

Altitude can cause readings to vary a bit, so be sure to note the reading when no vacuum is applied. Find a vacuum source on the intake manifold (not the carburetor) and "tee" into it with a three-way hose connector.

With the engine warmed to normal operating temperature, put the transmission in park (automatic) or neutral (manual). Set the parking brake and chock the wheels.

A healthy stock Oldsmobile engine usually generates about 18 to 22 in-Hg at idle. There should not be any significant fluctuation on the gauge. High-performance engines with long-duration camshafts will generate less vacuum. Also, engines manufactured during the "smog era" (1972 and later) sometimes have lower vacuum due to differences in valve and ignition timing.

The following are typical readings that are encountered when checking vacuum. Keep in mind that a reading might indicate multiple problems.

A vacuum gauge is an essential diagnostic tool. It can indicate a myriad of problems in the engine, as well as in the ignition, fuel, and exhaust systems.

Connect the vacuum gauge to the intake manifold vacuum with a tee fitting. Make sure there are no disconnected hoses during the test because they can affect the readings.

Low and Steady Needle

If the reading is low and steady, it indicates a vacuum leak, retarded ignition timing, or incorrect valve timing. Vacuum leaks are commonly caused by disconnected or deteriorated vacuum hoses or poor sealing at gaskets, such as at the carburetor base or intake manifold-to-cylinder-head joint. Check for vacuum leaks and that ignition timing is correct. If you still can't find the problem, check for timing chain slack, as described in this chapter.

Low and Fluctuating Needle

If the needle is low and fluctuates about 3 to 8 inches, the problem is likely a vacuum leak at an intake port.

Needle Drops at Regular Intervals

If the needle drops several inches at regular intervals, there is likely a valve leak. Check compression and also perform a leakdown test.

Needle Drops at Irregular Intervals

An irregular needle drop is likely caused by an ignition misfire or a sticking valve. Read the spark plugs and perform a compression check.

Needle Vibrates Rapidly

If the needle rapidly vibrates within a range of about 4 in-Hg at idle, the valve guides may be leaking. This reading is also associated with

Compression gauges are commonly available from auto parts sources. It is best to get one that includes hoses and adapters to fit different vehicles. Purchase a quality gauge because some of the inexpensive gauges can give inaccurate readings.

Disable the ignition system before beginning the compression check. If the engine is equipped with HEI (1975-and-later models), the easiest way is to disconnect the battery wire connector on the side of the distributor cap.

blue smoke in the exhaust, most pronounced on start-up. Other possible causes are a leaking intake manifold gasket, leaking head gasket, ignition misfire, leaking valves, or weak valve springs.

Needle Fluctuates Slightly

Slight fluctuation of about 1 inch or so often indicates ignition problems. Check the spark plugs, spark plug wires, and distributor cap/rotor.

Needle Fluctuates Greatly

A needle that fluctuates greatly usually indicates a head gasket leak or a cylinder that has serious problems. Check compression and perform a leakdown test.

Needle "Hunts" Slowly

If the needle slowly moves across a wide range, there may be a clog in the PCV system, incorrectly adjusted idle mixture, or a vacuum leak at the carburetor or intake manifold gasket.

Needle Returns Slowly After Revving

Accelerate the engine to about 2,500 rpm, then release the throttle quickly. Under normal conditions, the needle should drop almost to zero, then rise slightly above the normal idle reading before returning to the normal idle reading. Slow return of vacuum that also does not peak when the throttle is released indicates worn piston rings. If there is a long delay before the vacuum returns, there's a restriction in the exhaust, most commonly the catalytic converter.

Compression Check

A compression check can help to determine the condition of pistons, piston rings, valves, cylinder heads, and head gaskets. Before performing the check, run the engine until normal operating temperature is reached. If the engine does not run, the test can still be performed, although the results will not be as precise.

Caution: Exhaust manifolds or headers are very hot and in close proximity to the spark plugs. Be careful not to get burned. It's a good idea to wear heat-resistant gloves during the check.

Remove all of the spark plugs from the engine. Open the throttle and find a way to hold it in this position. Usually, it can be blocked or wired in the open position.

Disable the ignition system. HEI is an abbreviation for high energy ignition. On non-HEI systems (1974 and earlier), detach the coil wire from the center of the distributor cap and ground it on the engine block. On HEI systems, disconnect the battery connector from the side of the distributor cap.

Install the compression gauge in the number-1 spark plug hole.

Turn the ignition key to Start. An assistant may be needed to crank the

A remote starter switch allows the starter to be operated while you're under the hood and observing the compression gauge. Without it, an assistant is needed to turn the ignition key during the compression test.

A "wet test" can quickly determine if low compression is due to worn piston rings or upper-engine problems, such as a blown head gasket or leaking valves. Just add a few squirts of oil to the low cylinder and repeat the compression test.

engine while you observe the gauge. Another option is a remote starter switch. As the engine is cranked, the gauge needle should rise rapidly on the first compression stroke, then more slowly on successive strokes.

Crank the engine until the gauge needle stops moving, which is usually about five compression strokes. If the first compression stroke is low and gradually increases with each stroke, the piston rings are likely worn. If the compression starts low and remains low on successive strokes, the problem could be valves that are not sealing, a blown head gasket, or a crack in the cylinder head's combustion chamber.

Repeat the procedure for the other seven cylinders. Record each reading. In a healthy engine, the readings from all cylinders should be within 20 percent of each other. Compression readings can vary significantly from engine to engine, so don't be overly concerned if the readings are different than on another engine. Instead, look at how each cylinder compares to the others.

If any of the readings are low, repeat the test with a few squirts of oil added in each cylinder. This is known as a "wet test." If the oil increases compression, it indicates worn piston rings. If there is no increase in compression, the problem is in the top end of the engine. It could be bad valves, a blown head gasket, or a crack in the combustion chamber.

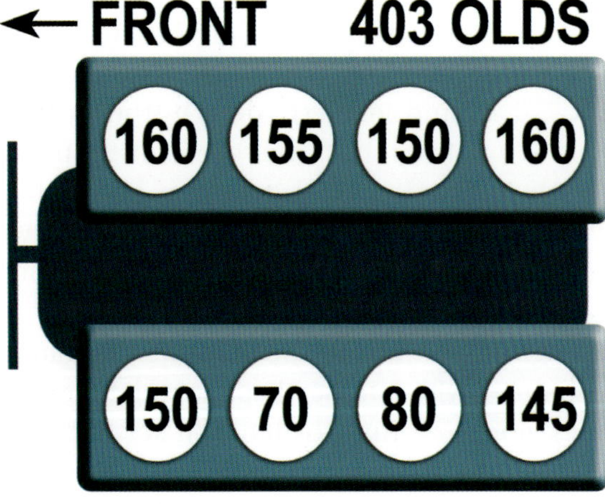

Carefully record the compression readings to compare them. The two low cylinders in this test are adjacent to each other (numbers 3 and 5). The problem turned out to be a blown head gasket between the cylinders.

Adjacent cylinders with equally low compression (much lower than the others) indicate a blown head gasket (blown between the cylinders). Another indication of a blown head gasket is coolant in the combustion chambers or oil pan. Coolant in the oil gives the oil a milky appearance.

If compression is very low (less than 100 psi) or varies greatly among cylinders, perform a leakdown test, which will give more exacting information about the source of the cylinder leakage.

Oil Pressure Check

Engine oil pressure is a good indicator of the condition of the main and connecting rod bearings. Excessive bearing clearance and/or damage leads to lower oil pressure. Low oil pressure can also be caused by a worn oil pump or low-viscosity (thin consistency) oil.

Remove the dipstick and check the condition of the oil. If it's dirty or seems very thin, change the oil before the check.

Remove the oil pressure sending unit and install a gauge in its place. Run the engine at normal operating temperature and note the reading at idle. In a healthy engine with the correct oil viscosity, the pressure shouldn't drop below 20 psi at idle.

valve is not seating. If you can hear air escaping into the intake manifold, an intake valve is not seating. Remove the oil filler cap and listen to check if air is escaping past the piston rings (commonly known as "blowby").

Test the remaining cylinders. Rotate the crankshaft clockwise exactly 90 degrees to get to the next cylinder in the firing order. It's important to mark the vibration damper carefully to ensure precision of rotation. Inexpensive degree-marking tapes are available that adhere to the outer circumference of the damper.

Cooling System Tests

An engine with a blown head gasket, a cracked block, or a cracked cylinder head will likely exhibit overheating, steam emanating from the exhaust, bubbling in the coolant reservoir, unexplained coolant loss, and/or coolant in the oil, which gives the oil a milky appearance. These problems are usually caused by severe overheating or coolant freezing in the engine block due to inadequate antifreeze protection.

Diagnosis starts with checking the oil on the dipstick. If the oil has a milky appearance, there's almost certainly an internal coolant leak, which also causes an unexplained increase in oil level.

With the engine cold, check the coolant in the reservoir and in the radiator. If oil is floating on top of the coolant, this is a sign of a blown head gasket. With the engine running, observe the coolant in the reservoir (if equipped). If there is bubbling, suspect a blown head gasket or a crack in the cylinder head or block.

Steam coming from the tailpipe after the engine is fully warmed up means coolant is entering the combustion chamber due to a blown head gasket or a crack in the cylinder head. Some steam is normal during warm-up due to condensation in the exhaust system. When the steam continues after warm-up, be concerned.

A cooling system pressure tester is a great diagnostic tool that will help to find internal or external coolant leaks. The tester is a hand pump with a gauge that connects to the radiator filler neck. With the engine cold, use the pump to pressurize the cooling system to the pressure indicated on the radiator cap. The gauge needle should remain steady at this reading.

If the gauge needle drops, there's a leak. External leaks are usually obvious, although a leak in the heater core can be hard to identify. If a heater core leak is suspected, pinch off the two heater hoses and see if the pressure now holds.

A cooling system pressure tester is not required but is helpful in finding coolant leaks. If pressure leaks down, there's a leak. If the leak is not external, it's inside the engine. The most common cause of an internal coolant leak is a blown head gasket.

A combustion leak detector can help identify a blown head gasket or a crack in the engine block or head. The tester draws gases from the cooling system through a special test fluid. If the test fluid changes color from blue to yellow, there is a combustion leak into the cooling system.

If testing indicates an internal coolant leak, remove the spark plugs and check their firing tips. If a firing tip is clean and/or wet with coolant, it indicates an internal leak affecting that cylinder. The plug tip is being steam-cleaned by the boiling coolant in the cylinder.

If it is determined that there is an internal coolant leak, remove the cylinder heads and inspect carefully. If the head gasket(s) are blown, check for cylinder head warpage and cracks in the heads and cylinder block.

If you suspect a blown head gasket or another internal leak, perform a combustion leak test. Testers are commonly available and work on the simple principle that combustion gases will change the color of the special test fluid.

ENGINE REMOVAL AND DISASSEMBLY

Caution: Removing an engine is difficult, dirty, and potentially dangerous. When under the vehicle, be sure that it's safely supported. When removing a heavy component, be sure to have a solid grip on it before removing the bolts. When removing transmission-to-engine bolts or engine mount bolts, be absolutely sure both the engine and the transmission are safely supported. Never position any body parts underneath heavy components as they are removed.

Engine removal requires some specialized tools and equipment (see Chapter 2) and can only be done on a level concrete or asphalt surface. Concrete is preferable, as jack stand bases will tend to sink into asphalt.

This is a messy job. No matter how careful you are, you will almost certainly spill coolant and likely some transmission fluid and oil as well. Be prepared with oil absorbent (or clay cat litter) and lots of rags. It's also a good idea to wear gloves, as old engines are greasy!

To make the job a little cleaner, spray the engine down with engine degreaser that's commonly available from auto parts stores. Allow it to soak in, then spray it off with a pressure nozzle on a garden hose. Better than a garden hose is a home pressure washer or the high-pressure spray wand at a self-service car wash. Just be sure that the cleaning methods do not violate any environmental guidelines.

Be organized! When the engine goes back together, you will need to remember where all the components attach and which bolts go where. It's best to keep bolts stored with their associated components. Use labeled plastic bags and boxes. Many times, components are secured by bolts of different lengths. Be sure to keep track of which hole each bolt goes in. Take lots of photos. You'll need them!

Before beginning, be sure to set the parking brake and block the rear wheels. Place the transmission in neutral to prevent a release of tension between the transmission and engine when the engine is detached.

The procedure described is for a typical car with an automatic transmission. If you have a manual transmission, remove the transmission and the clutch prior to engine removal.

The following photos and captions describe the job. Take your time and be sure each step is complete before moving onto the next.

Remove the Hood and Disconnect Components

1 ***Disconnect both terminals of the battery: negative first, then positive. Disconnecting the negative terminal first prevents accidental grounding when removing the positive terminal. Clamps like the ones shown are used on early models. Later models have side-terminal batteries that are disconnected using a 5/16-inch wrench or socket.***

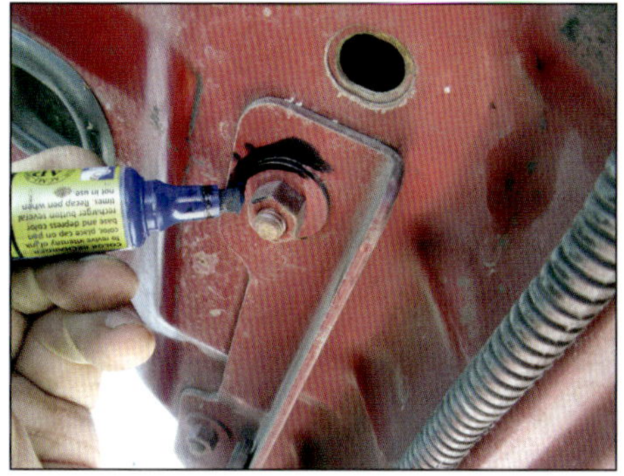

2 *Using a permanent marker or a scratch awl, mark around each hood attachment bolt so that you'll be able to correctly align the hood when it is reinstalled.*

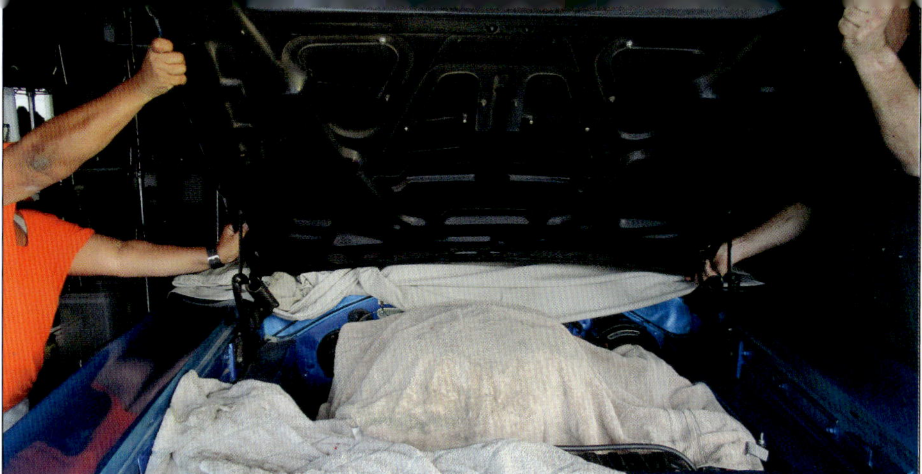

3 *Get help to remove the hood. Pad the rear of the hood to protect the windshield. Hold the hood securely at both sides and remove the front bolts first. The hood is heavy and will move after the last bolts are removed. Move the hood forward, then up. It can be stored vertically against a wall, front up, with padding at the bottom. Wire the latch securely to the wall. Storing the hood flat is asking for a dent!*

4 *Once the hood is off, start disconnecting all the wiring and hoses on top of the engine. The negative battery cable is usually connected to the engine. Sometimes there are secondary ground cables, so inspect carefully.*

5 *Many of the electrical connectors will simply pull off, such as this spade-type connector used for the oil pressure sending unit. These types of connectors tend to become corroded and loose over time. Note any connectors that are loose or damaged so that they can be replaced later. Make sure to label all wires as they are disconnected. You may think you will remember all of them later, but you probably won't.*

6 *Some connectors have tabs that must be pried away with a small screwdriver before the connector will pull off. Shown here is the battery wire at the HEI distributor used on later models. Models with tachometers will also have a tach wire next to it.*

7 *This later-style coolant temperature sensor has a tab that can either be pried with a screwdriver or lifted with a finger. These types of connectors can take a little effort to disconnect if they've never previously been disconnected. Take your time and gently rock the connector back and forth while pulling up gently with the tab lifted.*

8 *Later-model carburetors have an electrically assisted choke. Disconnect this wire at the right side of the carburetor.*

9 There are two electrical connectors at the back of the alternator: one larger wire (the output wire) that is secured by a nut (left) and a plastic connector with two or more wires (right). On later-style alternators, lift a tab to disconnect the plastic connector.

10 The 1974-and-earlier models have a separate cylinder-style coil. The large center wire and the two small wires must be disconnected, which often requires an 11/32 wrench or nut-driver. Be aware that this size is not included with most wrench sets!

11 You'll find many vacuumhoseson1971-and-later engines. Label them so that you can reinstall them correctly. It's best to replace all the hoses during reassembly. Old hoses don't seat well after they've been disconnected.

12 On most models, the throttle cable can be easily pulled or pried off. Shown here is an early type that requires prying up a safety tab on a clip while sliding it off. Most automatic transmission models also have a TV cable. Be sure both cables are detached from the carburetor and the brackets on the engine.

Drain Coolant and Disconnect Hoses

1 Use at least two large drain pans to avoid making a mess of your driveway and the environment. The pan used for coolant should be larger than a standard oil drain pan and capable of holding at least 2 gallons of coolant.

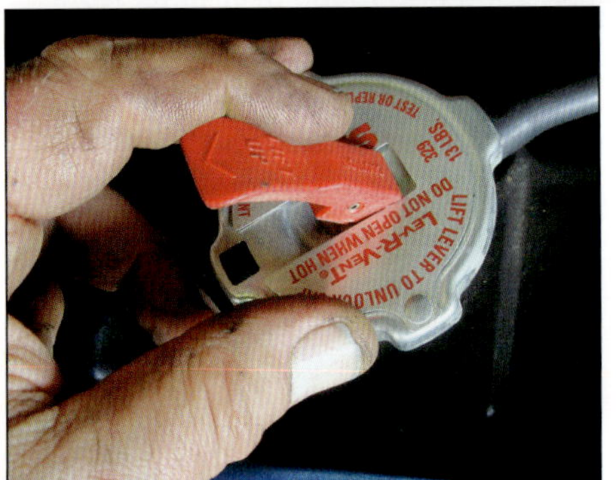

2 Now, it's time to drain the coolant from the radiator. First, remove the radiator cap, which will allow the coolant to flow out more quickly and steadily. If the cap is left on, the draining coolant will create a suction that slows coolant flow.

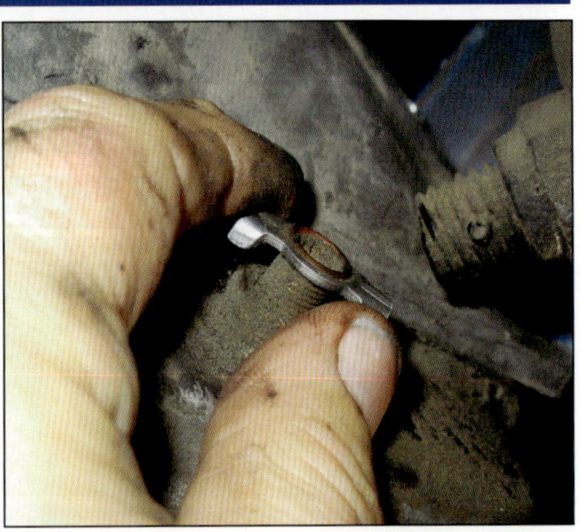

3 Place a large drain pan under the radiator petcock and rotate it counterclockwise until it is fully seated. Be sure all coolant has drained before disconnecting hoses.

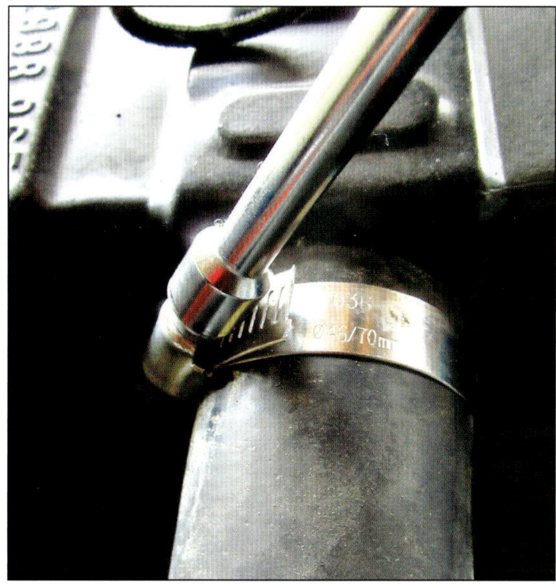

4 *Remove the upper radiator hose. There are usually aftermarket worm-type clamps on the radiator and heater hoses. They can be removed with a nut-driver, as shown here, or a flat-blade screwdriver. If you have a nut driver, it's a better choice because it won't slip.*

5 *Also disconnect the smaller-diameter heater hoses. One is on the water pump, and the other is attached to the heater control valve at the rear of the engine on the passenger's side.*

6 *Sometimes old hoses adhere to their fittings. It's easy to damage the fittings if you pull too aggressively. This special hook breaks the adhesion around the fitting, making the hose pull off more easily.*

7 *If you don't have the special tool, gently grip the hose with pliers and rotate the hose, which will often break the adhesion. Don't grip too tightly or you can damage the fitting.*

8 *As a last resort, the hose can be carefully slit with a sharp utility knife and peeled away from the fitting.*

9 *The fan and shroud should be removed together. First, remove the four bolts that attach the fan to the water pump hub. If the fan moves as you try to loosen the bolts, try tapping on the wrench with a soft-face hammer, which will usually break the bolt loose.*

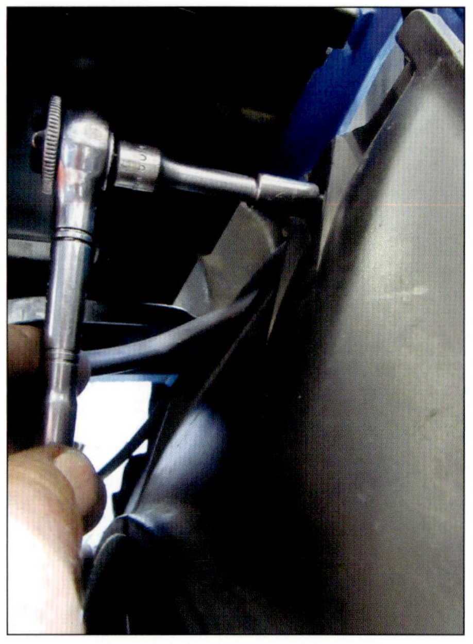

10 *Next, remove the four bolts that attach the fan shroud to the radiator or radiator support.*

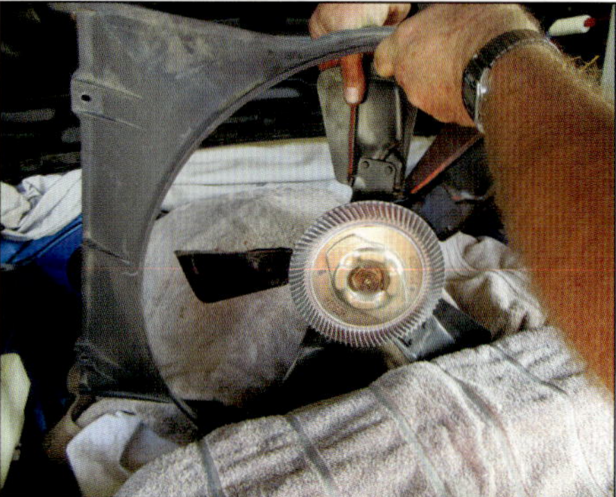

11 *Gently work the fan off the water pump hub and remove the fan and shroud at the same time. Do all of this slowly and carefully, as it's easy to damage the radiator that's made of thin aluminum or copper. With the fan removed, you can usually remove the water pump pulley, which will also release belt tension and allow the belt(s) to be removed.*

12 *Place a drain pan underneath the lower radiator hose and disconnect the hose from the radiator. Be ready for the coolant to splash everywhere. It usually does!*

Remove Radiator and Transmission Lines

1 *If the car has an automatic transmission, use an appropriately sized flare-nut wrench to disconnect the transmission cooler lines. It is best to buy a full set of these wrenches, as you'll need other sizes as you further disassemble the engine.*

2 *The automatic transmission cooler lines are attached to the bottom or side radiator tank. Sometimes, a backup wrench is needed to hold the fitting on the tank so that it doesn't damage the tank or twist the line. Keep a drain pan underneath and plug the lines to prevent further leakage.*

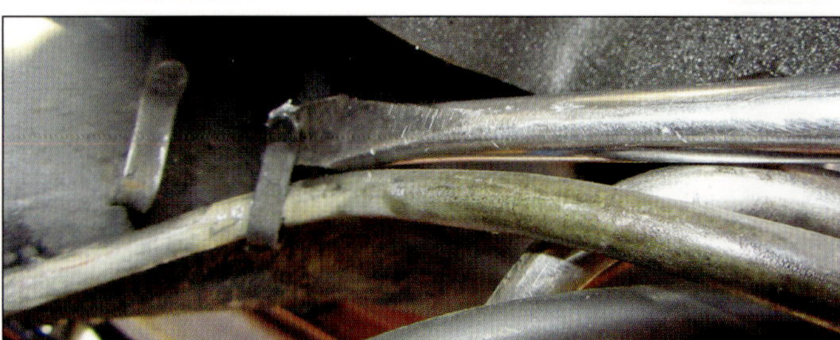

3 *The transmission lines are often clipped to the side of the engine. Disengage the clips so the lines don't get bent when the engine comes out. Sometimes it's easier to unclip the lines from below, in which case you can wait until you raise the car later in this procedure.*

4 *Remove the radiator mounting bolts (there are normally four) and carefully lift out the radiator. Most commonly the radiator is secured in place by a bracket above the radiator. Unbolt it and the radiator lifts out.*

Remove Accessories and Distributor

1 Remove the crankshaft pulley bolts and remove the pulley, disengaging any remaining belts. The center bolt can stay in place for now.

2 If the alternator bolts are easy to access, remove them and lift off the alternator. If they are difficult to get to, leave the alternator in place during engine removal (arrows).

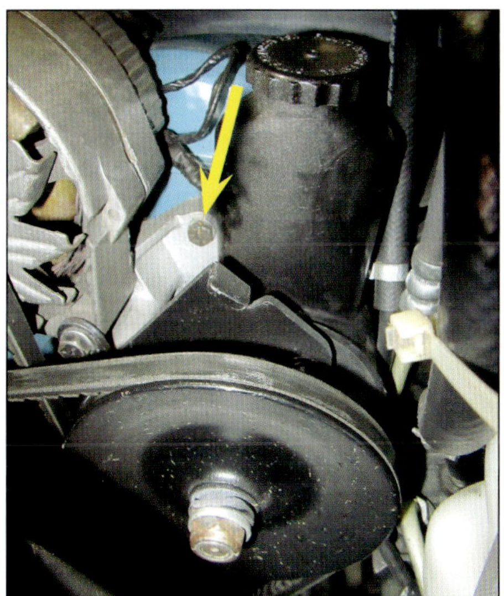

3 Unbolt the power steering pump, together with its bracket. Tie it up out of the way with the hoses still attached. Do the same with the air-conditioner compressor. This pump has one front bracket bolt (arrow) and a bracket nut at the rear of the pump. The photo shows the alternator installed, but it should already be removed. The AIR (smog) pump can be difficult to access. You can leave it in place for now.

4 Locate the distributor at the back of the engine and remove the distributor cap. It is secured by spring-loaded fasteners. Press a flat-blade screwdriver firmly down onto each fastener and rotate it 90 degrees counterclockwise. The 1974-and-earlier models have two fasteners. The 1975-and-later models have four fasteners.

5 Sometimes the distributor cap can be moved off the distributor and out of the way enough to remove the distributor. If not, remove the wires from the cap first. On 1975-and-later models, a wire retainer must be removed by prying open two clips.

6 The wire retainer then lifts off, providing access to the wires.

7 *Remove each wire by twisting and pulling at the boot.*

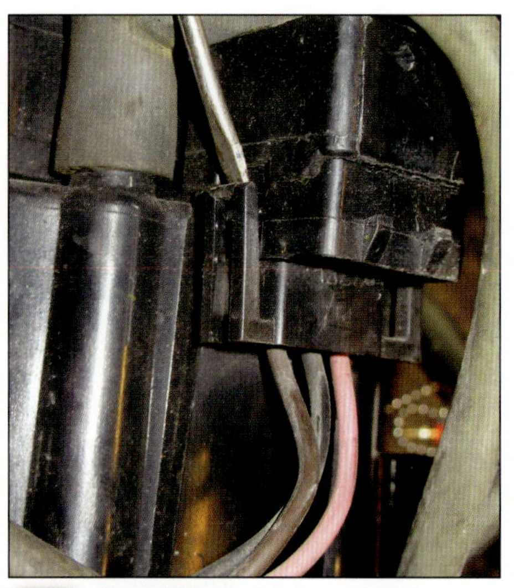

8 *On 1975-and-later models, remove this wiring connector, then remove the distributor cap.*

9 *Most cars from the mid-1980s on have an additional electrical connector on the distributor base. It is secured by a lift-tab that can usually be operated with a finger.*

10 *The distributor is secured to the engine by a bolt/clamp. While it can usually be removed with a 1/2-inch wrench or socket, a special tool with a cranked end (shown) makes the job easier.*

11 *If the distributor does not rotate freely with the bolt/clamp removed, it may need to be rotated with an open-end wrench on the distributor housing flats.*

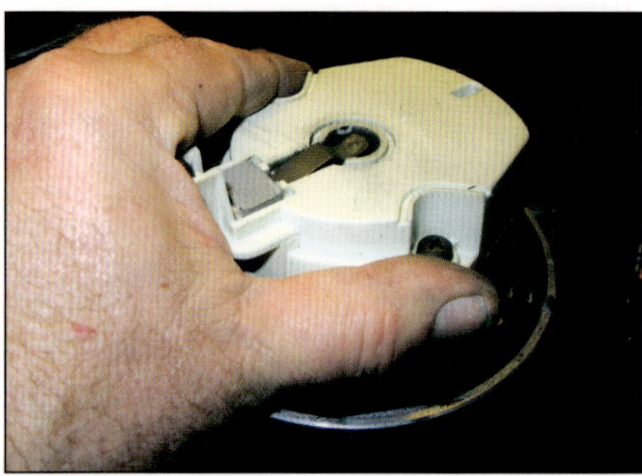

12 *The distributor should be able to be pulled straight up. Since the distributor drive gear is bevel-cut, it is helpful to turn the rotor counter-clockwise while pulling up on the distributor.*

13 *Plug the distributor hole in the engine to prevent fasteners and debris from falling in.*

14 *Raise the front of the vehicle and support it safely on jack stands.*

Drain Remaining Fluids

1 *Position a drain pan underneath the drain plug at the bottom of the oil pan, then unscrew the drain plug and allow the oil to fully drain. Screw the plug back in place to prevent perpetual dripping.*

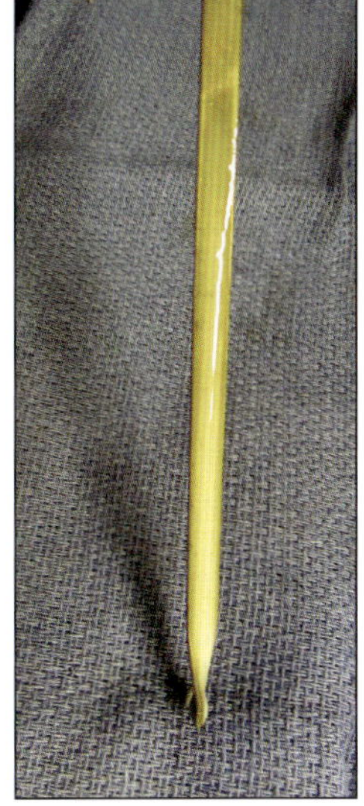

The condition of the oil can sometimes give a clue of problems within the engine. Milky oil like this generally indicates a blown head gasket or a cracked cylinder head.

2 *Use an oil filter wrench to unscrew the oil filter that's located at the right rear of the engine. Be sure there's a drain pan underneath, as oil will drain.*

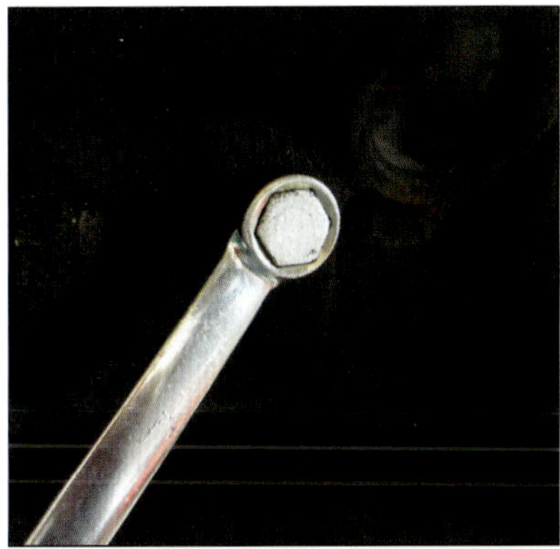

3 *There's a coolant drain plug on the left and right side of the engine block. If they're not too difficult to remove, it's good to do so as it will drain additional coolant that will otherwise spill when the engine is removed.*

Disconnect the Engine

1 *Disconnect the exhaust pipes from the exhaust manifolds on the engine. These bolts are often rusted in place. If they are rusted, apply penetrating oil to the threads and let it soak in for at least 30 minutes.*

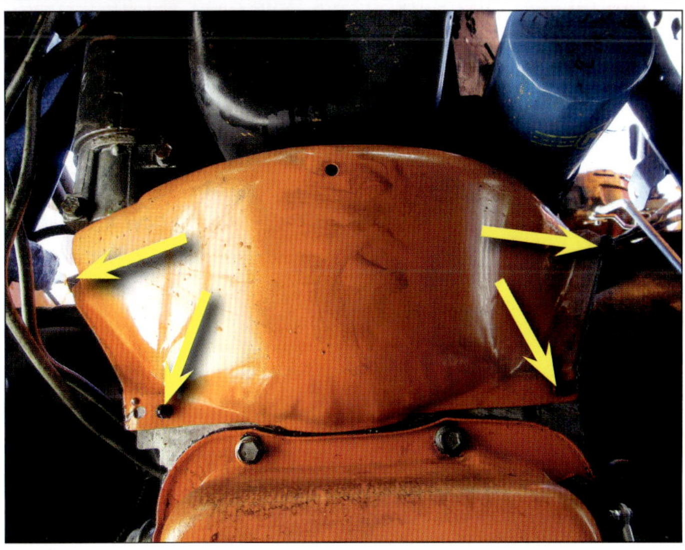

2 *Remove the four torque converter cover bolts (arrows).*

3 *Disconnect the wires from the solenoid on top of the starter. If they're difficult to access, sometimes it's easier to unbolt the starter and position it for better access to the wires.*

4 *Remove the two starter mounting bolts at the front of the starter (arrows).*

5 *Remove the rubber hoses from the fuel pump.*

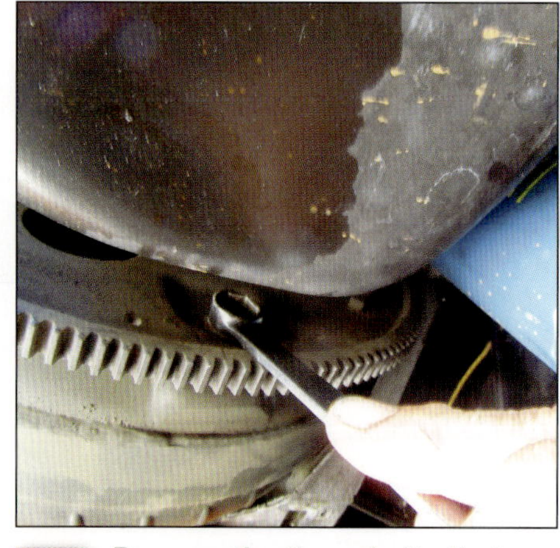

6 *Remove the three bolts that attach the drive plate to the torque converter. If steady force on the wrench causes the engine to turn, strike the wrench sharply with a mallet while holding the wrench in place at the bolt end. Use a 6-point box-end wrench for added strength.*

7 *Rotate the engine to access all the converter bolts. This can be done using a pry bar or a large screwdriver on the drive plate ring gear teeth.*

8 *After removing the last converter bolt, mark the relationship between the converter and the drive plate.*

9 *Slide the converter back, away from the drive plate to be sure it doesn't interfere with engine removal.*

10 Support the front of the transmission so it doesn't fall when the engine is removed. Here a chain is being used. Other options are to use a jack under the transmission pan or to secure the top of the transmission bellhousing from under the hood. If you use a jack, the vehicle will have to remain stationary after engine removal.

11 Remove the six bolts that attach the engine to the transmission. This is best done with a flexible socket and a 3-foot-long extension. In some cases, it might be easier to access the upper bolts from above the engine compartment.

Remove the Engine

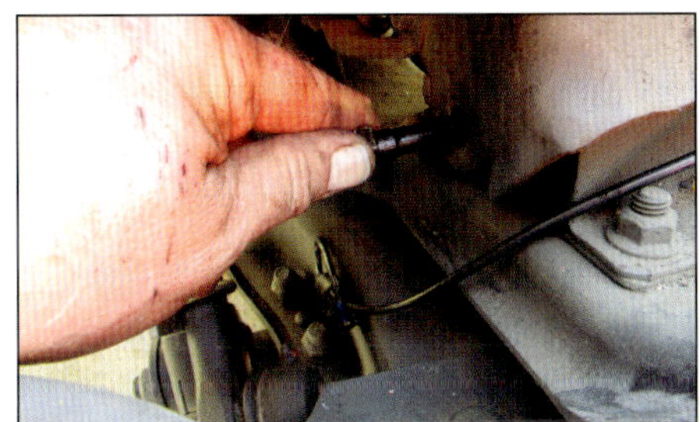

1 Remove the engine-mount through bolts. There are two of them: one on each side of the engine. Use a long punch and hammer to drive the bolt out far enough to remove by hand.

2 Bolt a heavy-duty chain to the engine. The usual method is to remove one bolt from the front and rear of the cylinder head or intake manifold, on opposite sides. Install longer high-strength bolts in their place through the chain ends, using thick washers. The bolts should be long enough to engage all the threads in the bolt holes.

3 A load leveler makes it easier to remove the engine, as it allows the engine to tilt to the perfect angle to clear obstacles during removal. If you use the single-chain method described earlier, just be sure to place the hook of the engine hoist as close as possible to the engine's center of mass.

4 *Another option for attaching the hoist to the engine is to use a lift plate like this. It attaches to the carburetor mount on the intake manifold. Use long, high-strength fasteners.*

5 *Now, lift the engine slowly and carefully. It's best to have a friend who can make sure the engine does not contact anything and that you haven't missed disconnecting anything. Here the cylinder heads were previously removed and the head bolts were used as mounting points for the chain. Unbolt and remove the drive plate from the back of the engine.*

6 *Carefully maneuver the engine to the base of the engine stand. Loosen the large bolts/nuts and position the arms to align with the upper and lower transmission mounting bolt holes. Install high-strength bolts (arrows) to attach the engine to the stand.*

Remove External Components

1 *Once the engine is mounted securely, start disassembly by removing the spark plug wires. If they are still attached to the distributor cap, leave them there and mark the spark plug end of the wires with the associated cylinder number. This will allow you to match up the lengths of the new wires. Don't cheap out and install old wires on a new engine!*

The spark plug on the left shows carbon fouling from a rich mixture. That's probably a carburetor problem. Seven plugs looked like the one on the left. The number-2 plug on the right shows oil fouling. Somehow oil was finding its way into the cylinder.

2 *Remove the PCV valve from the valve cover. The valve should rattle when it is shaken. A stuck PCV valve can cause rough running, noise, oil leaks, and excessive oil consumption. This PCV valve is bad but is not the source of the oil consumption in our number-2 cylinder. A stuck PCV valve would affect all cylinders, not just one.*

3 *Remove the vacuum hose from the EGR valve. To open this unique clip, use long-nose pliers.*

4 *Two bolts secure the EGR valve to the intake manifold.*

5 *Use a flare-nut wrench as well as a backup wrench when disconnecting the fuel line from the carburetor.*

6 *A flare-nut wrench and backup wrench are also required when disconnecting the fuel line from the fuel pump.*

7 *Starting in the late 1970s, most factory carburetors had an electric choke that also has a heat tube. Disconnect the heat tube with a flare-nut wrench.*

8 *On stock Quadrajet 4-barrel carburetors, the two front mounting bolts are at the top of the carburetor.*

9 *The two rear carburetor mounting bolts are at the base of the carburetor.*

10 *The choke heat tube is attached to the intake manifold by two bolts. Pull carefully up to remove it.*

11 *A variety of vacuum hoses and check valves are found on later models. Carefully note how they're installed. Take pictures, as you're likely to forget how they're connected by the time you're ready to reassemble the engine.*

12 *Now is the time to remove vacuum valves and other items that are threaded into the intake manifold. They're harder to remove when the intake manifold is off the engine.*

13 *The heater control valve (at the right rear of the engine) should be replaced during overhaul, as it's a common failure item and is difficult to replace when the engine is installed.*

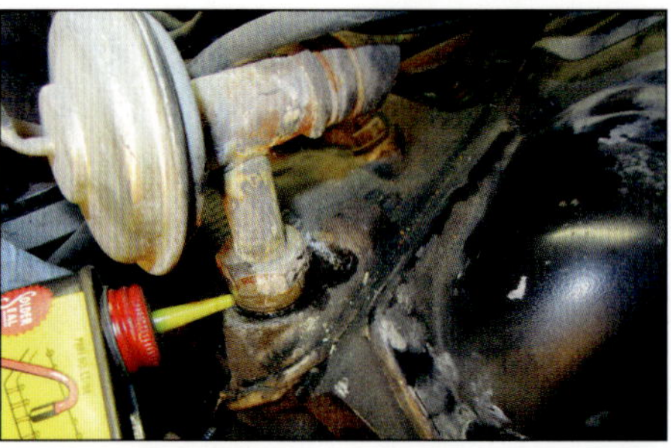

14 *If the heater control valve is difficult to remove due to corrosion, apply penetrating oil to the threads and allow it to soak in. If you don't have a large enough open-end wrench to unscrew the fitting, use a large adjustable wrench. Use care because it's easy to round off the corners on the fittings.*

15 *Don't remove the oil pressure sending unit at this time because the intake manifold is in the way.*

Remove Intake Manifold and Valve Covers

1 *Disconnect the hose from the tube attached to the thermostat housing.*

2 *Remove the two bolts from thermostat housing and lift it off.*

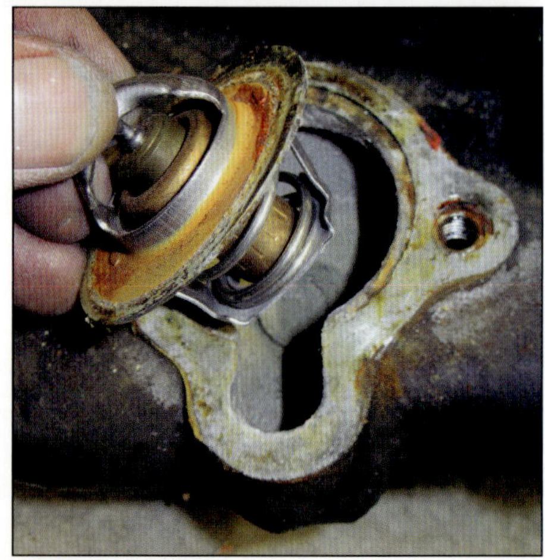

3 *Now, the thermostat can be pulled straight up.*

4 *The thermostat should always be replaced during overhaul, but inspect it for signs of failure. If it's stuck closed or not opening fully, it's a sign that the engine has overheated, likely blowing the head gaskets, warping the heads, and possibly cracking the cylinder heads.*

5 *Remove the nuts/bolts that secure each valve cover and lift off the covers. If needed, gently tap the covers to break the gasket seal. The 1977-and-later engines have 5 nuts/bolts per valve cover, while earlier models have 10 nuts per cover (arrows).*

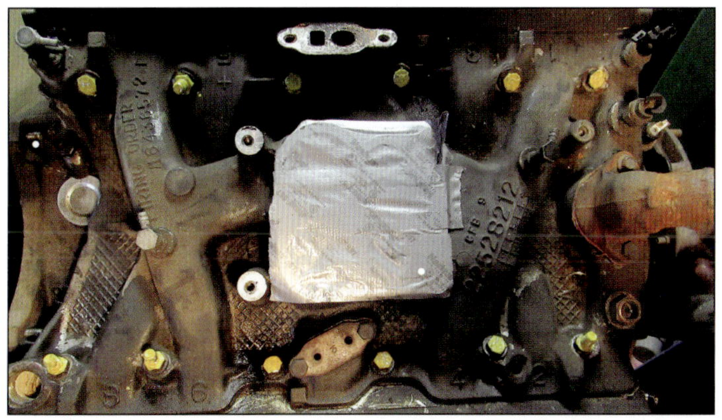

6 *Remove the 12 bolts attaching the intake manifold. If it sticks to the heads, pry gently, just not at a gasket surface. Some of the bolts have studs at the tops. Note their location so they can be correctly placed during reassembly.*

7 *Many engines have a tin valley tray that also serves as the intake manifold gasket. It should lift out easily.*

8 *Take note of cooling system corrosion that may have led to overheating.*

Here's why the number-2 spark plug was oil fouled. The number-2 intake port (left) is wet with oil, but the adjacent number-4 intake port is dry. Intake vacuum was drawing oil from the valley area through an improperly sealing intake gasket. This can be caused by uneven machining on the cylinder head or intake manifold.

9 *Now, you can easily unscrew the oil-pressure sending unit. Aren't you glad you waited? If the sending unit is stuck on tight, a special oil pressure sending unit socket can be used, as shown on page 91.*

Disassemble the Valvetrain

1 *Remove the rocker arm pivot mounting bolts. Loosen the two bolts at each pivot a quarter turn at a time, working back and forth, and don't apply too much force. The pivots are easily damaged.*

2 *Each rocker arm pivot serves two valves.*

Be very careful when removing the pivots, as they are aluminum and break easily.

3 Store the rocker arms and pivots in order so they can be returned to their original locations. Well-organized parts also allow for precise inspection that helps with failure diagnosis.

4 The pushrods can be pulled straight out. Note the tab, which should be at the top of the pushrod.

5 Organize the pushrods so they can be returned to their original locations on reassembly.

6 On later models with roller lifters, remove the bolts and lift off the lifter guide retainer.

7 On models with roller lifters, also remove the eight "dog-bone" roller lifter retainers.

8 The lifters will usually pull out easily. Use a pick-type tool to pull up gently on the wire clip.

9 *Store the lifters so they can be returned to their original locations. For conventional flat lifters, this is critical if the original camshaft and lifters will be reused. Mixing up the lifters on reassembly can lead to accelerated wear. Even if the plan is to install a new cam and lifters, keeping lifters in order can be helpful in diagnosis.*

10 *If the lifters do not easily lift out of their bores, a special tool like this can be used to pull them out. This tool is a slide-hammer that creates upward force. It's kind of the inverse of a regular hammer.*

Remove the Water Pump, Timing Cover, and Fuel Pump

1 *Remove the bolt from the center of the harmonic balancer. An impact gun works best for this, but you can also remove it with a breaker bar after securing the crankshaft so it doesn't rotate.*

2 *Now, pull the balancer off using a bolt-type puller. Use a large screwdriver between the puller bolts to lock the crankshaft in place as you tighten the puller draw bolt.*

3 *Remove the eight bolts that secure the water pump. The bottom four bolts secure the timing cover and are best removed after the water pump is off.*

4 *If the water pump does not pull off easily, tap it with a mallet to break the gasket seal. Hold the pump so that it does not fall.*

5 *Check the balancer hub for wear caused by contact with the crankshaft front seal. If there's a wear ridge that can catch your fingernail, either replace the balancer or fix it with a repair sleeve. Repair sleeves are commonly available from parts sources.*

6 *After the lower four timing cover bolts are removed, carefully separate the timing cover from the engine. The cover must clear two alignment pins (one shown here) before it will pull off. If the cover is difficult to remove, loosen the oil pan bolts one turn each.*

7 *Rotate the crankshaft until the fuel pump arm is positioned at the lowest point on the cam.*

8 *If equipped, remove the camshaft endplay button and spring from the front of the camshaft.*

9 *Remove the two bolts that secure the fuel pump.*

10 *Carefully guide the fuel pump arm out of the engine.*

Strip the Block

1 Remove the engine mounts that are each secured by two bolts.

2 Remove the oil filter adapter. It's secured by three bolts.

3 Remove the oil filler tube. It's press fit into the block, so it might take some effort to get it out. First, try rotating the tube.

4 If the tube still doesn't come out, pry it from the bottom while also trying to rotate it.

5 The dipstick tube is also press fit. If twisting and pulling doesn't get it out, use a hammer and chisel to tap it out at the base.

6 Turn the engine upside down and remove the oil pan. There will probably be some coolant and/or oil that drips out when the engine is flipped, so be prepared. Each side of the oil pan is secured by 2 nuts at the end and 7 bolts in between (18 total fasteners for the whole pan).

CHAPTER 5

Cylinder Head and Valvetrain Overhaul

The traditional valve job includes resurfacing the valve seats and faces as well as inspecting and measuring the valves and guides to determine if there's excessive wear. The valve springs are inspected and measured for pressure at the installed height and open height. The cylinder head is then reassembled with new valve stem seals, and the spring height is set as specified by the manufacturer. A complete rebuild of the cylinder heads should also include new springs and all-new valve guides that are correctly sized to the valve stems.

If this is your first time rebuilding an engine, it's probably best to leave the cylinder-head reconditioning work to an engine machine shop. It will have the equipment and expertise to perform this job correctly. Prices are usually reasonable compared to what you will otherwise spend purchasing the tools needed to do it yourself.

If you're willing to spend a little money on tools, consider doing the disassembly, cleaning, and visual inspections yourself. You might save some money at the machine shop, and you'll get to learn about cylinder heads in the process.

Keep in mind that reconditioned cylinder heads are commonly available on an exchange basis. Prices usually aren't much higher than the cost to have your existing heads rebuilt. This is where doing the inspections yourself can save you some money. If you find serious problems with the heads you have, it may be less expensive to exchange them than rebuild them.

Disassembly

If you plan to disassemble the cylinder head yourself, label and organize the parts carefully. This will help you with your inspections and also

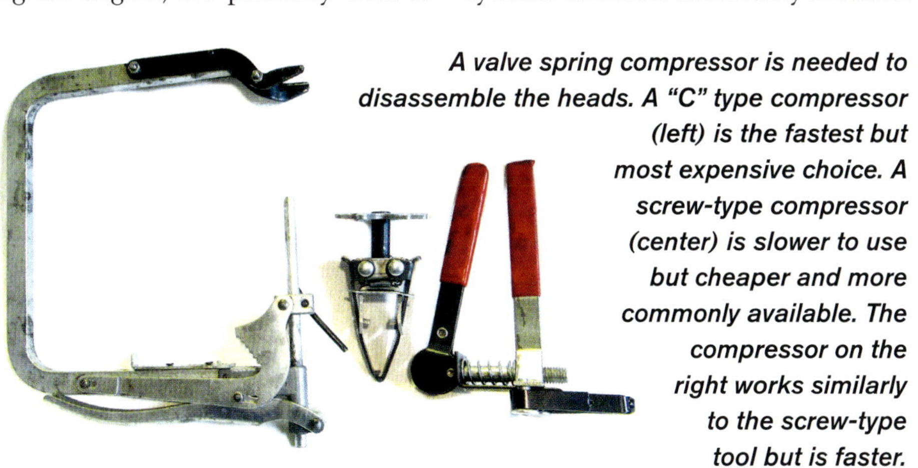

A valve spring compressor is needed to disassemble the heads. A "C" type compressor (left) is the fastest but most expensive choice. A screw-type compressor (center) is slower to use but cheaper and more commonly available. The compressor on the right works similarly to the screw-type tool but is faster.

Compress the valve spring fully, then carefully remove the two keepers (sometimes called "valve locks"). A small magnet is helpful. Be careful when using a valve spring compressor, as it can slip and cause the valve to release suddenly, which can result in injury.

Sometimes the keepers stick in place. If so, place the cylinder head on a bench and put a small block of wood under the valve head. Use a 9/16 deep socket and hammer to hit the retainer, which should jar the keepers loose from the retainer. If it is hit hard enough, the keepers might come loose, releasing the retainer. If not, reinstall the compressor. The keepers should come out easily now.

With the keepers removed, the valve spring and the retainer can be easily lifted off. Slowly release the tension from the spring and separate the valve, the retainer, and any shims that may be between the spring and the cylinder head.

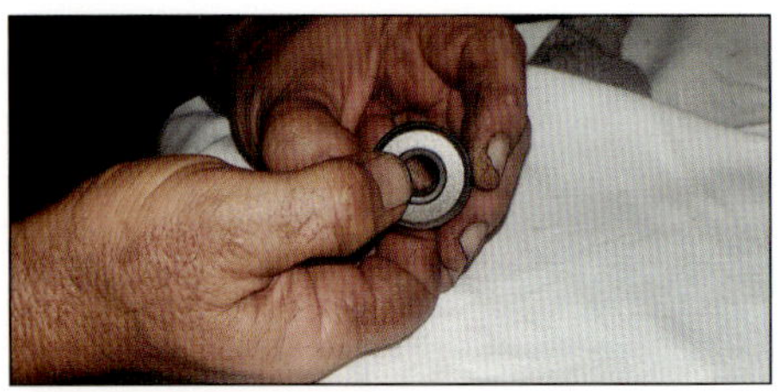

Often, the retainer incorporates a rotator. This allows the valve to rotate in operation to reduce carbon accumulation and avoid hot spots that can lead to a burned valve. Make sure the inner and outer portions of the rotator move smoothly against each other.

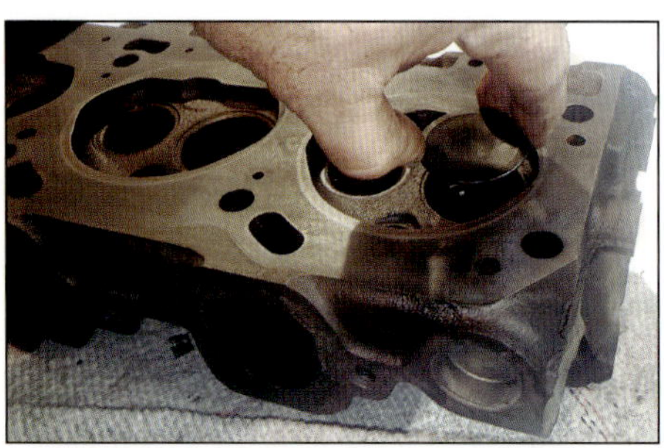

Grasp the head of each valve and carefully pull them from the cylinder head. If there's an "umbrella" type of oil deflector on the valve stem, slide it off the valve stem before removing the valve.

If the valve doesn't pull out easily, there's probably a burr at the top of the valve stem. Use a fine-toothed file to remove the burr. Rotate the valve stem as you do this.

If there are shims underneath the valves, note their locations so that they can be returned to their original locations. Shims are used to achieve the correct valve spring installed height. After the valves and seats are ground, an additional shim (or a thicker one) may be required.

It's easy to distinguish an intake valve from an exhaust valve. On the left is an intake valve, which is significantly larger than the exhaust valve on the right.

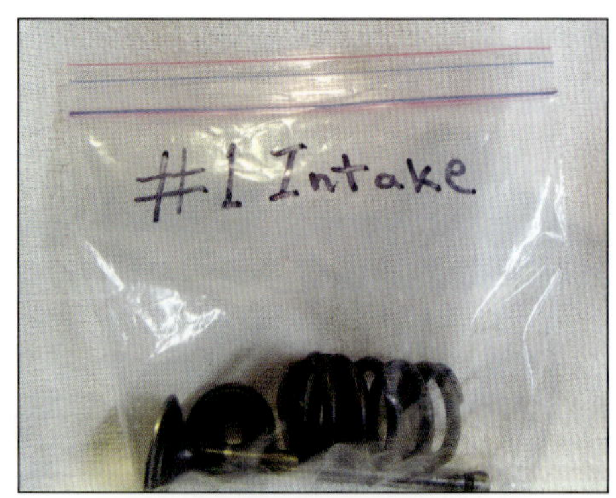

Keep the components for each valve together in a labeled plastic bag.

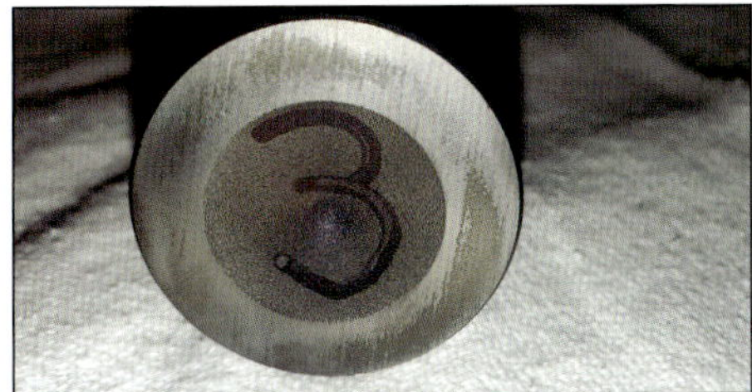

It's also a good idea to mark the head of each valve with a permanent marker. Make sure the valve head is clean before doing this.

Remove the valve seal from the top of the valve guide. The special tool shown makes this easier. If the seal is difficult to remove, cut it off. They will be replaced as a part of the overhaul.

help the machinist who will do the actual machine work. If you just bring in a box full of dirty parts, it's unlikely to save you any money versus bringing in the fully assembled heads.

Cleaning

If a machine shop is going to rebuild the heads, skip the heavy cleaning work. The machine shop will have much better cleaning equipment, and the cleaning is usually inexpensive when priced as part of machine work.

Cylinder heads and their components usually have two types of deposits on them after long service. The greasy, oily deposits should be removed first. This is best done in a solvent tank where the heads can soak and the deposits brushed away.

If you don't have a solvent tank, use engine degreaser or spray solvent. Foaming degreaser like this is very effective. After it soaks into the grease, hose it off. Use gloves and eye protection when using these caustic solvents.

Carbon is the other type of deposit that will have to be dealt with. A fine wire wheel on a bench grinder or rotary tool will help with the heavy accumulations. Avoid using such tools on gasket surfaces, which must remain smooth for proper gasket seating.

Spots of carbon and gasket pieces can be scraped off surfaces with a razor-blade scraper.

Mild abrasive pads on a rotary tool can be used to remove stubborn gasket material and dry deposits.

Most of the deposits on valvetrain components can be removed with solvent, but use a brush on a rotary tool to get the combustion chambers spotless. This way any cracks will be visible.

This same method is helpful for removing deposits within the ports. While cleaning, take note of any variation in the types of deposits that are found among the ports.

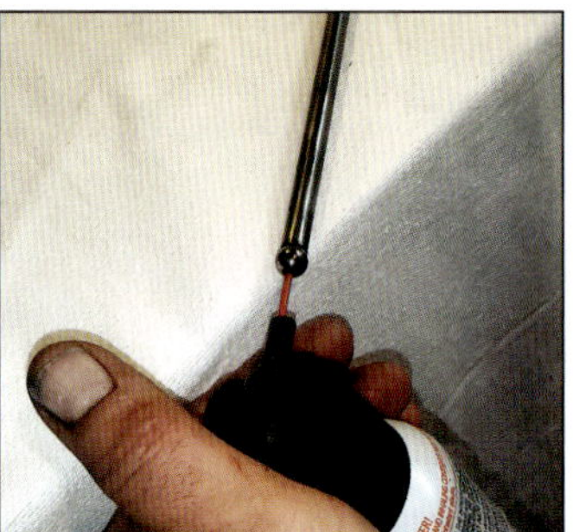

The pushrods carry oil to lubricate the valve and valvetrain components. Blow through them to be sure they aren't plugged up.

Inspection

With the components clean, do a thorough inspection to determine what parts will need to be purchased and if there are major problems that would make overhaul prohibitively expensive. In these cases, exchanging for remanufactured heads is an attractive option. Note that heads must be replaced in pairs.

Even heads with the same part number can have subtle differences, such as slightly different combustion chamber volumes due to previous machine work. This can lead to an imbalance in compression ratio among cylinders.

If the engine was severely overheated, the heads are probably warped. This can be checked with a precision straightedge, usually by a machine shop. Gaps beneath the straightedge greater than 0.003 inch across any 6 inches or 0.006 inch total means both heads will need to be resurfaced (and usually the intake gasket surface as well). This ensures the intake manifold will fit correctly.

Check the rocker arm pivots for wear. The surfaces where they contact the rocker arms should be smooth. If any wear can be seen, replace the pivots. The pivots are a common place to see wear, as they're made from aluminum.

Inspect the heads thoroughly. Look for cracks in the combustion chambers, particularly if the engine was consuming coolant. If one combustion chamber is cleaner than the others, coolant was probably leaking into that cylinder from a blown head gasket or crack in the head. Cracks can usually be seen, but machine shops have equipment that can pressure check and/or Magnaflux the heads to be certain there are no issues.

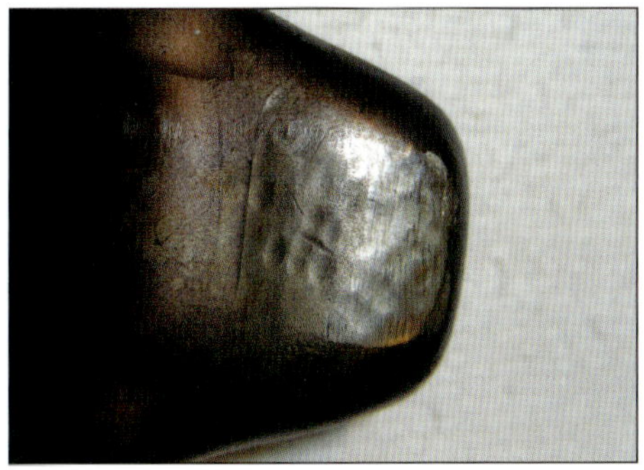

Inspect the rocker arms and pivots for scoring, wear, and blue spots from overheating. The valve tip and pushrod contact surfaces at the ends of the rocker arms should be smooth and shiny. If there's a rough surface, scoring, a wear ridge, or denting (as shown here), replace the rocker arms and fulcrums as a set.

Inspect for excessive wear on the pushrod ends. There should be a round, smooth, shiny area at each end that's smaller at the lifter end than at the rocker arm end. If there is a wear ridge or the surface is uneven in any way, replace the pushrods.

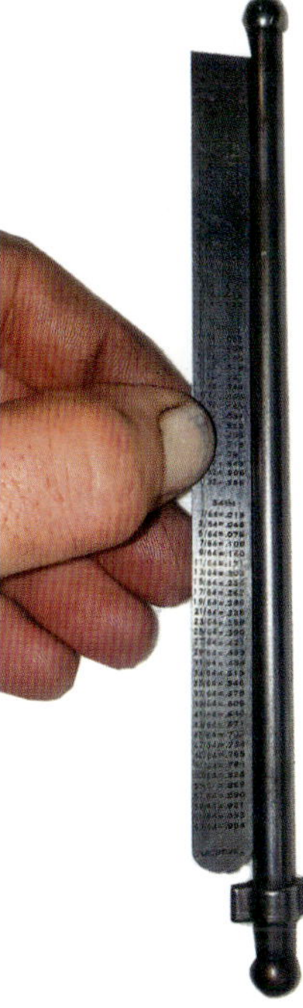

Check the pushrods for straightness. Hold each pushrod against a straightedge and rotate the pushrod against it. If light can be seen between them at any point while rotating the pushrod, replace it. It's best to replace pushrods as a set.

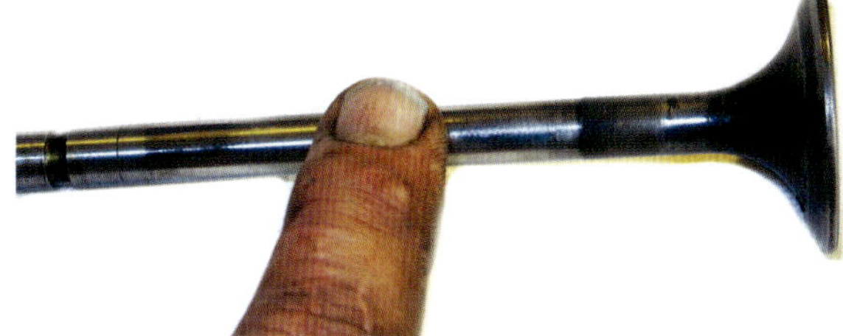

Check valves for straightness. A valve can become bent through contact with a piston head. Even the slightest bend will cause the valve to not seat correctly. Roll each valve across a flat surface and look for a wobble. Also check the head of each piston for signs of contact with a valve. A valve that has struck a piston must be replaced.

Valves must fit in their guides without any significant side-play. Install each valve into its associated guide and pull it out about 1/4 inch off its seat. Move the valve head side to side. There should not be any significant side-to-side movement.

To precisely measure valve stem-to-guide clearance, mount a dial indicator as shown, with the probe perpendicular to the valve stem. Move the valve left to right. Divide the total amount the indicator fluctuates by 2 to obtain the stem-to-guide clearance. See the Appendix for the specification on your engine.

If valve stem-to-guide clearance is excessive, the valve guides will need to be reconditioned or replaced. Sometimes the valves will also need to be replaced to get the clearance correct. Valve guide reconditioning and replacement must be done by a machine shop, as special equipment is required. Here a guide is being cut to the correct length.

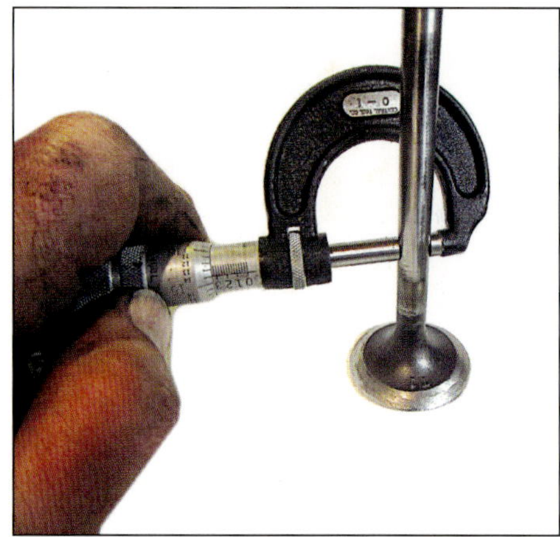

Measure the valve stems, particularly at the wear areas, which will appear shiny. Compare the measurements to the specifications in the Appendix. Replace the valves if worn excessively.

Inspect the keeper groove at the top of the valve stem for excessive wear, which usually shows up as sharp edges at the tops of the groove. If the grooves are worn excessively, you should replace the valves.

Check the tip of each valve for evidence of wear. Minor wear can be corrected by machining. If the wear is excessive, find the problem in the valvetrain that led to the wear. The severe wear on this valve tip indicates serious problems in the valvetrain.

Inspect the face of each valve seat. Look for wear and signs of erosion. This valve had been overheated, and erosion of the face is evident. Although the corresponding seat was not damaged, the damage shown caused low compression in the associated cylinder. Damage this severe will likely require replacement of the valve.

If not identified and corrected early, erosion from valve overheating will cause the valve to become "burnt." Damage like this will result in near-zero compression in the cylinder. It's usually an exhaust valve that gets burnt.

Carefully inspect the valve seats for signs of pitting, cracks, and wear. Minor wear and pitting will be removed during a "valve job" at the machine shop.

Valves and guides that are not severely worn can be reconditioned by an automotive machine shop. During this process, the seats and guides will be ground to precise angles, usually 45 degrees on the seat and 44 degrees on the valve. Grinding also ensures the worn seats and faces will be made concentric so they will fit together perfectly.

Check the "free" length of each valve spring. If one or more springs are shorter than the others, replace all of the springs. The Appendix has free-length specifications.

The ability of a spring to stand up straight without leaning one way or another is called "squareness." On a flat surface, rotate the spring while holding it gently against a precision 45-degree angle. If it leans more than 1/16 inch in any direction, replace the spring.

Valves must always have a "margin," which means there should not be a sharp edge around the face. The margin should be at least 1/32 inch on the exhaust and 1/64 inch on the intake.

It's best to replace the valve springs during overhaul, but if you're on a budget, try reusing the old ones. Inspect the springs carefully and replace any that have nicks or scratches. If one or more springs are shorter than the others, replace all of the springs. Keep in mind that valve springs are critical parts that can be worn or damaged in ways that cannot be seen.

A special tool is needed to check spring pressure at installed height and open height. The Appendix has specifications for stock rebuilds, but if you're upgrading the camshaft, use the specifications provided by the camshaft manufacturer.

Assembly

The shop doing the machine work on the cylinder heads will usually do the assembly. This is highly recommended, as the inexperienced are likely to make mistakes.

Before final assembly, check the valve spring installed height. With the valve installed in the guide, assemble the retainer and keepers on the end of the valve. Hold the retainer up tightly and measure between the valve spring seat on the cylinder head and the retainer. Compare the reading to the specification in the Appendix.

A more precise method of checking valve spring installed height is to use a special micrometer-type tool like the one shown here. Considering the greater precision and the time it will save, it can be a good investment.

Valve oil seals are usually included in upper-engine gasket kits. Valve-guide seals (right) are the most popular and work the best. Umbrella-type oil deflectors (left) were used on some early models. Umbrella deflectors are usually not as effective at oil control.

If installed height is excessive, shim under the spring to get it right. Shims are available in various thicknesses and are often necessary when the original valves and seats are reused. If new valves or seats are used, you might have too little installed height, in which case the valve/seat will need to be ground further or the spring seat on the head machined down.

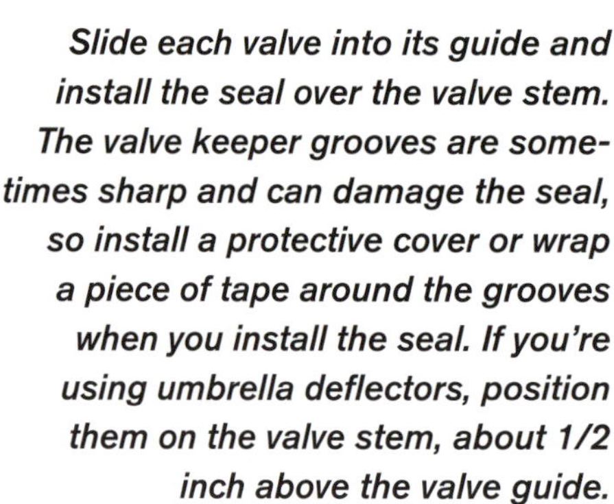

Slide each valve into its guide and install the seal over the valve stem. The valve keeper grooves are sometimes sharp and can damage the seal, so install a protective cover or wrap a piece of tape around the grooves when you install the seal. If you're using umbrella deflectors, position them on the valve stem, about 1/2 inch above the valve guide.

Valve guide seals must be tapped into place over the top of the valve guide. Use a socket that's a bit larger than the valve guide.

Compress the spring and install the valve keepers. It's often difficult to get the keepers to stay in place. Put a bit of grease on each keeper to make this easier.

Install the spring and retainer. Be sure the spring is centered and that it fits evenly on top of any shims installed.

With the heads reassembled, turn the head upside down and pour water into the combustion chamber. Check for leakage into the intake and exhaust ports. There should be a perfect seal with no leakage. If not, there is a leak between a valve and its seat.

Lapping will reveal problems with the valve seal. The process should leave an even ring on the valve and seat, roughly centered on the valve. If not, there is a problem with the valve job.

Valves that are not sealing properly can sometimes be corrected by lapping. With the spring removed, the valve is held by a suction-cup tool and rotated back and forth against its seat with a special abrasive compound between the valve and seat.

Engine Block Overhaul

The cylinder block contains the crankshaft, camshaft, pistons, connecting rods, and timing chain/sprockets. The block and its components need to be disassembled, cleaned, and inspected. The machine shop can handle this, but we recommend that you do the disassembly and basic inspection and wear measurements because these are things that can be performed at home without a lot of special tools. It will also help you understand any issues with the engine so that you can have an informed discussion with your machine shop about the reconditioning work to be done.

Machining operations will have to be done by an automotive machine shop. Do your research to find a shop with a good reputation. A bargain on machine work can be a false economy if the engine does not go together correctly or fails prematurely.

Reassembly can be done at home and is a way to save some additional money during the overhaul. If you're careful and take your time, you should be able to do as good of a job as the machine shop would do.

Disassembly

First, remove the timing chain and sprockets. These components are often

Remove the bolt from the center of the camshaft sprocket. This is best done with an impact tool, as the engine can rotate if it is loosened conventionally. For those without impact tools, a trick for these situations is to use a socket and a large breaker bar, tapping the end of the breaker bar with a hammer.

The fuel pump drive eccentric is normally replaced at overhaul time, but if it's not too badly worn, it can be reused. This eccentric has a shiny wear pattern and no wear ridge, which is what you want to see.

Pull out on the camshaft sprocket and rock it back and forth. Pry gently with a screwdriver, if necessary. If the sprocket comes loose but does not pull off the camshaft, the chain might be too tight. Pull the crankshaft sprocket out about 1 inch. Note that there is an alignment dowel in the camshaft. If you buy a new camshaft, this pin will need to be transferred over.

The crankshaft sprocket is often tight on the crankshaft and will need to be pried loose. Sometimes two pry bars are enough to persuade it.

Often it will be necessary to use a puller to remove the crankshaft sprocket from the crankshaft. Be careful to pull against the rear of the sprocket, not on the teeth of the sprocket, as they could be damaged.

Turn the engine block upside down, then unscrew the two bolts and lift off the oil pump. Note that there is a steel gasket between the block and the pump.

Remove the oil pump driveshaft. Look for excessive wear or twisting of the shaft.

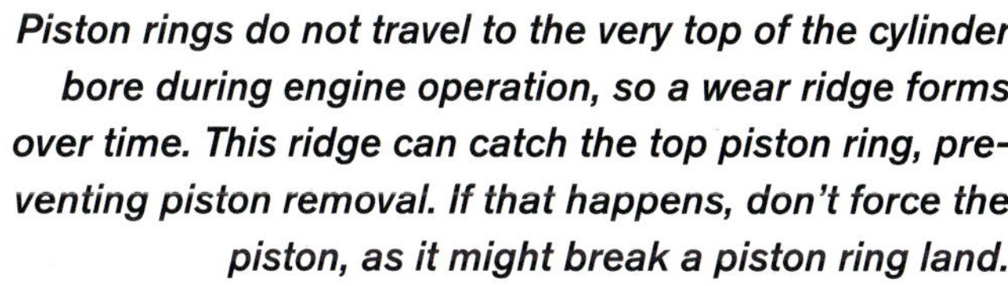

Piston rings do not travel to the very top of the cylinder bore during engine operation, so a wear ridge forms over time. This ridge can catch the top piston ring, preventing piston removal. If that happens, don't force the piston, as it might break a piston ring land.

stuck in place from years of varnish buildup. Some persuading will usually be needed!

The oil pump and pickup tube/screen are removed next. If debris and sludge are in the screen, damage is likely in the engine due to oil starvation. Look for pieces of white nylon in the screen. This debris comes from wear or failure of the camshaft timing gear.

Check for a wear ridge at the top of each cylinder. If there's enough of a ridge to catch a fingernail, it means that it will catch the piston rings when the pistons are pushed out the top of the bore. A ridge reamer is necessary to remove the ridge.

Ridge reamers can damage the cylinder bore if not used correctly, so we recommend that wear ridges be removed by the machine shop before the pistons are removed. If only a few cylinders have a significant wear ridge, the crankshaft can sometimes be removed with those pistons pushed all the way to the top of the bores.

Adequate connecting rod side clearance ensures that the connecting rods remain square to the crankshaft and perfectly centered in the cylinder bore. Excessive side clearance indicates wear on the side surfaces of the connecting rods at the "big-end" bore and/or wear at the ends of the connecting rod journals on the crankshaft.

Excessive side clearance is usually associated with excessive wear at the thrust surfaces of the number-3 main bearing. Wear in these areas (rod sides, rod journal ends, and thrust bearing) often indicates that the crankshaft is receiving excessive forward pressure. This can be the result of a torque converter being improperly installed.

On manual-transmission vehicles, pressure applied to the clutch pedal over many years of use will cause some wear. If a high-pressure (racing-type) clutch is used, the wear will be accelerated.

Loosen the connecting rod cap nuts a three-quarter turn, which will allow them to be pulled loose from the connecting rods. Rotate the crankshaft until the number-1 piston is near the bottom of its bore, which will allow easy access to the connecting rod nuts.

There is a bearing insert in each connecting rod cap. If it falls out during removal, be sure to keep it with its associated cap. Knowing where each bearing came from can help with bearing failure diagnosis.

Using feeler gauges, check connecting rod side clearance at each pair of connecting rods (four total points of checking). Firmly push both rods outward on the crankshaft journal and measure the gap between them with feeler gauges. The combined thickness of feeler gauges that will insert with a slight drag is the side clearance. Compare this to the specifications in the Appendix.

OEM rods and caps are usually not well marked. Mark them yourself with number-stamping dies or a hammer and punch (shown). The number of dots indicate the cylinder number. This is the number-2 cylinder connecting rod.

Remove each connecting rod cap. On later models, the nuts require a 12-point 9/16 socket. Pull up using a gentle side-to-side rocking motion. If a cap is stubborn, gently tap the bolts with a soft-face hammer and/or rotate the crankshaft slightly back and forth.

Check for marks where each connecting rod and cap meet. Aftermarket rods like the one shown here are usually marked clearly.

Put short pieces of rubber hose over the ends of the connecting rod bolts. This will protect the cylinder walls and crankshaft as each rod is removed.

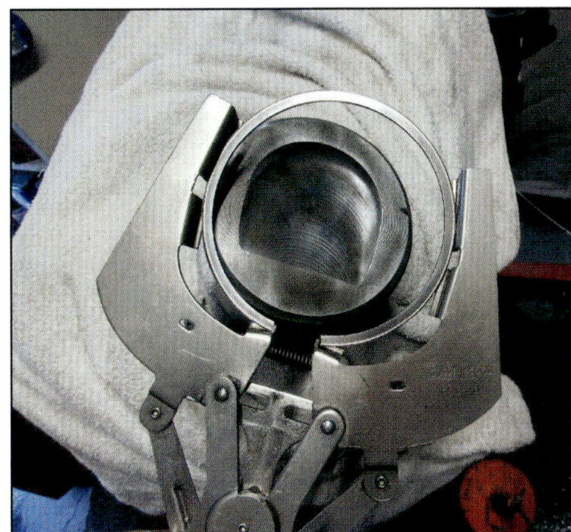

Remove the two compression rings, starting with the top ring. A special tool is required to do this without breaking the rings, which are cast iron and therefore brittle.

Before removing the crankshaft, check the endplay. Mount a dial indicator at the front of the engine with the probe directly in line with the crankshaft. Use a large screwdriver to gently pry the crankshaft to the rear, zero the dial indicator, then pry the crankshaft forward. Be careful where you pry so as not to cause damage. The total gauge reading is the endplay.

The oil control (bottom) ring is a three-piece design that can be removed by hand. Lift out and rotate each of the thin steel rails at the top and bottom. Use a feeler gauge to protect the piston against scratching.

If you don't have a dial indicator, pry the crankshaft forward, as shown in the photo above. Then, measure the gap between the crankshaft and the front surface of the number-3 (thrust) bearing.

The oil ring expander is easily removed at this point. Even though the rings need to be replaced, keep them all together in labeled plastic bags. This may help with diagnosis.

Once the connecting rod caps are removed, press firmly on the connecting rod to push the piston into the cylinder bore. Position a hand at the other end of the cylinder bore to catch the piston when it comes out of the cylinder. If the piston gets stuck at the top of the bore, it's because the top piston ring is encountering the wear ridge at the top of the cylinder.

Use moderate pressure to try to overcome the resistance, but if the piston is stuck, just leave it there for now. The crankshaft might be able to be removed with the piston in place; then, the piston can be removed from the bottom. If not, a machine shop can ream away the ridge to allow the piston to be removed from the top.

Repeat this procedure for the remaining piston/connecting rod assemblies. After removal, install each bearing cap back on its associated connecting rod and install the nuts finger-tight. This will keep all the associated parts together to aid

If the markings on the bearing caps are not clear, use a punch and hammer to mark them. It's critical that the caps be returned to their original locations with the correct end facing forward. Photos prior to disassembly are recommended.

Remove the bearing inserts by pressing on the side opposite the bearing tang. The bearing will roll out the other side. Sometimes the inserts are tight, particularly the thrust bearings. It might be necessary to use a plastic tool to help it along.

in failure analysis. Now, remove the piston rings from the pistons.

Check the crankshaft endplay. Endplay is an important check, as it will indicate the level of wear on the thrust bearing faces (and possibly the thrust faces on the crankshaft). If endplay is excessive, you'll want to determine why.

The main bearing caps should have cast-in numbers that indicate their orientation on the block. The numbers (1 through 5) begin at the front of the block.

Remove the bolts from the main bearing caps. They are very tight, so a

Unscrew the main bearing cap bolts. It's best to start loosening at the center cap and work out to the end caps. The caps are usually in the block very tight and will need to be rocked back and forth for removal.

It sometimes helps to use the loosened bolts as levers to help rock the caps loose. If a cap is already loose on the block, let the machine shop know. This might be a problem.

For more leverage, use a pair of punches, as shown here. Just be careful not to rock the caps excessively. Use punches that will not travel all the way into the bolt holes in the block.

The center (number-3) bearing is a thrust type that controls front-to-rear movement of the crankshaft. Inspect for wear on the vertical surfaces that contact the crankshaft. Excessive wear should be diagnosed. Thrust-bearing wear is most commonly found on vehicles with manual transmissions, due to the forward load transmitted by clutch actuation.

Lift the crankshaft up and out of the block. It's heavy, so be careful. If it's not lifted straight up, it will become stuck and won't lift higher. Lower the crankshaft and try again. A bit of light rocking might be necessary to find the sweet spot where the crankshaft will lift up easily.

Mark the upper bearing inserts as to their locations, then remove the rear seal half from the groove at the rear of the engine block. Also remove the other half of the seal from the rear main bearing cap. Shown here is a rope-type seal.

Engines with roller lifters will have a machined retaining plate and spacer that's held in place by the oil gallery plugs. First remove the plugs, then remove the spacer and the retainer plate, noting their orientation.

large breaker bar will be needed. Pull each cap off the block. The machined recesses in the block are an interference fit with the machined surfaces on the sides of the caps. The caps are tight to the block by design.

If you're short on space, store the crankshaft on its end against a wall (indoors) with the rear of the crankshaft down. Tie the top of the crankshaft securely to an anchor point on the wall. If it is stored in a garage with a concrete floor, place a piece of wood between the floor and the bottom of the crankshaft.

Now, remove the camshaft, as shown in the accompanying photos. The camshaft needs to be kept perfectly flat during removal; otherwise,

Carefully withdraw the camshaft from the block, keeping it as level as possible in the process. Thread a long bolt into the end of the camshaft and use it as a handle during removal.

Support the camshaft in the center with a coat hanger wire, which will help the camshaft stay straight during removal. As the camshaft is withdrawn, rotate it as you pull gently.

the lobes of the camshaft will scratch the camshaft bearings. The bearings will be replaced as part of the overhaul, but now is your chance to practice so that the new bearings will not be harmed during reassembly! Sometimes the center of the camshaft can be supported from underneath, but it will often need a heavy wire to support it through the opening in the valley area of the block.

Cleaning

Cleaning engine parts is the worst part of an overhaul. All dirt, grease, and carbon deposits must be removed; otherwise, it will be impossible to determine the condition of the parts. Cleaning the engine block itself is the most challenging task. Start by removing the plugs in the block, which will expose internal passages that will need special attention.

The first step in cleaning is to remove all the plugs. Some plugs are press fitted in the block, others are threaded. These two plugs at the front are for the main oil galleries.

At least one of the front oil gallery plugs should have a hole drilled in it to lubricate the timing gear and sprockets. If there's only one drilled plug, it's normally on the right side of the block. Note that the plugs are different sizes.

At the back of the block are two press-fit plugs. The larger plug is the camshaft plug. It can be knocked out by hammering a long rod placed through the camshaft bore at the front of the engine. The other plug provides access to a main oil gallery plug. Knock it into the block with a hammer and punch.

This threaded plug at the back of the block is for one of the main oil galleries. Threaded plugs are subject to rust and can be difficult to remove. Use penetrating oil to help loosen them. Here a box-end wrench is being used to provide extra leverage on the Allen wrench. Not a recommended method, but access to the plug is very difficult with the engine on a stand.

To access the other main oil gallery plug, reach through the opening at the back of the block with a long driver tool. The factory plug is a 5/16-inch square-drive. Here, the driver tool is just above the camshaft.

There are a total of six core plugs (sometimes called "freeze plugs") in the block: three on each side. Remove them by knocking them into the block with a hammer and a long round bar (such as a 1/2-inch-drive extension).

The core plug can now be removed by extracting it from the block with Vise-Grip pliers.

Here are some common engine cleaning chemicals. On the left is engine degreaser, which must be rinsed off after use. It is the most harsh and is usually used for large components, such as the engine block and cylinder heads. Spray solvent (center) can be used on the smaller parts. The green cleaner is environmentally friendly and also does a good job on grease. It should also be rinsed off, as it is water soluble.

There are two main oil galleries that have plugs at each end (four plugs total). They are threaded in place and are very tight. The driver-side rear plug is usually the most challenging. If there is a stubborn plug, soak it with penetrating lubricant and tap it with a hammer to make sure the lube penetrates deeply into the threads.

You don't need to do a perfect job cleaning the block, as the machine shop has special equipment to do the final cleaning. This is basically an oven that heats the block to high temperature, causing deposits to dry up and fall off.

Let the lubricant soak for at least 30 minutes before trying again to loosen it. The rear internal plug is usually a recessed square-drive plug. Even more annoying is that neither a 3/8-inch extension nor a 1/4-inch extension will fit. The size is 5/16 inch. You will need a special 5/16-inch square-drive tool to remove it. These are available, but it might take some effort to find one.

Once all of the plugs are removed, find a place outdoors with good drainage and start cleaning the block. This requires an effective cleaning solvent, wire brushes, heavy-duty gloves, and eye protection. Remove all the gunk and grime so you can do a thorough inspection. The stubborn baked-on deposits can be left if the machine shop is doing the final cleaning, which is highly recommended.

This machine is a media blaster, which takes cleaning to the next level. This is not a necessary step for a basic overhaul but will ensure all dried deposits are removed. The block comes out of the blaster looking new. The downside of this process is that the abrasive particles can become lodged in oil galleries and elsewhere in the block. Use great care when you do final cleaning of the block.

After the block has been scrubbed with solvent, spray it down with water to remove the deposits and solvent residue. Dry it immediately because cast iron rusts quickly. Compressed air will blow off the moisture. After drying the block, give it a light coat of WD-40, which will disperse the remaining moisture and protect the block from rusting. At this point, the block is clean enough that the machine shop can finish the job.

Use brushes and spray solvent to remove deposits from the oil holes in the block. Start first with the smaller holes before cleaning the main oil galleries, as debris removed from the smaller oiling holes will ultimately end up in the oil galleries.

When the block comes back from the machine shop, there's still more work to do. Make sure that there is no machining or cleaning debris in the oil galleries and other nooks and crannies of the block. For this job, a spray solvent and brushes are required.

Below the oiling hole at each main bearing is a passageway leading to the associated camshaft bearing. A rifle brush is great for cleaning these passageways.

Underneath the oil filter adapter are two oiling holes that must be carefully cleaned. They lead to the main oil galleries.

There is a small oiling hole at each lifter bore. These 16 little holes must all be brushed out prior to cleaning the main oil galleries. A small-bore rifle cleaning brush is perfect for the job.

The main oil galleries should be cleaned until every bit of grease and dirt are removed. Because they go all the way through the block, you can easily look through the galleries to locate debris.

Here's an example of the kind of debris that will be found during cleaning. This is abrasive material, most likely from a hone used to clean the lifter bores at the machine shop. Debris like this is very damaging. Normally, the oil filter would take care of this, but not when the abrasive is already on the parts.

Use taps and spray solvent to clean all the threaded holes in the block, particularly those for the main bearing caps and the cylinder heads. There is usually a bunch of gunk in these holes. If they're not totally clean, it can affect the torque readings on reassembly.

The same goes for the bolts. Each critical bolt should be cleaned with a die. Once the bolts and threaded holes are cleaned, the bolts should thread easily into their holes by hand.

The passages in the crankshaft should also be cleaned thoroughly. This is arguably the most important cleaning operation, as any remaining debris will go directly into the main and connecting rod bearings. Brush thoroughly and spray plenty of solvent through each hole. If the crankshaft journals were machined, there's an excellent chance that there are metal particles in these passages.

The two main oil galleries run the length of the block and feed oil to all internal components. They must be spotlessly clean, which can be observed by shining a flashlight through one end while looking through the other.

The internal parts will require more thorough cleaning, as there can be no deposits on parts that will receive precision measurements. The drilled holes in the crankshaft will need to be cleaned with solvent and a rifle-cleaning type of brush that fits snugly in the passageways. These passageways transmit oil to the main and connecting rod bearings, so any deposits remaining will be immediately sent into the new bearings and cause damage.

The piston/connecting rod assemblies are usually the hardest items to get thoroughly cleaned. The pistons are made of aluminum, so wire brushes can scratch and erode the material. The steel connecting rods can be cleaned more aggressively. Scrapers and wire brushes may be needed to remove the deposits from the piston heads. This must be done very carefully, testing a small area first to be sure the aluminum will not be damaged.

Cleaning the individual parts is best done in a solvent tank where the parts can soak and then the grease and deposits can be brushed away.

Most of us are not lucky enough to have a solvent tank at home, so an oil drain pan, spray solvent, and brushes will have to do.

Solvents and scrubbing will not usually remove the most stubborn deposits and bits of gasket material, so a scraper is also needed.

A fine wire wheel on a bench grinder can be used on steel parts and sometimes even on aluminum piston heads. Use a light touch and don't use a wire wheel on the sides of the piston.

Inspection

It's imperative that the block be inspected carefully and completely, as problems are not always obvious. Cracks in an engine block usually appear between the main bearing saddles, between the core plugs, or at the bottom of the cylinders. They can be hard to see, so it's best to have the machine shop inspect the block. If the condition of the block is questionable, it may be worth having the block Magnafluxed. A Magnaflux check will reveal cracks that are not otherwise visible.

Cylinder Block

Inspect each cylinder bore carefully, looking for cracks and scoring. Measure the bore diameters at the point of maximum wear (usually just below the wear ridge, parallel to the crankshaft). Also measure perpendicular to the point of maximum wear and note the difference between the two measurements, which is the out-of-round dimension. Cylinders should not be out of round by more than 0.001 inch.

Measure the cylinder at the point of minimum wear (at the bottom of the bore) and subtract this measurement from the maximum wear dimension. The difference between the two measurements is the cylinder taper. Taper should not exceed the specification listed in the Appendix. Excess taper causes the piston rings to expand and contract slightly but rapidly as the piston moves up and down. This causes the rings to lose tension prematurely.

If the block is seriously worn and/or damaged, consider starting with another used block in better condition. Extensive machine work can get expensive, and used blocks can often be found at reasonable prices. Of course, if the block is numbers-matching to a valuable car, do what you can to preserve the original block.

A large micrometer and telescoping gauges (sometimes called "snap gauges"), can check the cylinder bore diameters in a home garage. Telescoping gauges are tricky to use, as you must find the point of maximum diameter, which is usually just below the wear ridge with the gauge parallel to the crankshaft.

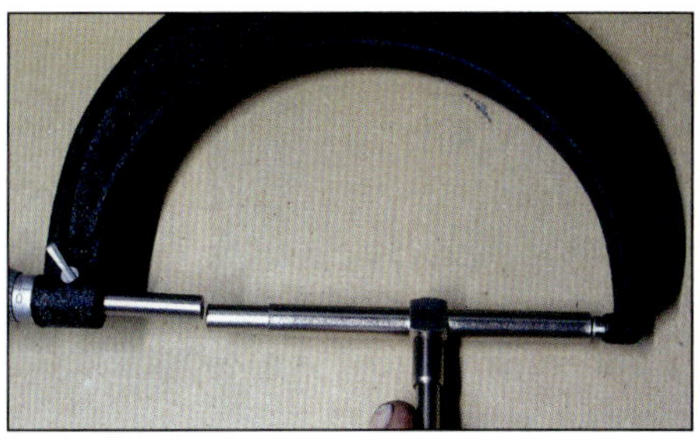

Measure the telescoping gauge with a micrometer to determine the cylinder bore diameter.

Crankshaft

The crankshaft bearing journals should ideally be shiny with no scratches. This is seldom the case. Over its life, the crankshaft is subjected to dry starts and oil contamination, which leave scratches. Unless the engine had a problem with low oil pressure or metallic debris in the oil, the scratches are usually light and not of much concern.

The most accurate way to check the diameter of the cylinder bore is with a cylinder bore gauge. This is an expensive tool that the machine shop will already have. There's no need to purchase one unless you're planning to get into engine rebuilding in a serious way.

Visually inspect the bearing journals on the crankshaft. Light scratching, like what is shown here, can be polished away by the machine shop. Deeper scratches will require grinding the crankshaft undersize and using oversize bearings.

Run a fingernail over any scratches on the journals. If the fingernail gets caught on them, the crankshaft will probably need grinding. An old mechanic's trick is to rub a penny across the bearing surface. If copper is left on the surface, it means the scratches are deep and sharp. Again, the crankshaft will likely need grinding.

Measure the diameter of the five main journals on the crankshaft and compare the readings to the specifications in the Appendix. Since the crankshaft journals are large in diameter, calipers cannot be used.

There are four connecting rod journals with two connecting rods attached to each. Measure both sides of each journal. The very center of the journal is a point where there should be no wear. If you have an accurate pair of calipers, you might be able to use them to obtain a measurement, but the calipers will not be as accurate as a micrometer.

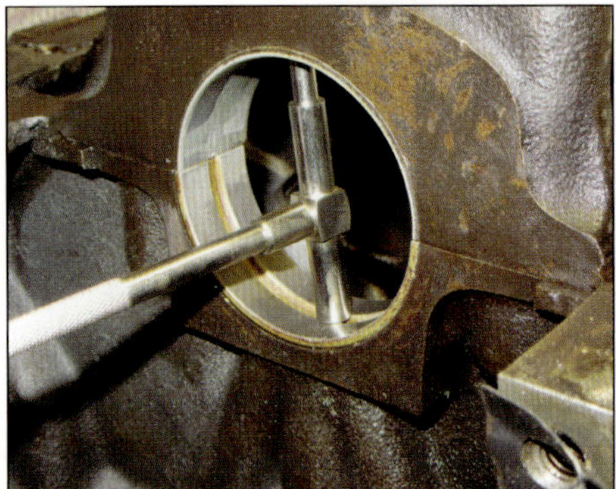

Measure the main bearing bores on the engine block with the bearing inserts installed and the caps torqued to specification. Subtract the journal diameter from the bore measurement to obtain the bearing clearance. On reassembly, you'll check this clearance again using Plastigauge.

If there are is no serious scratching on the crankshaft journals, proceed to measuring them with a micrometer. Check each journal in multiple places to determine if there is journal taper or out-of-round.

Now, check the main bearing oil clearance. As mentioned previously, snap gauges are finicky, so you'll probably need several practice tries.

The crankshaft has three different ways of controlling oil leaks at the rear seal. On the left is a larger-diameter section called an oil slinger that sheds most of the oil using centrifugal force. To the right of the slinger is a knurled surface that drives oil away from the seal as the crankshaft rotates. The pointer identifies where the seal contacts the crankshaft. A wear groove at this point will likely result in an oil leak.

To check crankshaft runout, put the crankshaft in place with only the upper main bearings installed. Set up a dial indicator over the number-3 (center) main bearing. Rotate the crankshaft. There should not be any variation of the dial indicator reading. If it's more than 0.0005 inch, there is likely a problem.

Visually inspect the camshaft for wear and damage. This camshaft has normal wear. The line around the center of each lobe is the lifter contact point, which should be centered. If the surface is not absolutely smooth, replace the camshaft and lifters.

Measure the snap gauge on each try. When the measurements are consistent, you've most likely got it right. The oil clearance will almost certainly be excessive when compared with the specification in the Appendix. New bearings will be installed, which will tighten up the clearances.

Inspect the rear main seal contact surface carefully to determine if there is any scratching, roughness, or a wear groove from contact with the oil seal. This area is critical and a common point of leakage. There's nothing worse than starting up your new engine and finding a drip at the rear of the engine. To fix it, you'd have to raise the engine and remove the oil pan in the vehicle. Spend a little extra time to be sure to get it right the first time.

If there is any reason to suspect a bent crankshaft, check for crankshaft runout. A bent crankshaft will also leave uneven wear patterns on the main bearings. Oldsmobile crankshafts rarely bend under normal operating conditions, but it sometimes happens during an engine seizure.

Camshaft

Inspect the camshaft lobes and journals. After cleaning, they should appear shiny with no scratching. The tops of the cam lobes are the most critical points for inspection. You should see an area down the center of each lobe where the lifter is in contact. If it's not centered, there's a problem with camshaft alignment, possibly the cam plug was installed too deep.

Measure each camshaft lobe at the smallest diameter (called the "base circle").

Also measure each camshaft lobe at its maximum height. The difference between these two diameters is the camshaft lobe lift. Most importantly, the lift should be equal among all the lobes. Any significant variance indicates camshaft lobe wear.

Look for scratching, pitting, and chipping at the lobes. A bad cam lobe will usually have deep scoring and appear dull rather than shiny. The lobes should be uniform in appearance.

Measure each camshaft lobe across the top of the lobe and at the base diameter (often called the "base circle"). The difference between these two measurements is the camshaft lobe lift. Keep in mind that the intake and exhaust lobes often have different lift specifications, so it's common to find eight lobes that are one height while the other eight are another height.

Lifters

Most Oldsmobile engines were equipped with conventional, flat lifters, which require careful inspection. The most important areas to inspect are the foot and sides. If there are problems shown on the lifters, there is usually damage to the camshaft as well. You want to see a circular wear pattern on the lifter feet. If not, the camshaft lobe may have worn flat.

Camshaft lobes are ground at a slight angle and are designed to impart spin to the lifters. If a cam wears to the point where it is flat, it can cause the lifters to stop spinning. Other possible causes of a lifter not rotating are a too-tight valve adjustment or the lifter fitting too tightly in its bore.

Roller lifters are simpler to inspect. The main area of concern is the roller itself, which should turn smoothly with no rough areas. Roller lifters are held by "dogbone" lifter guides that prevent the lifter from rotating in its bore and potentially scuffing the camshaft. Make sure the dogbone fits tightly over the lifter with no more than 0.001-inch clearance. As with conventional lifters, the sides should be smooth with no signs of deep scratching or galling.

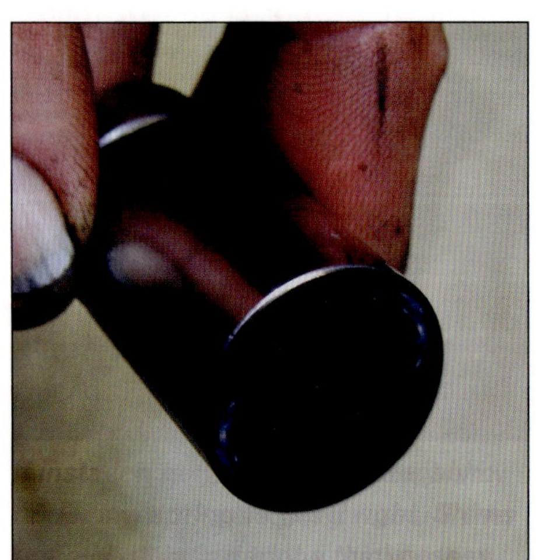

If you have conventional lifters, check each lifter foot for signs of wear. They should be shiny with an even circular wear pattern. If there is scratching across the foot of a lifter, it means the lifter was not rotating properly in its bore.

The sides of the lifters should be relatively smooth with no scratching or galling.

Lifter feet appear flat, but they are actually slightly convex. This prevents scuffing and allows the lifter to rotate in operation. Put one lifter foot against the side of another lifter and try to rock the foot against the side. If a lifter foot is flat or concave, replace all the lifters and the camshaft.

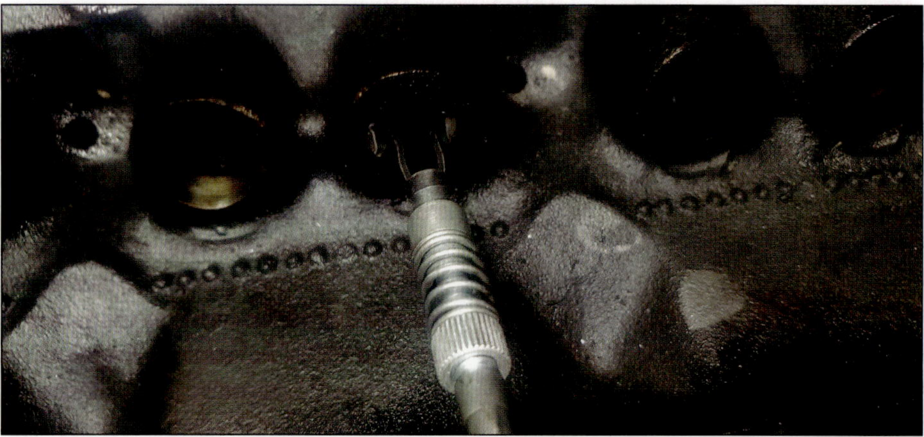

If a lifter fits too tightly, it might be necessary to hone the lifter bore just a bit. The idea here is to remove just the glazed deposits that are restricting the lifter's movement. Do not remove metal.

The hydraulic components within each lifter often get plugged up. To remove the internal components, remove the clip and tap the top of the lifter on a bench to remove the internal components.

On roller lifters, each foot must spin freely without any roughness or excess sideplay. If you feel differences among the lifters, it is best to replace them. A failed roller lifter can spread tiny roller bearings throughout the engine and cause significant damage.

It's best to replace the lifters at the time of overhaul, but if you want to take them apart to inspect and clean them, push down on the pushrod seat with a pushrod, then remove this clip.

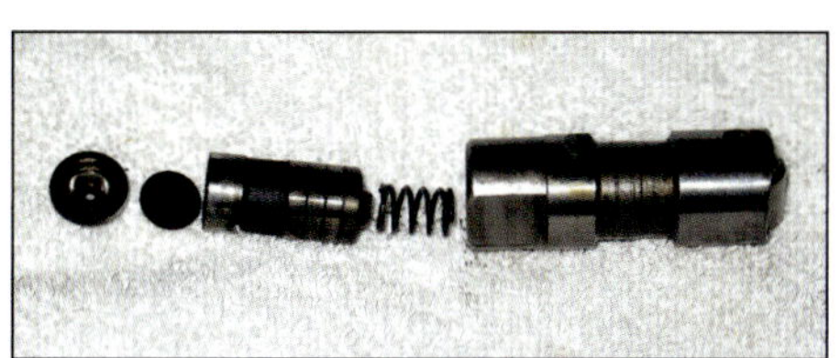

Here are the parts that are inside each lifter. Keep the parts from each lifter in a separate plastic bag. It's easy to lose them or get them mixed up.

Pistons

Piston wear and damage is sometimes obvious and sometimes subtle. A piston may have a hole in the head or a broken skirt. You would have already known there was a serious problem because the engine was running horribly. Less-obvious problems are wear in the ring grooves or excess clearance in the bore. These problems would have presented as knocking sounds, excessive oil consumption, or a drop in compression.

Visually inspect the piston for any signs of cracking, scuffing, deep scratching, or galling. Unlike scratching, galling is a wider stripe of roughness caused by seizure. Pistons that have been seized must be replaced, as they were most likely overheated. Make sure the oil return holes in the lower groove are not plugged.

Inspect each piston for signs of obvious damage. This piston shows mechanical damage (the skirt is broken). Whenever there is damage like this, other damage is likely to be found in the engine.

Damaged or broken piston heads can be the result of foreign objects in the cylinder, as shown at the left. Foreign objects will usually damage the cylinder walls as well. Eyebrow-shaped dents in the piston head are the result of contact with a valve, which likely means a problem in the valvetrain. Severe detonation can cause the piston head to melt, as shown on the right.

Observe the wear pattern on the piston skirts. The wear pattern should be centered. If the wear pattern is not centered, it's a sign that the connecting rod might be bent. The machine shop will have equipment that can test rods for straightness. Make sure the piston is tight on the pin and that the pin is tight on the connecting rod. The connecting rod should move smoothly through its arc with no binding or noticeable looseness.

Most Oldsmobile piston pins are locked to either the connecting rod or the piston with a press fit. Because of this, they cannot be removed from the rods without a hydraulic press. This is a job for a machine shop.

Measure the piston diameter. Subtract it from the bore diameter that was measured earlier. This gives the piston-to-bore clearance. Compare this to the specification in the Appendix.

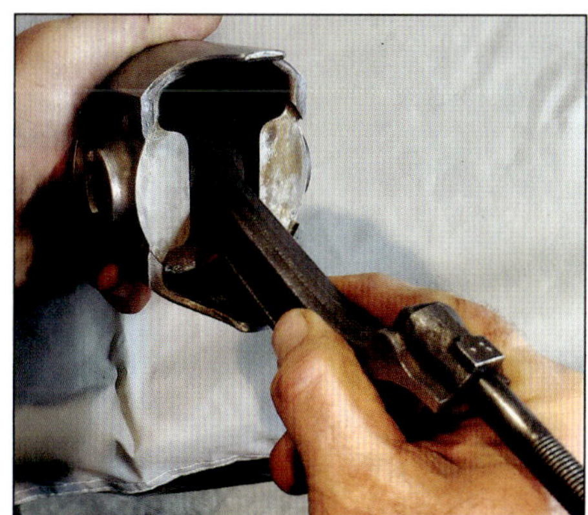

Try to rotate each piston against its connecting rod. There should not be any detectable movement. If there is any movement, the connecting rod pin is probably loose within the piston due to wear or damage. Let the machine shop know.

Measure the piston with a micrometer perpendicular to the piston pin and just below it. It's important to measure the piston at the right place because the top of the piston is slightly smaller in diameter than the bottom. This is to account for piston expansion during operation.

This lower connecting rod bearing shows the result of engine overloading, or "lugging."

To clean the compression ring grooves, break an old piston ring and use the sharp edge to scrape out the carbon. Special ring groove cleaning tools are available but usually aren't necessary. Be careful not to scratch the ring grooves.

The pistons should have already been cleaned with solvent and brushes, but carbon in the ring grooves will remain, which can lead to inaccurate measurements of the ring groove side clearance. Clean the ring grooves until there are no signs of carbon remaining.

With the ring grooves now clean, place a ring into each ring groove and try to slip a feeler gauge between the ring and the groove. When you find a feeler gauge that fits in with light resistance, you now know the ring side clearance, which should be within the limits listed in the Appendix. Keep in mind that new rings will tighten the gap a bit.

Bearings

If the bearings exhibit anything other than normal wear, determine the cause of failure before putting the engine back together. Common causes of bearing failure are lubrication issues, dirt, excessive loading, corrosion, and metallic particles from problems elsewhere in the engine.

Issues with bearing lubrication aren't always the result of low oil pressure alone. When an engine is badly overheated, the oil becomes less viscous and cannot protect the bearings properly. Loading an engine excessively at low engine speed can contribute to lubrication issues.

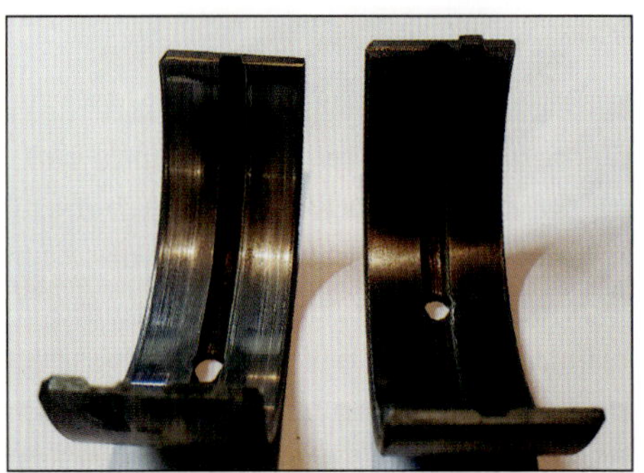

The bearing on the left shows normal wear. The bearing on the right has its overlay wiped out from excessive wear.

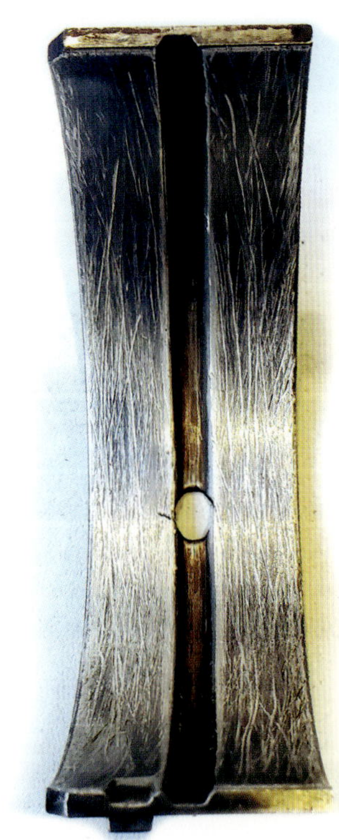

The scratches on this bearing are the result of sharp debris circulating in the oiling system.

This bearing shows corrosion, most likely caused by acidic contamination in the oil. This kind of damage can also be caused by an engine sitting for long periods of time without being operated or by coolant contamination.

To disassemble the oil pump, first remove the four screws and lift off the cover plate. The underside of the cover will show two circular wear patterns, but they should be smooth. The pump fails inspection if there are any scratches or grooves on the cover.

Inspect the oil pump gears for signs of scoring or other damage. These gears are in good shape.

Misalignment of oil holes in the block due to improper bearing installation can lead to insufficient oil delivery to the bearing surface. In the most severe cases of lubrication failure, the bearings will overheat so much that the steel backing of the bearing will turn blue.

Oil Pump

Normally, the oil pump should be replaced at the time of overhaul, and it is useful to inspect it as a part of diagnosing engine problems.

Machine Shop Inspections

The machine shop should have special equipment to check a block for cracks. Have the block checked if the engine has been severely overheated, the block has been frozen, or there was a phantom leak that was never identified. Magnaflux is the most common method of checking for cracks.

The Magnaflux machine magnetizes the block (or a portion of the

Inspect the oil pump housing and cover for wear, damage, and scoring. This housing looks good, nice, and shiny. We could probably reuse our old pump, but we'll put in a new pump because it's relatively cheap insurance against oiling problems.

A precision straightedge is used to check main bearing bore alignment. With the bearing inserts removed, a 0.001-inch feeler gauge should not be able to be inserted at any point. If the bores are out of alignment, they should be align-honed, which is a good idea whenever an engine is rebuilt.

A precision straightedge and feeler gauges are also used to check flatness of the cylinder head deck surface. The thickness of feeler gauges that can be inserted at any point is warpage, which should not exceed 0.006 overall or 0.003 within any 6 inches.

block), then metal filings are applied to the magnetized area. If there's a crack, the filings will outline the crack. More advanced Magnaflux equipment uses fluorescent filings than are viewed under a black light. The fluorescent glow allows the filings to be seen more easily, so smaller cracks are more easily identified.

Engine blocks are subject to thousands of heating and cooling cycles, which can cause distortion over time. If the engine is overheated, the distortion will be greater. Machine shops have precision straightedge tools that can be used to check the block deck for straightness and also to check alignment of the main bearing bores.

Cylinder Boring

If the cylinder measurements are within tolerances, the cylinders can generally be honed and the original pistons reused (assuming they are in serviceable condition). If the cylinder measurements are not within tolerances, the cylinders will need to be bored oversize for the use of new oversize pistons. The most common oversizes are 0.030 and 0.060 inch. Your machine shop can make recommendations as to the oversize to use based on the amount of wear in the bores.

Cylinder Honing

Whether or not the cylinders are bored larger, they will need to be honed so that the new piston rings will seat correctly. Honing is best carried out by a machine shop, as it's important that the correct surface finish is provided for proper piston ring seating. Different ring types

Even if the engine does not require an overbore, it will need to be honed to ensure the new piston rings seat correctly. We recommend this job be handled by a machine shop.

Here's what the cylinder bores should look like after honing. The scratches from the hone should be light and intersect at about a 45-degree angle. The slightly rough surface aids in ring seating and carries oil across the ring and bore surface for cooling during break-in.

require different surface roughness factors (Ra).

If the surface of the cylinder walls is too rough, it can damage the piston rings. If it isn't rough enough, the rings will not seat correctly. The correct finish depends on the type of honing stones used, the pressure applied to them, and the rotational speed of the hone as it's lifted up and down in the cylinder bore.

Align-Honing

Over time, an engine block can become slightly distorted for a number of reasons, primarily the thousands of heating and cooling cycles it is subject to during its life. Align-honing corrects any misalignment of the main bearing bores that could cause uneven wear of the main bearings. If the engine has been severely overheated, seized, or shows uneven main bearing wear, align-honing is a requirement. Many machine shops align-hone cylinder blocks as a routine part of any engine overhaul.

Block Deck Resurfacing

Block distortion can cause warping of the surfaces where the cylinder heads attach (commonly called the "deck"). Deck warpage can cause the head gaskets to not seat correctly. Resurfacing the deck will restore a perfectly flat surface and ensure the head gaskets will not fail prematurely.

During the resurfacing process, it's essential that the block is set up on the resurfacing machine perfectly. Even a few thousandths of an inch variance front-to-rear or left-to-right is problematic and can lead to misalignment of the intake manifold or uneven compression. This is one of the reasons to pick a reputable machine shop!

Crankshaft Polishing and Grinding

Light scratches on crankshaft journals can be removed by polishing with a fine emery cloth. Machine shops have special equipment that can quickly polish each journal. This is normally done at a reasonable price and is a much better option than trying to polish the crankshaft by hand at home.

Deep scratches and damage are dealt with by grinding the journals to a smaller standard diameter or "undersize." This must be accompanied by oversize bearings to provide the correct oil clearance. If only the connecting rod journals are damaged, they can be ground separately so that they would only need oversize bearings for the connecting rods.

Main bearing journals can also be ground separately from connecting rod journals. When a crankshaft has been ground, the machine shop will usually mark it to be sure the correct oversize bearings are used. A common marking is 10/10, which means both the main journals and rod journals were ground 0.010 undersize.

Connecting Rod Reconditioning

At the machine shop, the connecting rods and pistons will be separated and the connecting rods will be checked for bending and twisting. The pin bore will be inspected and the bearing bore will be checked for out-of-roundness. New connecting rod bolts will be installed and the rod bearing bore will be honed to ensure it is perfectly round. After the rods are reconditioned, the machine shop will usually reassemble the pistons to the rods.

Camshaft Bearing Replacement

Camshaft bearings must be pressed into the engine block using a special tool. Even with the special

Camshaft bearings are routinely replaced at the time of overhaul, and this bearing definitely needs it! Replacing camshaft bearings is a precise operation that requires special equipment. A machine shop can handle this.

tool, properly aligning the bearings and oiling holes requires practice. Camshaft bearings have different diameters: the bearings at the rear of the block have a smaller diameter than those at the front. Each bearing requires a specific arbor to drive the bearing into place.

Reassembly

Now that all the machine work is done and the block and components have been cleaned to hospital level clean, we are now ready to start the assembly process.

Engine Block Plugs

Note 1: Access to the rear of the block is restricted when the engine is installed on a stand. It's best to install the camshaft plug, oil gallery plugs, and the small access plug before the engine is mounted to the stand for final assembly.

Note 2: On later models with roller lifters, the front oil gallery plugs also serve to secure the camshaft retainer plate. Do not install the front gallery plugs until the camshaft has been installed.

Begin reassembly by installing new oil gallery plugs. The rear internal gallery plug should have a small hole in it to lubricate the adjacent distributor drive gear. If there isn't a hole in the plug, the distributor drive gear or camshaft gear might fail prematurely. The passenger-side front gallery plug should also have a small hole drilled in it to lubricate the timing chain and gears.

Again, if there is no hole, the timing chain could fail prematurely, particularly if a stock-type nylon camshaft timing gear is used. Earlier engines have a hole in both of the front gallery plugs, presumably for even more lubrication on the timing chain and gears.

Spread non-hardening sealant onto the outside circumference of the camshaft plug, then drive it into place at the back of the engine block using a large socket and hammer. Drive the plug in until it is flush with the surface of the engine block. Do not drive the plug in too deep or it might not allow the camshaft to be installed to the correct depth.

Oldsmobile engines have six core plugs: three on each side of the block. Although the factory plugs were steel, we recommend replacing them with brass plugs to prevent rust that could cause the plug to fail. However, brass plugs are more likely to have trouble sealing correctly, so be sure to use plenty of sealant and make sure the plugs are square in their bores.

Camshaft

Lubricate the camshaft with thick assembly lube and carefully install it into the block. Be extremely careful because you want to avoid scratching the new bearings. Thread a long bolt into the end of the camshaft to use as a handle as the camshaft is slowly and carefully moved rearward. The camshaft must be kept completely level.

When the camshaft can be seen through the window in the center of the engine block valley area, fish a coat hanger wire beneath it to support it from that point. The camshaft can also be supported from below by reaching between the main webs. If there is any resistance as the camshaft is installed, move it backward slightly, rotate it a bit, and try again.

On later-model engines with roller lifters, lubricate the spacer and retainer plate with grease. Then, install them along with the two gallery plugs that also secure the plate.

The outer edge of the camshaft plug should be coated with non-hardening sealant prior to installation. If it doesn't seal completely, there will be an oil leak at the back of the engine.

Special tools are available to install core plugs, but they can be driven into place with a hammer, a large socket, and an extension.

Camshaft Installation Mishaps

Camshaft installation requires equal parts of patience and finesse. Also, never assume that everything will be correct. Camshaft bearings are sometimes installed incorrectly at the machine shop. It's also possible for there to be something wrong with the camshaft.

A personal anecdote is that I was installing a camshaft that wouldn't go all the way in. I spent a great deal of time trying to figure out what was wrong; then, I finally realized that the camshaft lobes protruded slightly above the rear camshaft journal! The camshaft lobes had been measured for lift, which was correct, but somehow the crankshaft grinding machine was set to grind the lobes on a larger base-circle diameter, which made the lobes too big overall.

I contacted the camshaft manufacturer, which said this was a one-off problem. I continue to purchase camshafts from this manufacturer and have never seen a problem like this again. In fact, I have never heard of this happening to anyone else. Nevertheless, this experience taught me to never assume a part is correct out of the box. Always confirm the dimensions of machined components. ■

Crankshaft

Prior to final crankshaft installation, the crankshaft bearing oil clearance should be checked using Plastigauge. First, turn the engine block upside down and install the upper main bearing halves into their saddles on the block. Be sure the saddles and undersides of the bearing shells are completely clean. Remember that the thrust bearing is installed on the center (number-3) bearing saddle.

Hopefully, you practiced camshaft manipulation during the removal process. Now, you need to be even more careful. New camshaft bearings have less clearance, so it will be even more difficult this time. If there is a lot of resistance, it's possible that the camshaft bearings were installed incorrectly.

Make sure the main bearing journals on the crankshaft are completely clean, then install the crankshaft onto the new bearings. Make sure the crankshaft is completely level as it is lowered slowly into place.

Cut off a piece of Plastigauge that's slightly shorter than the width of the number-1 main bearing. Lay it carefully into place parallel to the crankshaft.

Install the main bearing caps and torque the bolts to specifications. Be sure not to move the crankshaft in the process. Remove the main bearing caps and observe the Plastigauge, which should have been compressed when the main bearing caps were tightened. The amount the Plastigauge is compressed indicates the oil clearance.

Install the upper main bearings on the saddles in the engine block. Make sure that each tab aligns with the groove in the block.

Use the scale on the Plastigauge envelope to read the oil clearance

Place a piece of Plastigauge on the main bearing journal. Make sure it's as straight as possible along the journal.

The Plastigauge flattens when the bearing cap bolts are tightened. The width of the Plastigauge should be uniform across its length. If it's significantly wider on one end or the other, there might be a problem. Remove the bearing inserts, clean the cap and saddle, clean both sides of the inserts, and recheck the clearance.

by comparing the width of the Plastigauge to each of the bars on the envelope. The bar that most closely approximates the width of the Plastigauge indicates the oil clearance. Note that the Plastigauge envelope has both standard and metric measurements, so be sure to use the correct side of the envelope.

If the Plastigauge measurements are not within specification, the bearing insert(s) may not be seating correctly; they may be the wrong bearing sizes or there may have been an error made during the machining process. Remove the crankshaft and upper bearing halves, clean and inspect them thoroughly, and double-check that you have the correct bearing sizes.

Repeat the check. If the clearance is still not correct, contact the machine shop for advice. Do not proceed until the clearance is correct; otherwise, the new engine will likely be damaged.

Shown on top is a rope-type seal, which was commonly installed at the factory. The lip-type seal below is easier to install.

Install the lower half of the rear oil seal. This is a critical step, as a poor seal here will result in a leak that's very difficult to fix once the engine is in the car. There are two types of seals used on these engines: rope and neoprene lip-type. We recommend using the lip-type seal, as it's a simpler installation that is generally easier for the do-it-yourselfer to accomplish.

If a lip-type seal is used, insert one of the halves into the groove in the block with the lip facing toward the front of the engine. Make sure the groove is completely clean, as dirt can lead to leaks.

Position one end of the seal so that it is protruding about 1/4 inch above the block surface. The idea here is to offset the seal parting lines so that they are not aligned with the edges of the cap. This can help reduce the possibility of leaks. Wipe a bit of engine oil on the seal lip. Avoid getting oil on the ends of the seal.

Rope-type seals are trickier to install. However, some say that they seal very well when they are installed correctly. As mentioned earlier, we prefer the lip-type seal. Lay one of the rope pieces on a bench and roll a large socket across it until it has been flattened enough to fit into the seal groove on the block.

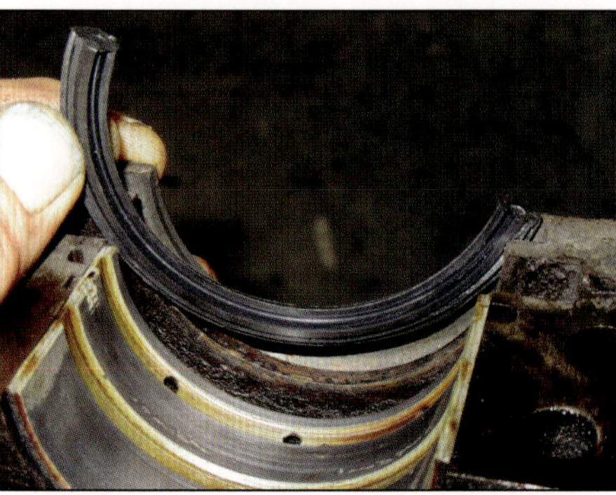

A lip-type seal is simply inserted into the groove in the block. Just make sure the lip faces forward and that one side protrudes slightly above the block.

Install the other seal half into the cap with 1/4 inch protruding at the opposite side as in the block. Again, make sure the seal lip faces forward.

Press the seal into the seal groove, then roll the large socket across the seal until it is flattened and fully seats in the groove. Using a sharp razor blade, trim the seal flush with the block surface on each side. There should not be any bits of rope hanging off and the rope ends should not appear uneven—in other words, a clean cut.

After the upper bearings are installed in their saddles and lubricated, reinstall the crankshaft, making sure not to disturb the rear seal in the process.

Use a large socket to roll the rope seal half into place in the seal groove. Tap on the socket with a hammer to help seat the seal in the groove.

When trimming the rope seal, there should be nothing protruding above the block or cap surface, and the cut needs to be absolutely clean. Use a brand-new razor blade and a slight sawing motion.

Apply a small amount of non-hardening sealant to the areas shown on the block. This will seal any oil that tries to sneak between the main bearing cap and the block.

Prepare the rear main bearing cap for installation. First, make sure the mating surface of the cap and the block are completely clean. Wipe the surfaces with a bit of brake cleaner or acetone to be sure they're completely clean. Install the other seal half into the cap.

If a lip-type seal is used, offset the seal about 1/4 inch on the side opposite of what was done on the other half in the block. If a rope-type seal is used, roll it into place in the cap and trim the edges as was done on the other half of the seal.

Install the lower main bearing inserts into the caps. Remember that the center (number-3) bearing is the thrust bearing. Lubricate the bearings, then install the rear main bearing caps and torque the bolts to specification.

Rotate the crankshaft by hand. The thick assembly lube provides initial resistance, but once the crankshaft is rotating, it should turn easily with no spots of resistance.

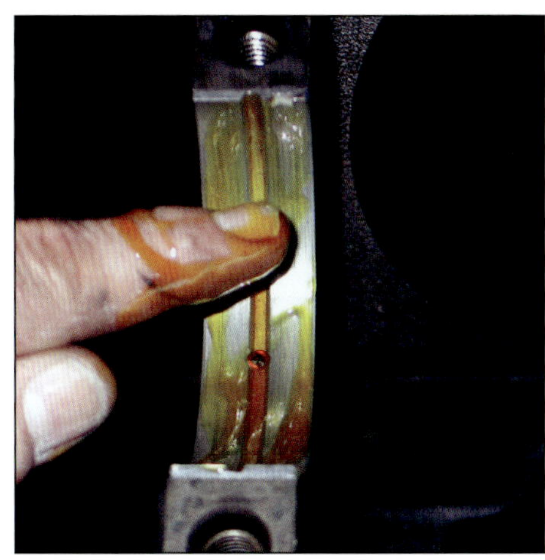

Before installing the crankshaft for the final time, coat the bearings in the block with thick assembly lube designed for engine assembly.

Again, check the crankshaft endplay as you did during disassembly. With new thrust bearings installed, the endplay should now be within the specification listed in the Appendix.

Piston Rings

The first step in installing the piston rings is to check the ring end gap of the compression rings. This is done to be sure you have the correct rings and that the machine work has yielded the correct bore size. First, insert a compression ring into the number-1 cylinder and square it in the bore.

Using feeler gauges, determine the piston ring end gap and compare it to the specification (see the Appendix). If the gap is too small, the ring ends will need to be filed down until the gap is correct. A gap that is too small can cause the rings to contact each other in operation and damage the cylinder walls and piston.

If the gap is larger than specified on a stock engine, it won't cause an issue unless it exceeds approximately

0.040 inch. On a high-performance or racing engine where every tiny bit of compression is desired, match the gap to the specification provided by the ring manufacturer for the type of usage intended.

Apply thick assembly lube to the main bearing inserts in the caps.

Square the piston ring in the bore by pressing against it with an overturned piston. Installing an old compression ring in the second groove can ensure that the piston won't be cocked in the bore.

Repeat the end gap check for each of the two compression rings in each cylinder. The top and bottom compression rings are usually of different designs. Do not mix up the rings among the cylinders, as there could be slight differences in the bore sizes.

Install the oil ring expander in the lower groove, then install the side rails. Do not use the piston ring expander tool on the oil ring side rails. Unlike the cast-iron compression

Measure the piston ring end gap with feeler gauges. The correct gauge is the one that slides through the gap with light resistance.

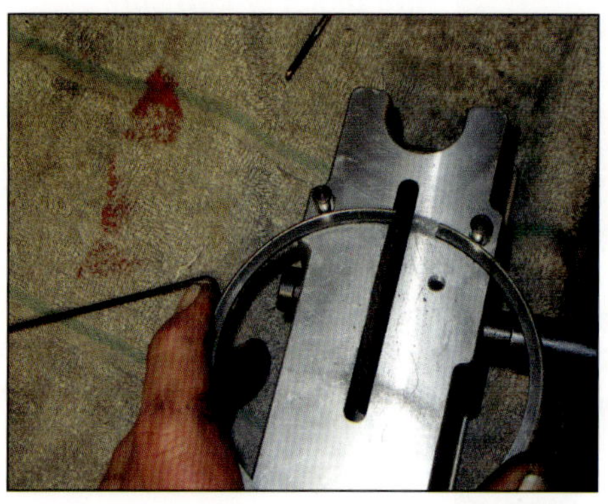

If the piston ring end gap is too small, use a tool like this to file down the ends. We do not recommend using standard files, as they do not always cut square and have more of a tendency to leave burrs.

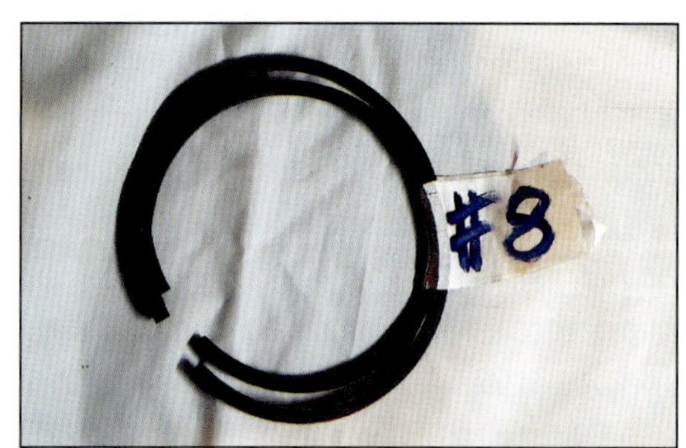

Keep the compression rings for each piston together and mark the number of the cylinder where they belong.

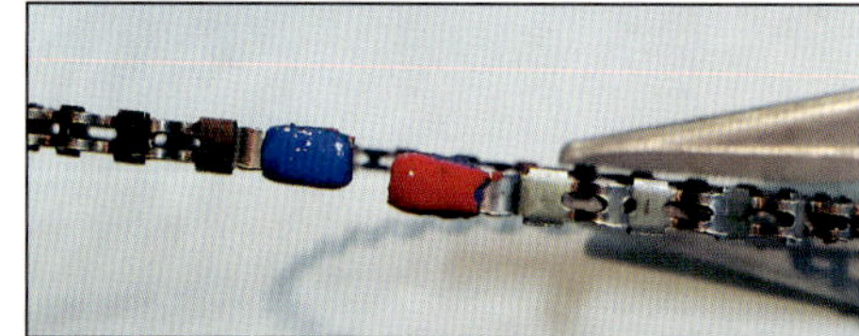

When installing the oil ring expander, make sure the two colored ring ends are next to each other like this. If you can't see both ends, it means one end has slipped underneath the other. Pay attention to the ends as you install the side rails. It's common for the ends to become overlapped during the process.

Hold one end of the side rail while winding the other end into place. Install the lower rail first. Use a feeler gauge to avoid scratching the piston during this process.

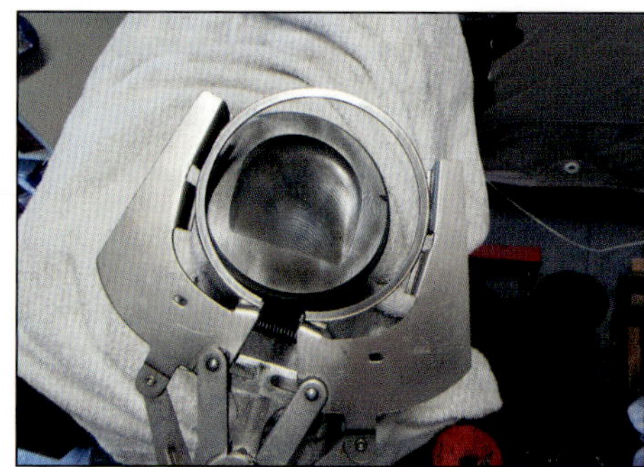

Use the piston ring expander tool to open the ring just enough for it to fit over the piston and into the lower ring groove.

rings, the oil ring side rails can be twisted lightly during installation. Put one end of a side rail in the lower rail, below the expander, and hold it there. Next, carefully wind the expander into place. Do the same for the upper side rail.

Note that the side rails are all the same, so they don't have to be installed with a particular orientation (up or down). With the side rails in place, make sure that both colored ends of the expander can still be seen. If not, remove the side rails, reposition the expander, and reinstall the side rails. With the oil ring assembly properly assembled, position the gaps of the side rails so they are each 90 degrees offset from the ends of the expander and 180 degrees opposite of each other.

Next, install the lower compression ring. The piston ring package should identify which ring is for the upper groove and which is for the lower groove. Also, there will be a dot on each ring, which must face up. Repeat this process for the upper compression ring.

Position the compression ring gaps so the lower ring is aligned with the colored ends of the oil ring expander. The upper ring gap should be 180 degrees opposite of the lower ring.

Pistons

Coat the inside of the number-1 cylinder with engine oil. Do not use assembly lube because it could delay piston ring seating, which requires the friction from direct contact with the cylinder walls during break-in. Rotate the crankshaft until the journal for the number-1 cylinder is positioned opposite the cylinder (bottom of piston stroke).

Remove the bearing cap from the number-1 connecting rod and install

When installing the pistons, note that the notch on the top must face the front of the engine.

Use a hammer handle to gently drive the piston into its bore. Go slowly, as it's easy to damage a piston ring if it pops out of the ring compressor.

a bearing insert into the connecting rod, aligning the tab with the notch in the connecting rod. Put short sections of rubber hose over the connecting rod bolts to protect the crankshaft as the piston is installed in the bore. Do not lubricate the bearing at this point.

Apply oil to the piston rings and position the piston so the notch faces forward. Install the piston in a piston ring compressor tool with the bottom of the piston skirt protruding from the bottom of the tool. Tighten the tool to compress the rings and slide the bottom of the piston skirt into the cylinder bore. Align the bottom of the tool with the block deck. It is critical that there be no gap between the tool and the block deck.

Gently tap the piston into the cylinder bore. Each tap should move the piston just a little bit at a time. If there is any resistance, it's probably because the ring compressor is not tight enough or a piston ring has popped out between the tool and the block. Remove the piston and try again. It's common for oil ring side rails to pop out during installation, and they are very easily bent.

After the piston has cleared the compressor tool, continue to tap the top of the piston while carefully guiding the connecting rod bearing onto the crankshaft journal. When the bearing is tight on the journal, install a piece of Plastigauge on the journal and install the connecting rod bearing and cap over the bolts, making sure to align the markings on the rod and cap.

Install the connecting rod nuts and tighten them to specification. Remove the bearing cap and check the connecting rod oil clearance by comparing the width of the crushed Plastigauge with the envelope. Compare this measurement to the specification in the Appendix. If the measurement is not within specification, either the incorrect bearing was used or there is a problem with the machine work. Once the oil clearance has been checked, scrape off the Plastigauge with a piece of plastic, such as a credit card.

After determining that the connecting rod bearing oil clearance is correct, push up on the connecting rod. This is most easily done by pushing on the rod bolts. Push up far enough to allow lubrication of the upper bearing half. Use thick lubricant designed for the engine bearing assembly.

Rotate the crankshaft so the crankshaft journal presses against

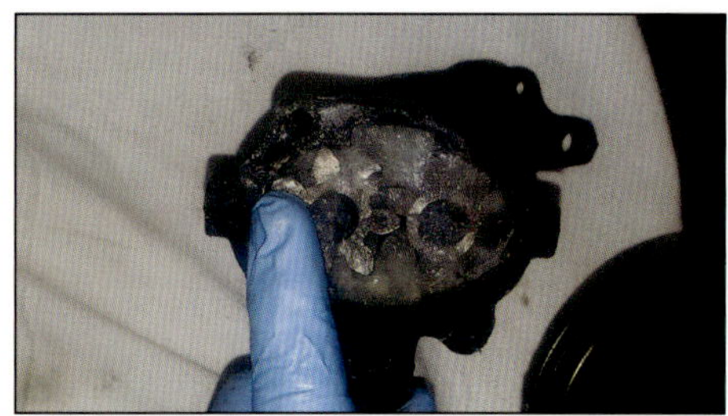
Remove the cover from the new oil pump and pack it with petroleum jelly. This will allow the pump to prime quickly.

Install the oil pump driveshaft.

Install the oil pump and gasket, making sure that the hex on the shaft properly engages with the hex recess in the oil pump. Tighten the bolts to the torque listed in the Appendix.

the connecting rod bearing. Put a bearing insert into the connecting rod cap and install the cap and nuts, aligning the markings on the cap and rod to be sure the cap isn't installed backward. Torque the nuts to the specification listed in the Appendix.

Oil Pump

Always use a new oil pump at rebuild time. Why take a chance of ruining the new engine? For a standard rebuild, it isn't necessary to use a high-volume pump. That will just raise the oil pressure and create extra friction. High-volume pumps are only recommended on racing engines that run extra bearing clearance that reduces pressure.

Timing Chain and Sprockets

Reinstall the woodruff key at the front of the crankshaft. Align the groove of the crankshaft sprocket with the woodruff key and press on the crankshaft sprocket. Tap lightly on the sprocket to get it to move. Do not seat the sprocket completely. Instead, press it on until it's about 1/2 inch from the fully seated position.

New timing chains are usually very tight, sometimes making it difficult to seat the camshaft sprocket on the camshaft. Follow this procedure to make this process easier:

1. Rotate the crankshaft until the mark on the crankshaft sprocket faces straight up.
2. Temporarily place the camshaft sprocket on the end of the camshaft and rotate the camshaft until the timing mark on the camshaft sprocket faces straight down.
3. Remove the camshaft sprocket and drape the timing chain over the sprocket with the timing mark still facing down.
4. Lower the sprocket and chain as an assembly, looping it under the crankshaft sprocket.
5. Pull the chain tight and attempt to press the camshaft sprocket over the end of the camshaft. If the small hole in the camshaft sprocket is not perfectly aligned with the dowel pin in the camshaft, rotate the camshaft slightly to obtain perfect alignment.
6. Press both sprockets into place, each a little bit at a time, keeping the sprockets aligned vertically.
7. As the camshaft sprocket gets close to the end of the camshaft, try to fit it into place. If it does not fit, tap both sprockets a little at a time until it does fit.
8. Once the camshaft sprocket is in place, check the alignment of the marks, which should point exactly toward each other.

Install the fuel pump eccentric and camshaft bolt, then tighten the bolt to the torque specification listed in the Appendix.

Align the timing marks as shown. The mark on the camshaft sprocket should face straight down, and the mark on the crankshaft sprocket should face straight up.

Final Assembly

We're now rounding third base and heading home! In this chapter, we're going to assemble the components that have been so carefully overhauled. All parts should be prepared for assembly, all bolt holes clean and a complete engine gasket set available. Take stock of the gaskets that were purchased to be sure they are correct for the engine and that all the correct gaskets are included. If not, purchase additional gaskets.

Here are the gaskets and seals that are needed for assembly:

- Valve cover gaskets
- Cylinder head gaskets
- Intake manifold gaskets
- Thermostat cover gasket
- Exhaust manifold gaskets
- Front engine cover gasket
- Water pump gasket
- Oil filter adapter gasket
- Distributor gasket or O-ring seal
- Fuel pump gasket
- Front crankshaft oil seal
- Rear crankshaft oil seal
- Oil pan gasket set

Strongly consider replacing the following components at the time of overhaul:

- Camshaft thrust button and spring
- Oil pump
- Cylinder head bolts (particularly if the engine was overheated)
- Water pump (highly recommended)
- Thermostat (absolutely essential!)
- Fuel pump
- Distributor (with a new or rebuilt unit)
- Oil pressure sending unit (strongly recommended)
- Coolant temperature sending unit (strongly recommended)

Assemble the engine in the following order:

- Oil filter adapter
- Oil gallery plugs
- Oil pressure sending unit
- Oil filler tube
- Engine front cover
- Water pump (immediately after front cover)
- Oil pan
- Vibration damper
- Fuel pump
- Cylinder heads
- Valvetrain
- Intake manifold
- Thermostat and housing
- Distributor
- Valve covers
- Engine mounts
- Exhaust manifolds

Oil Filter Adapter

Apply some Gasgacinch to the mounting surface of the oil filter adapter and stick the gasket to the adapter. Let the Gasgacinch dry a bit, then put a light coat of RTV sealer on top of the gasket. Install the adapter and three bolts. Tighten them to the specification listed in the Appendix.

Oil Gallery Plugs

Inspect the block thoroughly to ensure all coolant and oil plugs are in place on the block.

The front oil gallery plugs are different sizes. One of them (usually the passenger's side) has a small hole that serves to lubricate the timing chain and sprockets. If there is no hole, or if it's plugged, the chain and gears could fail prematurely. This is particularly true if a factory-type nylon camshaft gear is used.

As a review: There are four main gallery plugs on the engine, two at each end. The front gallery plugs are next to the camshaft bore. At the rear, one gallery plug is external and the other internal, next to the distributor drive gear on the camshaft. The internal gallery plug has an access hole in the rear of the block that must be sealed by a small steel plug.

Make sure the internal plug has a small hole in it for lubrication of the distributor drive gears. Put a little non-hardening sealant around the outside edge of the access plug before driving it into place. The external rear oil gallery plug should be wrapped with Teflon tape prior to installation.

Sealing Tips

Modern engine designs use machined gasket surfaces and high-technology gaskets. Unfortunately, that's not the case with Oldsmobile engines that were designed more than half a century ago. Back then, cork, paper, and rubber were the primary materials available. Stamped sheet-metal covers were the norm, which are prone to warpage and leakage.

When assembling the engine, great care must be taken to ensure that there will be no leaks. All sheet-metal gasket surfaces should be inspected for bending and warpage.

Although factory service manuals do not recommend some of the techniques that are included here, keep in mind that some of the sealers that we recommend were either not available or not thoroughly tested when the engine was manufactured. The quality of RTV, for example, has improved dramatically since the 1970s.

Consider using a light coat of RTV for many gasket installations, even in situations where it might not be absolutely necessary to achieve a good gasket seal. This is done for insurance against potential issues related to imperfections in gasket surfaces that may have scratches or dents that can't easily be seen.

In some cases, we call out sealants by brand. This does not represent any kind of brand endorsement. These are sealant brands common to the industry that we have experience with. Alternatives are available. Use what you know and trust. For example, some people use weatherstrip adhesive to attach gaskets to surfaces instead of Gasgacinch. Weatherstrip adhesive will work. We just think weatherstrip adhesive is more difficult to work with and harder to remove on disassembly.

Gasgacinch (or an equivalent) holds gaskets tightly in place, preventing them from moving or deforming during component assembly.

Don't be influenced by purists who sometimes say, "The factory didn't use those sealants, you don't need 'em." When the engine was originally built at the factory, all the parts were brand new with perfectly flat gasket surfaces and assembled by people who were well practiced in the techniques necessary to make a leak-free engine. Even then, leaks were common. ■

RTV sealant (sometimes called silicone) is great for filling scratches or uneven surfaces, particularly on sheet-metal covers.

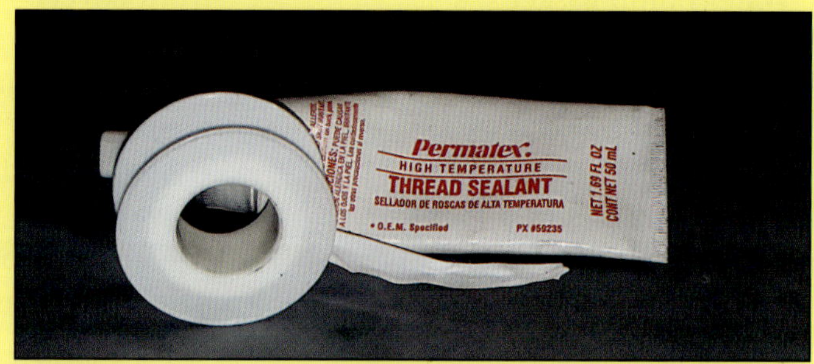

Teflon thread sealant (either in tape form or liquid type) is used to prevent leaks at threaded fittings, such as on sending units and oil gallery plugs.

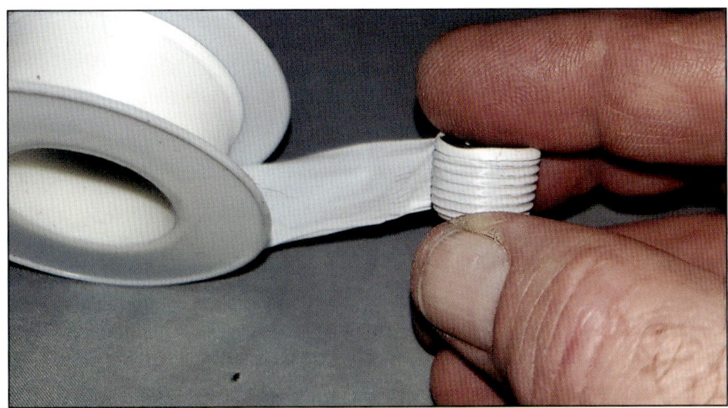

Plugs that are exposed to the outside of the engine should be sealed with Teflon sealant, otherwise oil can seep out through the threads. Keep in mind that the oil behind these plugs is under high pressure.

Put thread sealant on the threads of the oil pressure sending unit, then install and tighten it securely. Shown is a special socket designed to fit over the end of the unit and fully engage the unique contours of the sending unit. A socket is not always required. A standard deep socket usually works so long as the sending unit is not overtightened.

Oil Pressure Sending Unit

The oil pressure sending unit is threaded into a hole at the top front of the engine block. Use a new sending unit, as old sending units cannot always be relied upon. Put some thread sealer on the threads to avoid an oil leak. Some say not to put sealant on the sending units since they ground electrically through the threaded fitting. In practice, the tapered pipe threads will force metal-to-metal contact at the top of the threads when the sending unit is tightened securely.

Oil Filler Tube

The oil filler tube is a press fit. You must thoroughly clean the tube and the hole in the engine block to be sure varnish does not interfere with installation. Put a bit of RTV sealer around the tube, then tap it into place with a hammer and a wooden block. The RTV not only seals, it lubricates as the tube is knocked into place.

Drive the tube into place with a hammer and a wood block. Firm taps should move it down a little with each hit. If not, stop and inspect the surfaces again. Sometimes, a light sanding on the tube is needed so that it fits properly. Do not pound hard, as that will damage the tube.

Spread some RTV sealant over the bottom area of the oil fill tube. This will help seal the tube and also make installation easier.

Engine Front Cover

The front cover should be cleaned thoroughly and inspected. Look for dents, deformation, and rust at the gasket surface. Lay it on a flat surface to be sure it's totally flat. New covers are commonly available, so if there are any doubts about the condition of the cover, replace it.

There are four threaded holes in the cover that must be in good condition, as they are for the upper and lower water pump bolts. If the threads

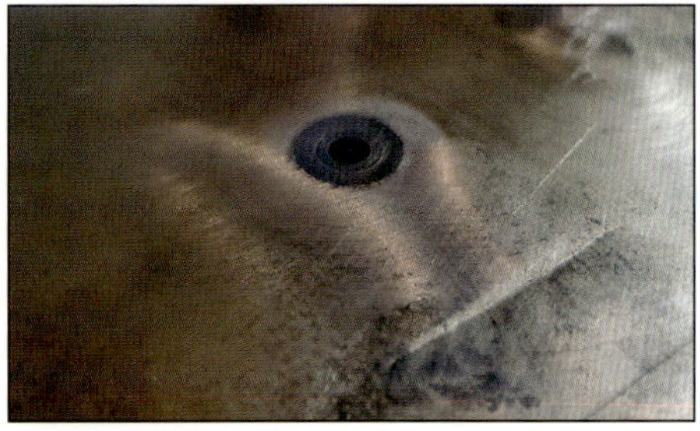

If equipped with a thrust button, the inside surface of the front cover will have a mark where the endplay button was contacting it. Ideally, it should be shiny and not have deep wear grooves. If there's deep wear, replace the cover. Also try to determine what caused the excessive wear.

Use a hammer and a block of wood to drive the front seal into place. This is better than using a socket as a driver because the front seal will need to be flush with the cover surface. The wood block will keep the seal flat as it's being driven into place.

With the front cover supported on blocks, drive the old seal out with a punch and a hammer. Work around the seal, which will keep it from getting hung up in the bore.

Apply oil to the seal lip. This is important, as otherwise the seal will be dry on initial start-up, causing heat-generating friction that could damage the seal material and lead to leaks.

Put a light coating of RTV sealant on the outside edge of the front cover seal. This will help seal imperfections in the seal bore and also help lubricate the new seal as it's driven into place.

are stripped, it's best to replace the cover. You can drill and tap the holes for 5/16 inch oversize, but the water pump bolt holes will be too small to accommodate them. You would have to also drill the four water pump bolt holes oversize.

Replace the front oil seal in the engine front cover. To do this, place the front cover on blocks of wood and drive the seal out using a hammer and a dull punch.

Turn the front cover over and inspect the bore. It should be clean and not deformed, bent, or noticeably out of round. If it is badly damaged, replace the cover. Replace the front cover seal.

After the seal is installed, it's time to attach the front cover to the engine block. Double-check the valve timing marks on the camshaft and the crankshaft gears to be sure they're perfectly aligned.

If equipped, install the camshaft thrust button. Also, install the oil slinger. In case you're wondering about the purpose of the oil slinger, it "slings" oil away from the front seal, keeping the seal cooler and also keeping it from being overwhelmed by oil during engine operation.

Don't forget to install this part, but if you find it on your bench after the engine is installed in the car, don't panic. The seal will generally still do its job, probably for a long time. Just don't expect it to remain supple and leak-free after 200,000 miles!

Make sure every bit of old gasket material is removed from the block and the front cover. Then, attach the

It's best to use a new camshaft thrust button on reassembly. Put a bit of assembly lube on the end that contacts the front cover and make sure the spring end is tight inside the fuel pump eccentric. You don't want this falling out during installation.

Many an engine builder has forgotten to install this oil slinger and then found it on the bench after the engine is in the car! This is your official reminder.

Also apply a thin layer of RTV sealant to the outer surface of the gasket to ensure a good seal. Only a tiny bit is needed.

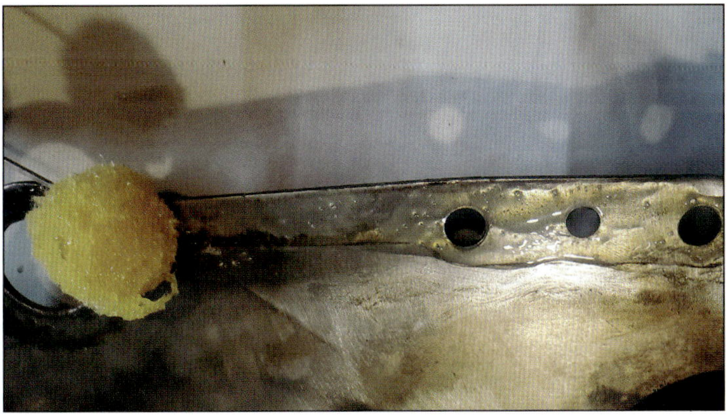

Secure the timing cover gasket to the timing cover with Gasgacinch, which will hold it in place while the cover is being installed.

front cover gasket to the front cover.

Now, place the front cover on the engine, guiding it over the alignment pins. Install the four lower bolts and the ignition timing scale. Leave the bolts finger-tight for now. Proceed immediately to water pump installation.

Water Pump

A new water pump should always be installed during an overhaul. The last thing you want to do is overheat your new engine, which will be running warmer than ever during break-in. Nevertheless, there will be a few people who will want to save a few bucks by not replacing this critical item. If you don't replace it, make absolutely sure that there is no looseness in the shaft, that the impeller is tight to the shaft, and that there are no signs of leaking out the weep hole underneath the pump.

Attach the water pump gasket to the water pump with Gasgacinch, then put a very thin coat of RTV on the gasket. Place the water pump against the front cover and install

The front cover and water pump share bolts, so installing the two parts is really one operation to ensure the gasket sealer on the front cover doesn't dry before the water pump is installed.

The larger front cover and water pump bolts thread into blind holes in the block, so they don't require sealant. The two smaller bolts at the bottom of the water pump thread through the cover and therefore are exposed to oil on the other side. Use some RTV sealant on the threads to prevent oil leaks.

the four bolts at the left and right sides of the pump. There's no reason to put sealant on these bolts, as the holes they thread into are "blind," meaning they are not exposed to coolant or oil.

Now, tighten all eight of the larger bolts: the lower cover-to-engine bolts and the water pump-to-engine bolts. Once the large bolts are installed, install the four small bolts that attach the water pump to the front cover. The lower two bolts are exposed to oil at the rear, so use RTV sealant to prevent leaks. Tighten all bolts to the torque specified in the Appendix.

Oil Pan

The oil pan gasket sealing surfaces must be free of any gasket material. The oil pan itself cannot have bends or dents at the gasket sealing surfaces. Deformation at the bolt holes from previous overtightening of the bolts can be removed with a ball-peen hammer.

Oil pan gasket rails are commonly deformed, particularly at the bolt hole areas. Check for uneven surfaces on the rails with a straightedge. Dents at holes can be removed by using an appropriately sized socket and extension as a driver. Do this on a solid flat surface, such as concrete.

A common area of leakage is at the corners where the oil pan end seals meet the pan rail gaskets. Use a dab of RTV at all four corners.

Turn the engine upside-down and install the gasket to the engine block with Gasgacinch. Install the front and rear end seals to the main bearing cap and front cover. Then, apply a small bead of RTV sealant to the four points where the gaskets meet the seals.

Vibration Damper and Hub

Inspect the hub for signs of a wear ridge from contact with the front seal. This is a common issue, and there are repair sleeves available to repair the seal surface. The repair sleeve slides over the end of the hub, creating a new seal surface.

The vibration damper itself consists of two steel components bonded together with rubber. The outer ring can become loose from the hub, resulting in a knocking noise and

A tool like this is needed to press the damper into the crankshaft far enough to get the crankshaft bolt installed. Do not hammer on the damper during installation, as it is possible to deform the front surface of the crankshaft thrust bearing.

also inaccuracy of the timing marks on the damper.

Install the vibration damper using a special tool to push it into place on the crankshaft far enough to engage several threads of the crankshaft bolt. Install the crankshaft bolt and tighten it to draw the hub to its final resting place on the crankshaft.

Tighten the crankshaft bolt to the specification listed in the Appendix. Note that on some later models the hub and damper are separate components. First, install the hub using the procedure described above, then install the damper, tightening the bolts to the torque listed in the Appendix.

Fuel Pump

Note: If the crankshaft has not been disturbed since the timing marks were aligned, the fuel pump eccentric should be pointing away from the pump arm and will allow the pump to be installed easily. If the crankshaft has been disturbed, reposition the eccentric by rotating the crankshaft; otherwise, it will be very difficult to press the fuel pump into place on the engine block.

The fuel pump should be replaced routinely at the time of the overhaul unless it had been replaced very recently and was working properly. Even if the old pump was working okay, it might not be operating at full efficiency and might have even been one of the reasons the engine was running poorly.

Apply Gasgacinch to the fuel pump gasket and put it in place on the fuel pump. Apply a light coat of RTV sealant on the top surface of the gasket. Spread grease across the top of the fuel pump arm, put the pump in place on the engine, install the bolt and nut, and tighten them to the torque listed in the Appendix.

Apply grease to the fuel pump arm when you install it. This will prevent friction with the fuel pump eccentric until oil gets to it. If the pump does not sit flush against the block, rotate the crankshaft until it does.

Cylinder Heads

Make sure the cylinder head gasket surfaces on the block and cylinder head are completely clean of any bits of gasket material or oil. Wipe down the gasket surfaces with brake cleaner prior to gasket installation to ensure ultimate cleanliness. The head gaskets are a common failure item, so don't rush through this part of the job.

Position the cylinder head on the block. Be very careful not to allow the edges of the cylinder head to nick the gasket. It may be necessary to rock the cylinder head back and forth until it seats solidly on the head gasket.

Unlike engines from other manufacturers, Oldsmobile engines have blind cylinder head bolt holes, so there's no reason to put any sealant on the cylinder head bolts. Put a small amount of oil on each bolt

Position the cylinder head gasket on the block, over the dowel pins at the upper part of the block. Make sure all of the passages and bolt holes align with the gasket holes. If you're using a composition gasket, no sealer is required. Both the head and block surfaces must be completely clean. Steel shim gaskets require a sealer. Use the sealer specified by the gasket manufacturer.

Tighten the cylinder head bolts in the sequence shown. Do not apply full torque to the bolts all at once, as you want the clamping force on the gasket to be applied evenly. Go through the sequence in three stages, increasing torque each time until the final torque is reached.

and thread it into place. Don't use too much oil; otherwise, the oil holes will fill with oil and cause the bolts to hydro-lock and not torque down correctly.

If the bolts do not thread in easily by hand, there's a problem. Look down into the bolt holes to see if there's a problem with alignment of the gasket or between the cylinder head and block. If the issue cannot be corrected with the head in place, remove the head and inspect it carefully.

Once the bolts are threaded down against the head by hand, use a socket and breaker bar to gradually tighten the bolts a half turn at a time in the proper sequence. When the bolts start getting tight, switch the socket over to a torque wrench and tighten the bolts in the proper sequence to the torque listed in the Appendix.

Valvetrain

Note: Do not prime the lifters with oil at this time. Check the lifter preload first. The lifters will be primed later in this procedure.

Install a lifter into each lifter bore to ensure it slides easily up and down and that the fit is the same among all bores. The lifter should not be able to move side to side when it is in the bore.

Assemble the pushrods, rocker arms, and fulcrums onto the cylinder heads. Be sure the tabs on the pushrods face up. Tighten the bolts securely.

Check the lifter preload. This is important even if you're using the same engine block, cylinder heads, pushrods, and rocker arms. Machining of the cylinder heads or block deck or even a different gasket thickness will change the preload.

Set the number-1 piston to TDC on the compression stroke. If you

Align the ignition timing marks and be certain that you're at top dead center on the number-1 cylinder. This can be confirmed by looking at the positions of the number-1 cylinder lifters. They should both be at the bottom of their travel.

The pushrods have tabs that must face up during installation.

It's important that the lifter preload is within range. Too little preload can allow clearance to develop, which leads to lifter clatter and potential damage. Too much preload can lead to lifter "pump-up" at higher RPM, which can hang the valves open, possibly even causing them to contact the piston heads.

On conventional lifters, lubricate the feet with thick assembly lube that's designed for camshafts and lifters. Lubrication of the feet on conventional lifters is critical, as severe damage can occur if the wrong lubricant is used. Put the lube only on the feet. The sides of the lifters should be lubricated with a light film of engine oil.

The "dogbone" guides on roller lifters keep the rollers aligned with the camshaft lobes. If the rollers aren't perfectly aligned, they might fail early. The clearance between the lifter and the guide should not exceed 0.001 inch.

If preload is not within the acceptable range, select pushrods that will correct the issue. Use an adjustable pushrod to obtain the correct preload, then measure the adjustable pushrod to determine what pushrod length is needed.

have not rotated the crankshaft since installing the front cover, rotate it exactly one turn clockwise, aligning the ignition timing marks. In this position, the intake and exhaust lifters for the number-1cylinder should both be positioned on the base circle of the camshaft. You'll know this because the lifters will be at the lowest point of their travel. In this position, check the preload at the number-2 and number-7 intake lifters and number-8 and number-4 exhaust lifters.

To check lifter preload, use wire-type feeler gauges, such as those that are used for checking spark plug gaps. Position the feeler gauge between the lifter plunger and the retaining clip at the top of the lifter. The clearance should be 0.020 inch to 0.060 inch. Check the preload for the remaining lifters, rotating the crankshaft a half turn (180 degrees) clockwise between each adjustment. Follow the chart provided.

After checking preload and making any corrections necessary, place the crankshaft back to the number-1 TDC position. This position is needed for installing the distributor.

Remove the lifters and lubricate them for final installation. For conventional lifters, coat the foot of each lifter with thick assembly lube designed for break-in of conventional lifters. The lube should contain a

Lifter Preload Checking Sequence

	Intake Number	Exhaust Number
TDC number-1 cylinder, check	2, 7	8, 4
Rotate 90 degrees, check	1, 8	6, 3
Rotate 90 degrees, check	3, 4	7, 5
Rotate 90 degrees, check	6, 5	1, 2

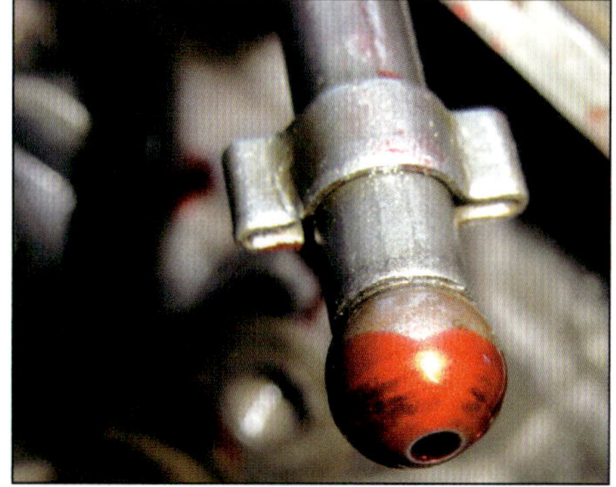

Lubricate both ends of the pushrods with thick assembly lube.

high-pressure anti-scuff additive.

Do not put assembly lube on the sides of the lifters, as conventional lifters need to spin in their bores at start-up or the camshaft and lifters could be damaged. A light coat of oil on the sides of the lifters is all that's needed.

For roller lifters, no special precautions are necessary regarding the lifters other than making sure the dogbone guides and retainers are reinstalled correctly. Make sure the dogbones fit tightly against each lifter. A loose fit can cause misalignment of the lifter to the camshaft. Even just a little bit of misalignment can cause the lifter to fail early.

Put a bit of assembly lube on the top and bottom of each pushrod, then install the pushrods, making sure the tabs face up. Now, install the rocker arms and fulcrums. Apply assembly lube to the rocker arm-to-fulcrum contact points. Torque the fulcrum bolts to the specification listed in the Appendix.

Intake manifold gaskets usually come with end seals designed to be used between the ends of the intake manifold and the front and rear block rails. These seals are a common source of leakage. Instead, use RTV sealant on the end rails. Dimple the end rails with a hammer and a punch. This will help the RTV stick better.

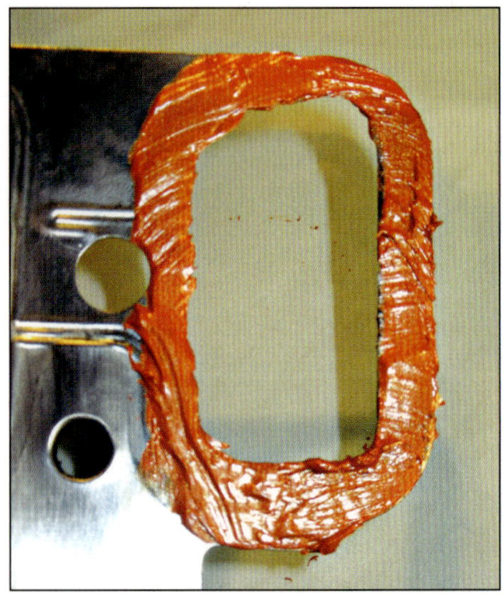

Apply RTV sealant at the four coolant passage openings at the ends of the intake manifold gaskets. The RTV should also be applied around the coolant passages on the cylinder head.

Intake Manifold

The intake manifold is one of the most common sources of leaks, particularly vacuum leaks at the port areas. On disassembly of our project engine, we found that one of the intake ports was sucking oil from the valley area through a leak at an intake port. Problems like this are very hard to diagnose, so it's best not to get them in the first place!

Any issues with machining of the cylinder heads or intake manifold can lead to misalignment of the parts. It's a good idea to have a "dry run" to fit the intake in place and check for any misalignment. Be clean and meticulous when installing the intake manifold.

Clean the gasket mating surfaces thoroughly and clean the threads of the bolt holes with a tap. Also run a die over the bolts. Remember that if you make a mistake installing the intake manifold, you could end up with a vacuum, oil, or coolant leak. Maybe all three!

Over the years, Oldsmobile engines came from the factory with different intake manifold gasket designs. Most engines used paper-type gaskets, which do a good job of sealing the intake if the proper methods are followed.

Later models used a steel gasket with an integral valley tray. This design helped keep hot oil off the bottom of the intake manifold, which allowed the manifold to operate slightly cooler and therefore allow the intake air to be slightly cooler and thus more dense. That's the theory at least. For most engine builds, this should not be a significant consideration. Any gain in performance or fuel economy will be unnoticeable.

Before installing the intake, dimple around the end rails on the cylinder block with a hammer and punch. This is a trick used by Mondello Performance to prevent oil leaks. Also make sure the gasket surfaces on the cylinder head and manifold are spotlessly clean.

Paper Gaskets

On paper gaskets, use Gasgacinch to secure them to the cylinder head. Align the gasket to the ports rather than the bolt holes to the gasket. If necessary, trim the gasket around the bolt holes with a razor blade. After the gasket is installed, apply Gasgacinch around the intake ports and RTV sealant around the water ports at the front and rear of the block (two on each head, four total).

Apply a thick bead of RTV sealant on the block end rails. Be sure the RTV gets into the corners where the block and heads meet.

Tighten the intake manifold bolts to the torque listed in the Appendix, following the sequence shown here. Don't tighten the bolts all at once. Instead, work up to the final torque in three stages, increasing torque each time through the sequence.

The two center bolts on each side of the intake manifold (four bolts total) are exposed to oil inside the engine. Apply RTV sealant to these bolts when installing them.

Valley Tray Gasket

If you're using a steel gasket assembly with a valley tray, apply a thin coat of RTV sealant around each intake port and a slightly thicker coat at the water ports at the front and rear of the block. Put the gasket in place.

New gaskets usually have alignment tabs that will help hold the gasket in place on the manifold surface. Apply another thin layer of RTV to the outside of the gasket in the areas around the intake ports and a thicker layer around the area of the water ports.

All Gaskets

Apply RTV to the end rails of the block. While end seals are included in gasket sets, they are not as reliable as properly applied RTV.

Carefully lower the intake manifold in place. Since some of the bolt holes are exposed to oil, put a bit of RTV sealant on the bolt threads.

Tighten the bolts by hand, then use a socket and breaker bar to gradually tighten the bolts about a half turn at a time in the proper sequence. When the bolts start getting tight, switch the socket over to a torque wrench and tighten the bolts in the sequence shown to the torque listed in the Appendix.

Thermostat and Housing

Place a short section of 3/4-inch heater hose on the tube at the top of the water pump. Clamp the hose in place and trim it to a length that's correct to join it to the tube attached

The advent of powerful flashlights has provided a new leak-detection tool. Attach the end of a flashlight to an opening in the engine using duct tape to prevent light from escaping, then, in a darkened room, inspect for light showing through at gasket surfaces.

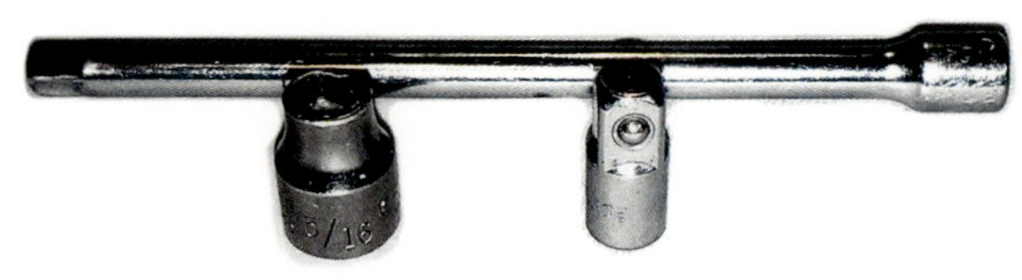

Pre-oiling the engine primes the oil pump and circulates oil through all the passages in the engine. This means instant oiling on start-up and also allows you to check for leaks before installing the engine in the vehicle. This requires a heavy-duty drill, a long extension, and a 5/16-inch socket.

to the thermostat housing. Slide a second clamp loosely over the hose.

Attach the thermostat housing gasket to the thermostat housing with Gasgacinch. Place the thermostat in place in the intake manifold and spread a thin coat of RTV sealant on top of the gasket. Position the thermostat housing over the thermostat while simultaneously sliding the tube into the hose. Install and tighten the thermostat housing bolts, then slide the hose clamp up and tighten it.

Thoroughly inspect the exterior of the engine, looking for points of potential leakage. It's easy to miss installing a plug or forget to tighten something. In a darkened room, use a bright flashlight directed into openings such as the distributor opening. Look carefully at all gasket sealing points at all angles. If a little light is getting through, it'll probably have a leak.

Pre-Oiling the Engine

It is strongly recommended to pre-oil the engine prior to installation in the vehicle. To do so, fill the engine with oil and install the oil filter. This brings us into the discussion of what type of oil and/or additives to use during engine break-in, which is covered in Chapter 8.

To monitor oil pressure during the pre-oiling process, connect a mechanical pressure gauge in place of the oil pressure sending unit.

For pre-oiling, you will need a 5/16-inch socket, a long extension, and a powerful variable-speed reversible electric drill. Attach the socket to the extension using duct tape to prevent it from falling off the end of the extension and into the engine.

Carefully lower the socket on the extension into the distributor hole on the engine and engage the socket onto the end of the oil pump driveshaft. Now, chuck the extension into the drill.

Set the drill to operate in reverse (counterclockwise), then operate the drill, using a slow speed at first. This is precautionary, as oil will spray everywhere if there is a leak. Run the drill at low speed while inspecting all

Secure the socket to the extension to prevent it from dropping into the engine, attach the drill to the extension, and run the drill in reverse (counterclockwise). If the drill's chuck does not open large enough to accept a 3/8-inch extension, use a reducing adapter at the end of the extension, reducing it to a smaller 1/4-inch-drive extension.

When oil is flowing into the rocker arms, the oiling system is developing good pressure. It may take a while for this to happen, and likely the oil won't flow evenly on every rocker arm. Rotate the crankshaft periodically, which should even things out.

When installing the distributor, mark the aluminum base below the terminal for the number-1 cylinder. Align the rotor with this mark during distributor installation.

around the engine to be sure there are no leaks. Now, raise the speed of the drill to about three-quarters of the full-speed setting. You should feel strong resistance as you do this.

Continue operating the drill for several minutes, looking for oil to appear around the lifters and at the pushrod end of the rocker arms. If there is no oil at the rocker arms for a minute or two, that's normal. Also, there might not be oil at all at the rocker arms. That is also normal. You'll usually need to rotate the crankshaft to obtain oil flow to all of the pushrods and rocker arms.

Oiling at all the rocker arms is important to verify, as there is always a possibility that there is a plugged passageway or other problem in the block. The rocker arms are the high point in the lubrication system, so if oil is there, assume that there is oil throughout the engine.

Distributor

If you have not disturbed the crankshaft since you installed the valvetrain, the number-1 piston should be at its TDC firing position. This is where it should be when installing the distributor. Mark the distributor housing underneath the number-1 wire terminal, which is usually at the left rear of the cap.

Install a new gasket or O-ring on the distributor housing. If a gasket is used, attach it to the distributor with Gasgacinch.

The distributor drive gear is ground at an angle, so the rotor will move a bit when lowering the distributor into place. The installation process is complicated further by alignment of the oil pump driveshaft. The driveshaft may have to rotate a bit to get the distributor to seat completely.

Installing the distributor always takes some trial and error. The end result you're looking for is that the rotor is pointing to the mark on the distributor base, which should be at the rear of the engine, slightly to the left. Once that is done, install the distributor hold-down clamp but leave it loose at this time.

Rotate the crankshaft slightly counterclockwise while observing the ignition timing marks. Position the timing marks to indicate 15 degrees before top dead center (BTDC). Realign the distributor rotor with the mark on the base, then tighten the hold-down clamp securely. Don't overtighten the clamp bolt, since it will be loosened again after the engine is started. Install the distributor cap.

Valve Covers

Install the valve covers. Do not overtighten the nuts; otherwise, the cover could be dented and the gasket could be crushed. The factory torque specification is only 7 ft-lbs.

Engine Mounts

Install new engine mounts. They're relatively inexpensive and difficult to replace once the engine is in the car. The new engine will probably have more torque than it did before, so a mount might end up breaking the first time that you step on the gas hard. It's better to be safe than sorry! The mount bolts do not have a specific torque value. Make sure they're good and tight.

Exhaust Manifolds

If you're using the original exhaust manifolds, the mounting face might be warped or the bolt holes may no longer line up correctly. Surface warpage can be accommodated by using a thick exhaust gasket. Misalignment of bolt holes can be corrected with a reamer to make the holes bigger.

If the manifolds are badly warped, we recommend replacing them. They are available new for reasonable prices. You can also probably find a good deal on used manifolds, so long as they are not high-performance-style manifolds, which are now rare and expensive.

Engine Installation and Start-Up

Finally! The overhaul project is complete, and it's time to get that beauty installed and running. Once again, take your time and make sure everything is right as you move through each step. The work being done now is just as critical as any of the engine work that has been done previously.

Oldsmobile used a variety of colors when painting its engines over the years. For an enthusiast, the color is important, as it can give indication as to the era the engine was built and sometimes the performance level of the engine. The Oldsmobile gold and bronze colors are beautiful but difficult to find at the auto parts stores. You can also find them online.

Preparing the Engine

The assembled engine should be spotlessly clean, and now it can be painted. Depending on the year and model, Oldsmobile engines came

Engine paint has a higher temperature rating than normal household paint or even standard automotive paints. It's usually rated to handle 500°F or more. That's enough for the engine block and heads but not enough for exhaust components. Never use standard paint on an engine. It will not last.

Header paint (right) is available in different colors, but the most popular colors are silver and black. Header paint can handle 1,500°F and can be used on exhaust manifolds as well. Exhaust manifold paint (left) is designed to handle 1,200°F and provides a thick, durable coating. It is available in a gray color that simulates the original raw cast-iron look of an exhaust manifold.

Such a beautiful new engine. Why put it in that ugly engine compartment? Thoroughly clean the engine compartment with engine degreaser, being careful not to get the wiring connectors wet when spraying the degreaser off with water. Hit any rusty spots with sandpaper.

Give a fresh coat of paint to the firewall, fender liners, and the crossmember. This is not just for looks. Fresh paint will help in tracking down potential leaks. Engine paint is not required for these areas, but use quality paint. Flat black is usually the best choice. When painting the engine brackets, use engine paint, as anything attached to the engine will be getting very hot.

from the factory in a variety of colors: gold, bronze, metallic blue, red, and even black on later models.

Do some research to determine what color was used on your vehicle. Of course, don't be constrained by originality! Engine paint comes in a rainbow of colors. For practicality, darker colors are better, as they don't show dirt as much as light colors.

Preparing the Engine Compartment

Use engine degreaser to get rid of all the gunk in the engine compartment, particularly on the crossmember under the engine. It will be important to have all areas around the engine clean to help in diagnosing any possible oil leaks.

The engine compartment should also be organized. Move tubes, hoses, and wiring harnesses out of the way to accommodate engine installation and to allow for easy identification of connectors after the engine is installed.

Flush the radiator with water. Put a garden hose into the top radiator hose fitting and let water flow out the bottom radiator fitting until the water comes out clean.

If yours is a collector car, do the correct engine compartment detailing. It will be easier to do with the engine removed.

On any car, paint under the hood to give the engine compartment a fresh look and to prevent rust. This will also help in identifying leaks, particularly coolant leaks, as they tend to leave dry residue on paint. Before painting, be sure to mask all around the engine compartment, particularly the hood, fenders, and the front of the vehicle. You'd be surprised how far overspray can travel, even with a spray can!

In a full vehicle restoration, all wiring, hoses, and other components in the engine compartment are removed and replaced with new or restored parts when the vehicle is reassembled. For most rebuilds, these items will stay in place. This can create challenges when masking prior to painting.

Masking tape and newspaper can be used to cover most components, but it is difficult to apply to hoses and wiring. Also, masking tape is often difficult to remove from hoses and wiring after the paint has dried. Household aluminum foil is perfect for wrapping around these awkwardly shaped items.

Paint the accessory mounting brackets that bolt onto the engine. Here you will need to use engine paint because components that are directly attached to the engine can reach high temperatures.

Installing the Engine

Before installing the engine, take some time to check everything over once again to be sure fasteners are tight and that all vacuum hoses and fuel lines are properly connected. You've already checked that there were no serious oil leaks when it was pre-oiled, right? However, there is still the possibility of a coolant leak if you forgot to install a coolant plug, sending unit, or other thermostatic control switch. Hopefully you took a lot of photos during engine removal, which will be very helpful at this point.

Automatic and Manual Transmissions Tips

If the vehicle has an automatic transmission, remove the torque converter and have it inspected at a transmission shop. If there's any doubt about the condition of the torque converter, replace it. While the torque converter is out, replace the front seal and the bushing that goes behind it. It's common to find that there is a leak at the front of the transmission that's gone unnoticed due to leaks from the engine. You don't want to find the leak after the engine is installed.

If the vehicle has a manual transmission, inspect the clutch pressure plate, the clutch disc, the flywheel, the release bearing, and the pilot bushing. It's usually a good idea to replace the clutch components and have the flywheel surfaced at the time of an overhaul. You won't be able to enjoy the smooth power of a new engine if you have a slipping clutch. ■

It's common for the transmission front seal to develop a leak over time. Remove the torque converter to get to the seal. Behind the seal is a bronze bushing that should also be replaced, since a worn bearing contributes to seal failure. Also note the two lugs that drive the transmission front pump.

The torque converter hub has two cutouts that engage the lugs on the transmission pump. When you reinstall the torque converter, make sure it is fully engaged on the transmission input shaft, the stator shaft, and the pump drive lugs. These three engagements are usually felt separately as the converter is pushed and rotated into place. Getting the converter engaged can take some time and effort.

Decide which accessories and other external components to attach to the engine during installation. Most people want to keep momentum going and finish assembly while the engine is on the stand. It makes for nice photos on social media accounts! However, be strategic. Some components are easier to install while the engine is on the stand, and other components can make it more difficult to guide the engine into place and are not any harder to install in the engine compartment.

We recommend leaving the carburetor off the engine at this point, since it's relatively fragile and the

We recommend leaving the carburetor off the engine during installation. There is a chance of damaging the carburetor that outweighs the slight amount of extra effort involved with installing the carburetor while the engine is in the vehicle.

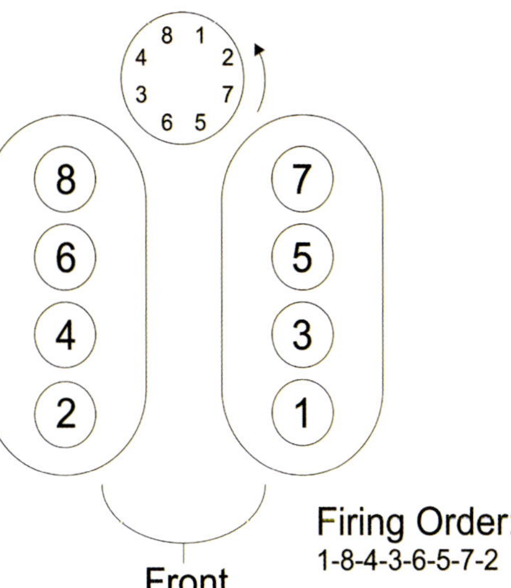

When routing the spark plug wires, refer to this chart.

engine hoist chain will be near it during installation.

Since it's at the back of the engine, the distributor cap is vulnerable to damage during installation. At minimum, disengage the distributor cap retainers so the cap can move if it contacts the firewall or other obstructions during engine installation. However, it is a good idea to install the spark plugs and route the spark plug wires at this point. It's much easier to do this on the engine stand.

Use clips to be sure the wires are kept away from the headers or exhaust manifolds, which are soon to be very hot! Don't forget that the distributor shaft on an Oldsmobile engine rotates counterclockwise, unlike many other engines.

When you're ready to put the engine into place, raise the vehicle, support it securely on jack stands, set the parking brake, and block the rear wheels.

Caution: We want to remind you again how important safety is when dealing with the maneuvering of heavy components. It's easy to get a finger trapped between a loaded engine mount and bracket or between the engine block and transmission—and these are minor compared to the severe injuries that you will have if the engine, transmission, or vehicle are not safely supported at all times.

Place a floor jack under the transmission bellhousing and raise the transmission until it is at or above its normal height with the engine installed. Remove any supports that were in place for the transmission and exhaust components. Allow the pipes to hang freely.

Take a final look over the engine compartment to ensure all hoses, lines, electrical wiring, and connectors are positioned out of the way and will not interfere with removal. It's common for electrical wires to get caught up in the engine during installation, leading to broken wires and connectors. Hoses and lines are also common places for the engine to get hung up. An engine should lower into place evenly. If that's not happening at any point, inspect carefully at all points, including underneath the engine, to be sure the engine is free to move.

The final stages of engine installation are precise. The engine must fit tightly and evenly against the transmission bellhousing. Rotate the engine a bit to make it level to the transmission. Watch the mounting surfaces of the engine and the transmission, and make sure they are aligned vertically.

The transmission can be lifted up and down with the floor jack to get this alignment correct. Apply some pressure at the front of the engine to get the engine and transmission to seat against each other. There are dowel pins on the engine to help with this. What usually gets the dowel pins into place is a combination of light rearward pressure on the engine, slight rotation of the engine, and small up-and-down movements of the transmission.

Once the transmission is in place on the dowel pins, install two transmission-to-engine bolts: one on each side. Make sure to engage at least three threads of the bolts with only the force of your fingers. At this point, the final seating of the engine against the transmission can be done by tightening the bolts.

Double-check that there are no wires or hoses trapped between the engine and transmission. Then,

Installation Safety

Have an assistant available during engine installation so that the process can be carefully monitored. One of you should be watching every inch of movement to ensure there are no obstructions and that the front of the engine is in alignment with the engine mounts and the transmission bellhousing.

Installation is not always straight down. Often the engine will need to be maneuvered to clear obstacles and angled to properly fit over the engine mounts and sit flush with the transmission mounting surface. While lowering and maneuvering the engine, it commonly sways. Hold it tightly during these times to prevent it from hitting vulnerable components such as the wiper motor. ■

slowly tighten the bolts, moving back and forth between them, a half turn at a time. If there is resistance, stop and find the obstruction. The bolts should pull the transmission up against the engine very easily without much more force.

Once the engine and transmission are flush, install and tighten the remaining transmission-to-engine bolts and tighten them to 35 ft-lbs. Remove the floor jack.

Now, guide the engine mounts over the brackets on the frame. A little rearward movement of the engine/transmission will usually be necessary. Sometimes it's difficult to get both mounts to seat evenly over the brackets so that both through-bolt holes align. In this case, position the engine to install one of the through-bolts. Then, use the hoist to position the engine so the other bolt will go into place. Tighten the bolts to 50 ft-lbs.

With the engine now solidly in place, install the remaining components by reversing the disassembly procedures outlined in Chapter 4. Refer to the Appendix for torque specifications.

Fill the cooling system with a 50/50 mixture of coolant and distilled water. Most early models used conventional ethylene glycol coolant, while later models, starting in the late 1990s, used red Dex-Cool. Since you're starting fresh, you can pretty much use any coolant you want.

Long-life coolants such as Dex-Cool or an equivalent have a service life up to 100,000 miles. However, they are more expensive and more prone to coagulation from excess air intrusion into the cooling system due to leaks.

Check for leaks in the cooling system. If there is the slightest drip now, it will become a significant leak after the engine gets warm and the cooling system develops pressure. Fix any leaks now, as you won't want to stop the engine until the 20-minute break-in procedure is complete.

It is advisable to pressurize the cooling system to the listed cap pressure rating to ensure there will be no leaks. This test requires a cooling system pressure tester. While a tester like this can be a bit pricey, it will be useful in the future for diagnosing coolant leaks.

Choosing Oil

Note: Do not use synthetic oils during the break-in period. Even if you plan to run synthetic oil, start out with non-synthetic oil for at least the first 1,000 miles.

Engine oils are rated as to their service grade and viscosity. The American Petroleum Institute (API) has a rating system for service grade that rates the ability of an oil to operate properly under high-stress conditions. The rating system has progressed over time, starting with SA in the 1930s, continuing through SN at the time of publication. The farther along in the alphabet, the better the oil. However, the latest API formulations do not have zinc, which is essential for break-in and for conventional lifters.

Viscosity is an oil's resistance to pouring. The higher the number, the thicker (or more viscous) the oil. Oils with a higher viscosity result in higher oil pressure. Select an oil with the viscosity that has the best chance of achieving the oil pressure specified for your engine (listed in the Appendix).

Bearing clearance plays a big role in oil pressure. The more bear-

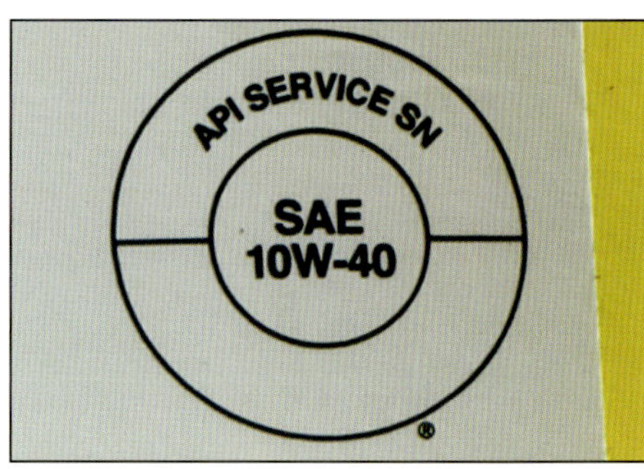

The American Petroleum Institute (API) rates oils as to their ability to handle high temperatures, neutralize contaminants, and resist molecular breakdown. The newer grades do not have high levels of zinc (ZDDP or ZDTP) as a part of their additive packages because it's assumed that the oil will be used in newer engines with roller lifters. This can create an issue if an engine has conventional flat-foot lifters.

If you have conventional lifters, it's best to use oil with zinc over the life of the engine. While it is somewhat more expensive than standard oil, it's cheap insurance considering the catastrophic damage that can happen if a camshaft or lifter fails, sending debris throughout the engine.

Even with roller lifters, a break-in additive is recommended for the first oil fill. Break-in additives supplement the oil with zinc and other high-pressure lubricants that are needed during the initial high-wear start-up phase.

ing clearance it has, the less pressure can be developed by a particular viscosity of oil. For break-in, SAE 30 oil will be appropriate for a stock rebuild with bearing clearances within new-engine tolerances. This assumes a standard-volume oil pump.

If the bearing clearances are more than stock, an oil with higher viscosity is needed, such as SAE 40. If in doubt, the machine shop should be able to provide a recommendation based on your bearing clearances.

After break-in, select a multi-viscosity oil that allows the oil to flow better at lower temperatures, such as when you first start your car on a winter day. For most engines, 10W30 or 10W40 will work well. An engine with stock bearing clearances will probably like 10W30, while an engine with more bearing clearance might prefer 10W40.

If the engine has conventional flat-foot lifters, you have something else to consider. Modern automotive oils do not contain high-pressure additives that are required for conventional lifters. The missing additive is zinc, which was removed from modern oils due to environmental concerns. But oils containing high-pressure lubricants are still available.

An early solution was to use heavy-duty diesel oils, since they still contain zinc. But diesel oil is formulated differently than automotive oils. There are now many specialty automotive oils available that contain zinc and are designed for use with conventional lifters.

When first starting your new engine, use a break-in additive. Break-in oils contain supplemental additives that will further protect the camshaft and lifters.

Starting the Engine

The big moment! The main event! This is where all the hard work pays off. You're eager to turn that key, but be sure to take enough time to prepare your engine—and yourself.

Have at least one assistant with you during your first start-up. He or she will provide another set of eyes to identify any issues once the engine starts. Ideally, this is someone with mechanical knowledge, who can identify problems and make adjustments.

Perform one final inspection of the engine compartment. Look for tools, rolls of tape, dipsticks, filler caps, or anything else that might have been left under the hood. Make sure the battery is fully charged. Check the fluids one more time.

It's common to find the coolant level low after it sits for a while. This is due to trapped air finding its way out of the engine. The coolant level often drops more after starting when coolant circulation brings out more air. It's best to have an assistant monitor the coolant level for a few minutes after starting before installing the radiator cap.

If you can do it safely and easily, fill the carburetor float bowl with gas. Here we're filling the carburetor through the float bowl vent. Add fuel slowly. Most float bowls only hold a couple of ounces of fuel.

If it can be done safely, fill the carburetor float bowl with gas. This will allow fuel to flow immediately into the engine once you start cranking the engine. If this is not done, the engine will have to run for several seconds before the fuel pump primes and starts delivering fuel to the carburetor.

Leave the air cleaner off the engine and make sure a fire extinguisher is close by. It's often helpful to spray a bit of engine starting fluid into the carburetor. This is especially important if you are trying to start the engine with a dry carburetor.

Attempt to start the engine. It should start immediately. Bring the engine speed to about 2,000 rpm.

Note: If the engine has conventional lifters, it's essential to take the engine to 2,000 rpm immediately and vary the engine speed between 1,500 and 2,000 rpm for 20 minutes. This ensures oil will flow freely over the lifters and camshaft while the lifters are breaking in.

Continue running the engine at raised RPM for 20 minutes. Allow the engine to idle. Adjust the carburetor and ignition timing. Turn off the engine, check for leaks, and add fluids, as necessary. Change the oil and filter. If there are bits of metal in the oil, do not operate the engine until you figure out the origin of this debris and correct the problem.

If the engine does not start, make sure all the spark plug wires are in place and that the distributor cap is tight. If you can't identify the problem, test for spark using a spark tester.

Sputtering and backfiring can be the result of incorrect ignition timing or the ignition firing order being wrong. Double-check these things. If backfiring continues, check for vacuum leaks, then try advancing the ignition timing a few degrees.

If the engine makes excessive noise, shut it down and try to find the source. Clunking noises after a first start are often related to loose torque converter bolts or a loose vibration damper. A shrieking noise is most likely a loose belt. Check to be sure the fan bolts are tight. A loud whining noise is probably coming from the torque converter or power steering pump. It's common for these fluid levels to be low, since there's usually some fluid leakage from the transmission cooler lines and power steering pump during engine removal.

It's normal to hear clattering noise from the lifters during the first minute or two after start-up. This is caused by the lifters not having enough oil in them to work properly. The noise should go away quickly when the lifters fill with oil. If the clattering continues, it could be caused by low oil pressure. Shut down the engine and determine the cause of the low oil pressure.

Breaking in the Engine

Put a new filter and the appropriate oil in the engine. Choose a multi-viscosity oil, either 10W30 or 10W40. Base that decision on the oil pressure you noticed during break-in. If the oil pressure was well within specification, use 10W30. If the oil pressure was on the low side, use 10W40. Drive about 500 miles, then change the oil again.

Break-in is the process through which the new piston rings and honed cylinder walls wear into each other and create a tight seal. The process can be compared with polishing. During this process, the engine temperature is slightly higher than usual. This is a result of the friction created by the break-in process.

During break-in, don't drive the car hard, but don't baby it. Too much friction and heat can damage the rings and leave scoring in the cylinders. If not enough friction is created early on, a glaze can form in the cylinders that will cause the rings to seat poorly.

Oil Consumption

After an overhaul, oil consumption is usually a little higher than on an engine that's fully broken in. This is usually not very noticeable, but it is something to keep in mind. The reason for the oil consumption is that non-seated piston rings are more prone to allowing oil to get past them.

If oil consumption issues persist after the first thousand miles or so, there might be a problem. Common causes of excessive oil consumption after an overhaul are piston rings that were not installed properly, piston rings not seating correctly, an internal intake manifold vacuum leak, or valve seals not sealing correctly. Chapter 3 can help you with diagnosis.

Maintenance

After break-in, change conventional oil at intervals of no more than 5,000 miles. Always change the oil filter at the time you change the oil. Change the air filter, the PCV valve, and PCV filters at the interval Oldsmobile recommended for the vehicle. Replace the spark plugs every 12,000 miles if using a points-type ignition or every 50,000 miles if using an HEI ignition. Staying current on these basic maintenance items can greatly extend the life of your engine.

Engine starting fluid is made from ether, which is highly volatile, meaning it will mix with air more easily than gasoline. Open the choke and throttle plates, then spray starting fluid into the intake manifold for about a second. This virtually guarantees a quick start, assuming everything else is right. If the carburetor is dry, have an assistant ready to spray more starting fluid should the engine start to die from fuel starvation.

Performance and Economy Modifications

Most of today's Oldsmobile enthusiasts are primarily interested in maintaining the reliability and drivability of their classic automobile, which is the main focus of this book. However, many are also interested in improving the performance of their engine, and some are also interested in racing and street performance. This chapter addresses the need for speed!

We will also look at things that can be done to improve the fuel efficiency of your Oldsmobile engine for those long cruises. Some modifications can improve both performance and fuel economy and should be considered by all enthusiasts.

Keep in mind that the performance modifications discussed in this chapter primarily regard making power. This should be distinguished from modifications related to an engine surviving in service when it's pushed toward its horsepower limits, such as with a racing engine.

Durability modifications include forged pistons and connecting rods and a forged crankshaft. For extreme racing builds, engine block strengthening may also be necessary, such as the installation of main-bearing support girdles. Such modifications should not be needed for a typical street-performance build.

Why is it that Oldsmobile engines didn't come from the factory with the performance modifications that are detailed in this chapter? The answer is that engine design is based on many factors, and chief among them are cost and exceptional drivability under all conditions.

It is necessary to trade off some engine performance to achieve these design characteristics. Remember

Stock Oldsmobile engines offered good performance, smooth operation in all conditions, and legendary reliability. These characteristics were of primary importance for cars that were driven daily by millions of Americans.

Today's Oldsmobile enthusiast is more likely to prefer a snap of the neck versus a dead-smooth idle. There's plenty of power to be had, but some of it comes with reductions in fuel economy and street manners. It's important to understand the costs and trade-offs involved with your performance build.

that the average Oldsmobile was not purchased by an enthusiast but rather by someone looking primarily for reliable daily transportation. Perhaps sadly, most engines were destined for "your father's Oldsmobile."

Whatever level of performance upgrades are planned, search for expert advice. Parts manufacturers, as well as some online retailers, maintain a staff of experts to help buyers make the right decisions. What you see here are gearheads. They are less interested in upselling you than in making sure you are a happy customer.

Any engine is essentially a pump that sucks in an air/fuel mixture and exhales exhaust gases. Most modifications will improve horsepower by better enabling this essential flow of gases through the engine. The greater the flow, the higher the horsepower. The horsepower increase from such modifications comes through, allowing the engine to operate more efficiently at higher RPM.

Some modifications increase power through increasing engine displacement, which improves both horsepower and torque. Your neck will snap harder when you hit the gas, but your gas tank will be drained quicker.

Although this chapter discusses engine modifications separately, it is important to understand that modifications need to be matched for best performance. If the components don't match properly, power could be reduced and drivability could be worsened. It's like putting different sizes of tires and wheels at each corner of your car. No matter how good the individual tires may be, the car will not corner well.

So, when you're selecting parts, talk to performance experts and parts manufacturers to get their insights. Be sure that they understand your performance goals and the other modifications that you planned.

Cylinder Heads

The cylinder heads are the primary determinant of how much power the engine can generate. Airflow through the cylinder heads must make directional changes that slow the flow of the gases. The sizes of the ports in the heads are restricted in some areas to clear nearby components, and turbulence can develop in these areas. Performance improvements in cylinder heads will come primarily by straightening the flow of gases and reducing restrictions.

In days gone by, the only way to get more flow from Oldsmobile cylinder heads was to port the original factory heads. Porting Oldsmobile cast-iron heads is difficult and time-consuming. It is also a bit of a lost art these days. If the goal is to keep the factory look under the hood, porting the factory heads might be an option, but don't expect a huge improvement in airflow.

For a small-block engine, consider swapping the original heads for big-block heads that have larger ports and significantly better flow. Porting should be carried out by a shop that is an expert on Oldsmobile engines, such as Mondello Performance. Check the Source Guide for other options.

For most performance-engine builds, aftermarket aluminum heads are the way to go. Some aftermarket heads will flow better out of the box than the best ported cast-iron heads. Aftermarket heads can look like a bargain when considering the cost of porting factory heads.

In addition to flow improvement, aluminum heads are much lighter and can handle a significantly higher compression ratio without detonation. Aluminum heads can usually run between one and two additional points of compression. So, as an example, an engine might be able to run 10.5:1 compression with aluminum heads but be stuck with 9:1 compression when using the original cast-iron heads.

Edelbrock

Developed in collaboration with Mondello Performance, the Edelbrock Performer RPM aluminum cylinder head has become the standard for Oldsmobile performance engines. In stock, unported form these heads easily support a 450-hp street engine build. A big-cam street/strip engine can squeeze over 500 hp out of the same heads.

With expert porting and upgraded valves and springs, a pair of Performer RPM heads can feed a 700-hp race engine. Edelbrock heads have been proven over many years of service in many thousands of vehicles. The manufacturing quality of the Edelbrock heads is excellent, and top-quality springs and valve components are used. All this comes at a price, though. Edelbrock heads, while offering a great value for the price, are more expensive than some other options.

Speedmaster and ProComp

Speedmaster and ProComp heads can provide a substantial improvement in flow (and therefore power) while staying within a tight budget. Most engine builders are happy with the quality of the castings, although some say the valve components—particularly the springs—can vary in quality. Have a machine shop check them out prior to installation to be sure that the springs and valve components are adequate for the build that is planned.

Other Brands

There are a number of other brands offering Oldsmobile heads, many of which are based on castings from Edelbrock, Speedmaster, and ProComp. Rocket Racing and Wenzler heads are designed for maximum-effort race engines. They are pricey and require specialty components.

Displacement

More displacement equals more horsepower and more torque, which is why it's usually best to design a street-performance engine with the largest displacement practical. The downside is that more displacement usually leads to lower fuel economy, assuming all other factors are the same.

For most people, the budget of the engine build will be the main factor limiting displacement. Getting to 455 ci (and a little more with an overbore) does not add significantly to the cost of a build. There are stroker kit options that can get you in the 500-ci range, but these options will add thousands of dollars to the build. Nevertheless, if you are building a serious performance engine that will need a forged rotating assembly in any case, the additional cost of going stroker will be much less.

Aftermarket aluminum cylinder heads are the best choice for most performance builds. These Edelbrock Performer RPM heads are among the most popular and powerful Olds heads out there. They are reasonably priced and made in the USA. If you have some extra money to spend on your build, the cylinder heads are probably the best place to spend it.

Camshaft Selection

No single modification changes the operating characteristics of an engine as much as the camshaft. In simple terms, the camshaft is a mechanical computer that determines when the valves open, how much they open, and how long they stay open. It sounds simple, but the lobes on a camshaft are precision machined to accomplish a specific pattern of flow through the cylinder heads, as well as the intake and exhaust systems.

The profile and spacing of the camshaft lobes are determined through hundreds of mathematical calculations that determine how an engine will perform. It's important to understand that, as in any other aspect of engine performance, there isn't "good," "better," or "best." As an extreme example, a stock camshaft is completely unsuitable for racing, and a racing camshaft is unsuitable for street use.

Selecting the right camshaft for the build is critical to meeting performance and drivability goals. Before selecting a camshaft, know the planned engine displacement, compression ratio, and operating RPM range. Also, know which cylinder heads, intake manifold, and headers you're planning to use.

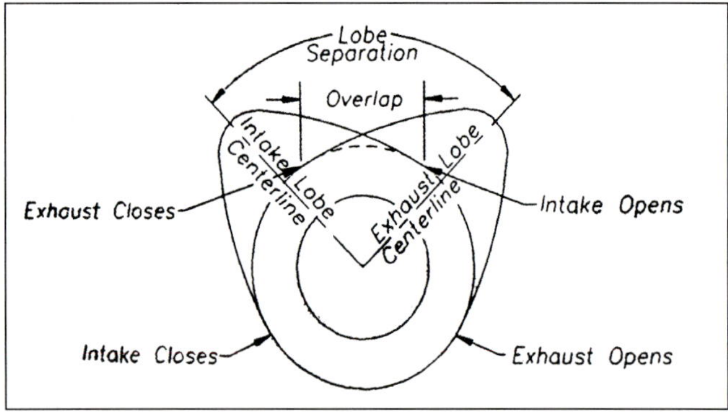

Camshafts might look simple, but they are extremely precise mechanical computers. This graphic provides a visual explanation of the terminology you need to know about.

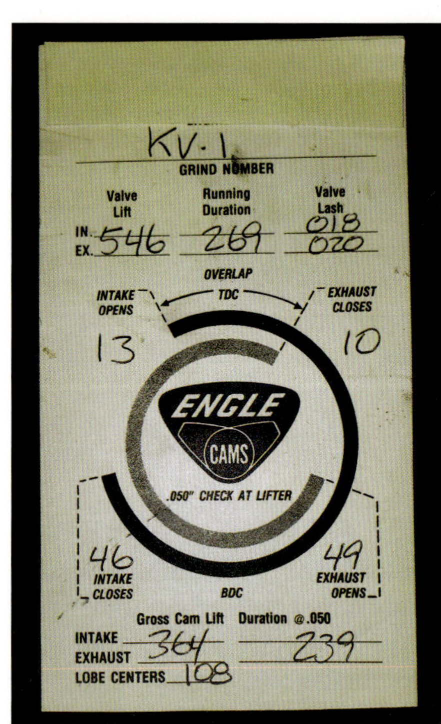

Every camshaft comes with a "cam card" that provides all the specifications of the particular camshaft. Don't throw this away! The other components in the engine build need to work within these parameters. If you make any substantial changes later, the cam specs will need to be considered again.

Camshafts are a compromise of a multitude of performance characteristics. Selecting a camshaft requires the consideration of all other components of the engine as well as the expected operating characteristics that you want from the engine.

Fortunately for Oldsmobile enthusiasts, all the major camshaft manufacturers produce camshafts for Oldsmobiles: COMP Cams, Lunati, Crower, Iskenderian, Crane Cams, Erson, and Howards Cams. Whether you're looking for a stock replacement cam or a maximum-effort race cam, plenty of options are available. Each manufacturer has its unique grinds, which can be difficult to compare. Consult with the tech departments of the major manufacturers, as well as other enthusiasts who have experience with the different brands.

Camshaft Specifications

When you shop for a camshaft, there are a number of specifications to contemplate. For the novice, they can be difficult to interpret. Fortunately, most camshaft manufacturers provide information about the operating characteristics that can be expected with their cam designs (sometimes called "profiles" or "grinds").

We recommend contacting the technical department of the camshaft manufacturer, which will help you select the right camshaft. Be prepared to provide all of the information about the engine build, including cylinder heads, intake manifold design, header/exhaust system design, and torque converter type (for automatic-transmission cars).

Certain specifications of the cam design can tell you a lot about how it will perform in an engine. It's helpful to review these specifications to select the right camshaft for your engine.

Lift

Lift is the maximum amount the valve is lifted off its seat during operation. A stock camshaft might lift a valve about 0.410 inch off its seat. Often, intake and exhaust valves have slightly different lifts for intake and exhaust (exhaust a bit higher than intake). A serious race engine might have lift as high as 0.700 inch.

Street-performance engines will generally have lift in the 0.500-inch range. Like so many other aspects of engine performance, more is not always better. Lift does not need to be higher than the point where maximum flow is achieved through the ports in the cylinder head.

Stock heads tend to max out flow at relatively low lift, so putting a 0.700-lift cam in a stock engine will not improve performance because lifting the valves more than the point of maximum flow is of no value. On the other hand, cylinder heads designed for high performance and racing tend to flow more at higher lifts, so 0.700 lift might be appropriate for an all-out race engine. The important thing to remember about valve lift is that it should be matched to the performance characteristics of the cylinder head.

Duration

Duration is the amount of time a valve stays open, which is measured in degrees of crankshaft rotation. Generally speaking, a cam with long duration will have better operating characteristics at higher RPM at the expense of low-end torque, fuel economy, and drivability on the street.

Camshaft manufacturers generally provide two duration measurements for their cams: "Advertised" duration and duration at 0.050 lift. The latter provides a more accurate way of comparing different cams, and we recommend seeking out the "at 0.050" duration for the cams you are considering.

Generally speaking, a stock engine will have a duration of about 200 to 210 degrees at 0.050. On a street-performance engine, you will see about 215 to 245 degrees at 0.050. Race engines tend to be in the 250 to 275 range.

Lifters for cams above 245 at 0.050 will almost always be solid (flat or roller). The reason for this is that even the best hydraulic lifters can become inconsistent at high RPM ranges, and racers prefer the strength and durability of solid lifters.

Overlap

All camshafts have overlap, which is the period of time during which the intake and exhaust valve are both open. To put it simply, this overlap time is needed to ensure efficient filling of the cylinder, particularly at high RPM. More overlap gives better high-RPM performance but results in lower compression and vacuum at low RPM, particularly at idle.

The familiar "lope" of a high-performance engine is caused primarily by high overlap. Generally, stock engines will have about 15 to 30 degrees of overlap, performance street engines have 25 to 55 degrees, and race engines 60 to as much as 100 degrees of overlap.

Overlap is closely related to other factors such as lobe separation angle (LSA), which cam manufacturers commonly give as a specification. A wide separation of the intake and exhaust lobes results in less overlap and therefore better low-RPM performance. Tighter LSA is associated with high-performance and racing engines.

Valve Lifter Types

Picking a camshaft also determines what type of lifter to use, as camshaft and lifter types cannot be interchanged. Nevertheless, it's important to understand the different lifter types because each has advantages and disadvantages that can become a part of your decision-making regarding the cam/lifter package that you select.

A roller lifter has a wheel at the end that rolls smoothly on roller bearings. Roller lifters are superior to flat lifters. They reduce friction and also permit the use of camshafts with faster ramps.

Conventional Hydraulic Lifters

Stock Oldsmobile engines came equipped with hydraulic lifters with a flat area of contact with the camshaft. This type of lifter provides a simple, reliable, and inexpensive way of transmitting motion to open and close the valves.

The main body of the lifter is essentially a hollow cylinder filled with pressurized oil (from the oil pump). A piston in the cylinder rides atop the column of pressurized oil that transmits the lift of the camshaft to the pushrod. The design of hydraulic lifters makes them self-adjusting. They do not normally require any servicing.

Additionally, hydraulic lifters tend to operate more quietly than solid lifters. The primary disadvantage of hydraulic lifters is that they are somewhat RPM-limiting. Their inherent operating characteristics are associated with a condition known as "pump-up," which contributes to unstable valve actuation at higher RPM (generally over about 5,500 rpm).

Solid Lifters

Solid lifters, sometimes called "mechanical lifters," are simply barrel-shaped, solid-steel components that ride on the camshaft lobes, raising the pushrods through direct mechanical action. Unlike hydraulic lifters, solid lifters do not compress or extend during operation and therefore provide stable, precise operation throughout the RPM range. Solid lifters are mostly used in high-RPM race applications and street/strip engines.

The main disadvantages of solid lifters are that they require periodic adjustment to maintain maximum performance, and they are prone to be noisy. Another disadvantage is that solid lifters operate more harshly than hydraulic lifters, so stiffer springs are required and valvetrain components tend to wear out more quickly.

Solid Roller Lifters

Solid roller lifters are used in the highest performance applications, usually racing engines. The most obvious advantage is that the spinning wheel at the foot of the lifter reduces friction versus the flat contact surface on lifters discussed previously. Equally (if not more) important is that the wheel allows more aggressive camshaft profiles to be used.

Roller lifters are known for their ability to operate on camshafts with fast "ramps," which refers to how much valve lift is delivered for a given amount of camshaft rotation. Flat-bottomed lifters are limited in terms of how much ramp speed they can handle before the edge of the lifter foot digs into the side of the cam lobe. Roller lifters can operate on camshaft lobes that are closer to being square in profile, permitting the valve to obtain high lift quickly.

Since solid roller lifters are used primarily on fast-ramp cams, one downside is that the associated rapid opening and closing of the valves leads to increased wear on valvetrain components, particularly valves and valve seats. Another disadvantage of roller lifters is that they are significantly more expensive than flat-bottomed lifters.

Hydraulic Roller Lifters

Hydraulic roller lifters represent the highest level of development for street-driven vehicles and are standard equipment on virtually all new vehicles with cam-in-block design. They offer the advantage of reduced friction and also the ability to use cams with faster ramps. They're also easier on valvetrain components and just as quiet as hydraulic flat-bottomed lifters.

Typically, a hydraulic roller cam will provide a smoother idle and better low-speed operating characteristics than a flat-bottomed lifter of the same specifications. The main disadvantage of hydraulic rollers is that they are more expensive. However, with more widespread use, the prices have come down to the point where they are an option for all but the most budget-oriented build.

Valve Springs

Camshafts with aggressive profiles designed to be operated at high RPM require upgrades to other valvetrain components. Most importantly, stiffer valve springs will be needed to keep the lifters tight against the camshaft lobes at high RPM.

A basic set of springs for a near-stock cam should provide about 100 pounds of pressure when the valve is seated and 250 pounds at maximum lift. A moderate hydraulic roller cam needs about 130 pounds of pressure seated and 350 pounds open. Solid lifter cams for racing often have 200 pounds seated pressure and 500 pounds open pressure.

Keeping within the guidelines from the camshaft manufacturer, err on the side of stiffer springs to prevent the valves from floating and potentially contacting the pistons. Just be sure all the other valvetrain components are up to the job.

Pushrods

Adequate pushrod strength is commonly overlooked during an engine build. Pushrods must be able to overcome the maximum spring pressure without deflection. Be sure that the pushrods you select are rated for the pressure of the springs that were selected.

Just don't go overboard, as stronger pushrods are also heavier, and excess weight can contribute to valve float at high RPM. Chrome-moly steel is a good compromise for strength and light weight, but chrome-moly pushrods are more expensive than pushrods made from standard steel.

Rocker Arms

If the valve springs will be significantly stiffer than stock, use upgraded rocker arms. Stock stamped-steel rocker arms can be overloaded easily, resulting in deflection and excess wear. Performance rocker arms provide better strength to avoid

A high-performance camshaft needs to be accompanied by upgraded valve springs. Springs need to be strong enough to keep the lifter on the camshaft lobe with no bounce at high RPM. The knock-on effect is that high spring pressures usually require stronger pushrods and rocker arms.

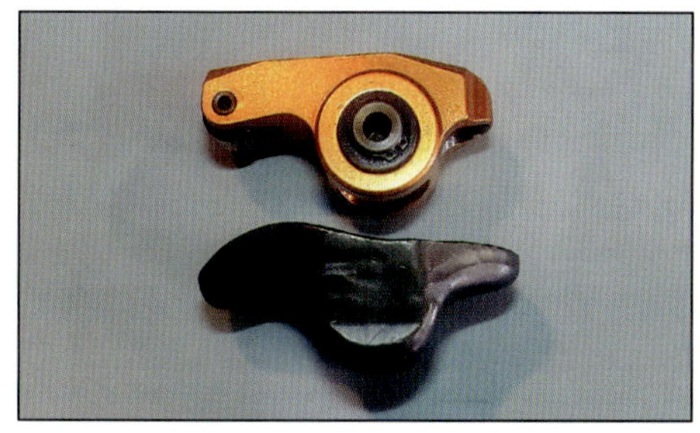

A stock stamped-steel rocker arm (bottom) is not strong enough to handle high valve spring pressures. In addition to being lighter in weight, a good aftermarket aluminum rocker arm (top) can handle spring pressures that would bend a stock rocker into a pretzel. The best rockers are made from high-strength aluminum and use roller bearings at the tip and the fulcrum point.

deflection. Most have roller tips, which offer greater precision and help to reduce friction.

The best rocker arms also have roller bearings at the fulcrum to reduce friction and handle high spring loads. Most modern performance rocker arms are made from aluminum, which offers lighter weight than steel rockers. As with pushrods, it's desirable to reduce the weight of valvetrain components in a high-RPM engine.

Another factor in rocker arm selection is the rocker arm ratio. Stock Oldsmobile engines had a 1.5:1 ratio, meaning that the rocker arm will multiply the camshaft lobe lift by 1.5. So, if a camshaft lobe raises the valve lifter by 0.400, the valve will be lifted 0.600 off the seat due to the lift multiplication provided by the rocker arm.

While most rocker arms have a 1.5:1 ratio, some have 1.6:1 or 1.7:1 ratios. Increasing rocker arm ratio is a way to increase the valve lift without moving to a cam with a higher lift. The aforementioned 0.400-lift cam would have 0.680 lift with a 1.7:1 rocker. Be sure to consider the specifications of all components when you design the valvetrain.

Critical Valvetrain Safety Checks

On a stock or near-stock engine where camshaft specifications run within narrow ranges, you can usually just install the valvetrain components and not worry about anything bad happening. However, high-performance engines vary greatly as to their camshaft specifications and valvetrain design. Thoroughly check the valvetrain to be sure there are no issues that will cause damage to the engine.

Valve Spring Coil Bind

Coil bind is when a spring's coils contact each other and stack solid at or before the point of full valve lift. With a high-lift camshaft, it's important to be sure this point will not be reached during engine operation or damage to the valvetrain will occur.

Spring manufacturers provide a specification for the height of the spring when it reaches the point of bind (sometimes referred to as "solid height"). Always check to be sure there is adequate clearance to avoid coil bind. To calculate, subtract the valve lift from the spring installed height (see the Appendix). The resulting number should be at least 0.060 inch more than the coil bind specification. The 0.060 inch is a safety factor that considers inertia effects at high RPM.

Valve Retainer-to-Guide Clearance

A similar phenomenon happens when a valve retainer contacts a valve guide before full lift is achieved. To check for this type of interference, install a valve without the spring in place and allow the retainer and guide to come into contact. Measure the distance between the valve spring seat and the retainer. This measurement should be at least 0.060 more than the spring installed height minus the valve lift specification.

Piston-to-Valve Clearance

High lift/duration cams can cause the valves to come into contact with the pistons. Camshaft manufacturers can tell you if there's a possibility of this happening with their cams, but there is no easy way to calculate this possibility. The only way to be sure is with a dynamic measurement method that requires the engine to be temporarily assembled.

With the cylinder head off, press modeling clay into the valve reliefs at the top of the piston. Install the cylinder head with an old gasket that has the same thickness as the gasket you're planning to use. Rotate the crankshaft through at least two full revolutions. Remove the cylinder head and use a razor blade to slice through the clay. Measure the thickness of the clay at its thinnest point. The measurement should be at least 0.100 inch to prevent potential valve-to-piston contact during engine operation.

Exhaust Manifolds

Oldsmobile engines left the factory with cast-iron exhaust manifolds that were designed to provide quiet, reliable operation. If you're planning a mild-to-moderate engine build, cast-iron manifolds have a number of advantages over tubular headers:

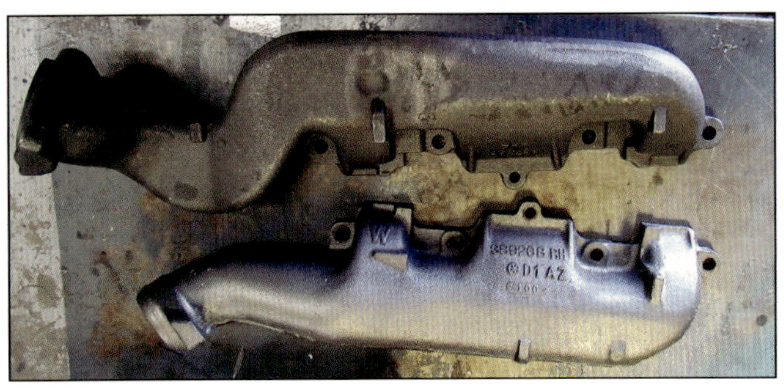

Factory exhaust manifolds maintain the original look of the engine compartment. They take less space, keep the engine compartment cooler, reduce noise, and are less prone to leaking. However, they should not be used in serious performance builds. Even these high-flow manifolds (full-size car, top; intermediate car, bottom) will become obstructive above 400 hp.

- Cast-iron manifolds do not become warped or damaged as easily as headers.
- Exhaust manifolds contain heat better than headers. Since headers have more surface area, they disperse more heat in the engine compartment. Manifolds do a better job of containing the heat and channeling it out through the exhaust system.
- Manifolds have less of a tendency to develop exhaust leaks.
- Exhaust manifolds tend to be quieter, reducing noise in the engine compartment.
- Headers are often difficult to install and occupy more space under the hood. This can make access to the starter and other components more difficult. Additionally, the starter's life might be reduced when using headers due to greater heat being generated in closer proximity compared to exhaust manifolds that give off less heat and are farther away from the starter.

The preceding points are not intended to keep anyone from buying a good set of headers. We just want buyers to make informed decisions and understand the trade-offs involved with headers. For a mild engine build, factory cast-iron manifolds may be the best choice. But if you plan to step up the horsepower more than 20 percent or so, the limits of most factory manifolds will be pushed.

Remember that performance is all about flowing as much air as possible through the engine. A restriction at any point will reduce overall flow, regardless of how capable the other components may be.

Headers

Most performance engine builds will benefit from steel-tube headers. They can increase horsepower without reducing fuel economy or affecting drivability. Headers allow exhaust gases to flow out of the engine more easily, using a phenomenon known as "scavenging." The gases flowing through the tubes create inertia that causes a low-pressure area at the exhaust port in the cylinder head. The low pressure pulls the exhaust out of the engine more efficiently.

Headers are available from a number of manufacturers and have different designs and sizes depending on the clearance available and the type of performance you're seeking. It's best to contact the technical departments of the manufacturers and discuss your build with experts who can help you choose the right design for your engine.

At the high end of the header price spectrum are American Racing and Hooker. They produce top-quality long-tube headers. Sanderson offers quality shorty headers at reasonable prices. Doug's has long-tube and Tri-Y designs that are good quality and reasonably priced. Some of the least expensive headers are from Hedman and Flowtech, and both offer complete lines of headers that will meet the needs of those on a budget.

Types

The most common type of header consists of four long steel

Four-into-one headers are the most common type. They vary in flow capacity based on tube diameter and length. Longer tubes with bigger diameters flow more exhaust. Note the comparison here with a stock exhaust manifold on the left. Looks kinda puny, huh?

tubes that join at a collector. Known as "four-into-one" headers, they produce high-RPM power but are a bit less effective in the low- and mid-RPM ranges.

Tri-Y headers are named for their appearance. The four pipes are paired into two pipes, which are again paired at the collector. Tri-Y headers sacrifice a slight amount of power in the high-RPM range as compared with four-into-one headers, but they provide excellent power and torque in the low- and mid-RPM ranges.

Short-tube headers (often referred to as "shorty" headers) are usually used when clearance is limited or emissions requirements won't allow the use of full-length headers. Shorty headers are often more efficient than stock cast-iron manifolds, but they do not perform at the level of long-tube headers.

Length and Diameter

As a general rule, longer tubes produce more power, although 40 inches is usually the longest you'll see. Shorter tubes are used where clearance is an issue or where emissions requirements do not permit long tubes.

Tube diameter is another important consideration, and it's not a "bigger is better" proposition. Instead, the tube diameter should be selected carefully based on the engine displacement and level of performance expected. As an example, a small-block engine built for street use will generally do best with a header tube diameter of 1⅝ inches. A big-block or high-performance small-block might do best with a 1⅞-inch tube. Engines built for racing often have a tube diameter of 2 inches.

Putting headers with 2-inch tubes on a street-driven small-block will result in reduced performance versus using a 1⅝-inch tube. This is because the exhaust flow is insufficient to allow scavenging in such a long tube. Again, it's best to consult with header manufacturers to determine what's best for your engine.

Buying Tips

Flange thickness is a significant consideration, as the thicker the flange, the better the cylinder-head-to-header flange will seal under high pressures. Cast-iron manifolds have a surface that's machined flat and will seal better than a header. Most headers are mild steel and have a thickness of 5/16 or 3/8 inch. It is best to choose a header with a thicker flange. It will hold its shape better, especially if the bolts get overtorqued.

Don't go cheap on header gaskets, particularly the flange gaskets. Headers are susceptible to leakage at this point, so choose gaskets that will resist blowout. Racers often use solid copper gaskets with a coating of high-temperature RTV at the ports. These will resist high pressures, particularly those run in turbocharged applications.

After installing headers, the air/fuel mixture is a bit leaner, so bigger jets may be needed in the carburetor. Use an air/fuel ratio gauge to determine if a jet change is needed.

Exhaust Systems

Most Oldsmobiles came from the factory with an exhaust system that compromised power and fuel economy to achieve quiet operation. The exhaust system components were adequate for the stock performance level, but increases in power will cause the pipes and mufflers to restrict the higher exhaust flow.

Most factory-installed exhaust systems have a two-into-one "Y" pipe. A single pipe carries all the exhaust to the rear of the car where the single muffler was located. This worked okay for a stock performance level, but a dual exhaust system will improve performance and economy on almost any application.

The higher the horsepower and exhaust flow, the more the car will benefit from an exhaust upgrade. However, there's no benefit to going overboard. Putting a 3-inch exhaust system with straight-through mufflers on a car with a mildly built engine will result in more noise but no more power. For most people, this extra money would be better spent elsewhere.

For performance and racing applications, pipe diameter should be at least 2¼ inches for moderate performance, 2½ inches for high performance, and 3 inches for maximum street performance and racing. Bigger pipes are often more difficult to fit on the car and can increase noise, but pipes that are excessively big for the application will not reduce performance.

Mufflers

There are a myriad of mufflers on the market that promise to improve the performance of the vehicle, and most will do that. When selecting mufflers, there are five major considerations: fitment, flow, noise level, tone, and price.

Fitment

Muffler fitment is the most important issue, as there needs to be room for the mufflers and they must fit well. Universal mufflers require you to modify and fabricate hangers. Better mufflers will be designed for precise fit on your car, but they tend to be more expensive.

Flow

The amount of exhaust gases that a muffler will flow is rated in cubic feet per minute (CFM). The major muffler manufacturers will provide this specification. Comparison of mufflers on the basis of flow will help with your decision-making.

Noise Level

Sometimes (but not always) the best performing mufflers are also loud. If it is a street-driven vehicle, be sure that the sound level (measured in decibels) is legal in your community. State noise laws are often more generous than local ordinances and rules by homeowners' associations. Be sure to understand the legal limitations as well as your neighbor's tolerance.

Tone

For many enthusiasts, the exhaust tone is one of the most important considerations. We want the car to sound as good as it performs. Once you've narrowed down your choices in terms of fitment, flow, and noise level, compare them on the basis of tone. Manufacturers provide sound clips of their mufflers on their websites, and other enthusiasts are usually happy to provide videos of their cars.

Emissions Considerations

The 1975-and-later Oldsmobiles were equipped with catalytic converters, which significantly reduce emissions. In many states, the car must retain a catalytic converter to be legal on the road. Be sure to consider this while planning the build. Even if you currently live in an area that does not have an emissions inspection program, laws can change, and you might move.

Most of the early catalytic converter designs were restrictive of exhaust flow. GM made common use of the "pellet" converter type, which is least efficient in terms of exhaust flow. Many aftermarket manufacturers offer monolith "honeycomb" designs that flow substantially better than the early GM converter types. Most of these converters are reasonably priced and should be considered when upgrading your exhaust system.

Starting in 1981, auto manufacturers were required to equip their cars with enhanced "three-way" catalytic converters. Earlier converters reduced carbon monoxide (CO) and hydrocarbons (HC). Three-way converters also reduce oxides of nitrogen (NOx).

Three-way converters are significantly more expensive than two-way converters. Both types are usually available as replacements, but some areas (California as an example) require you to retain the three-way functioning of the converter.

Ignition Systems

Pre-1975 model engines used point-type distributors. Standard models came with single-point distributors, while high-performance models sometimes had dual-point versions. If your engine has a point-type distributor, it will probably benefit from an electronic ignition system.

Electronic ignition systems such as those available in the aftermarket and those installed by the factory since 1975 make conventional point-type distributors outmoded. It's easy to convert from point-type ignition to electronic ignition, particularly if you use the reasonably priced kits available.

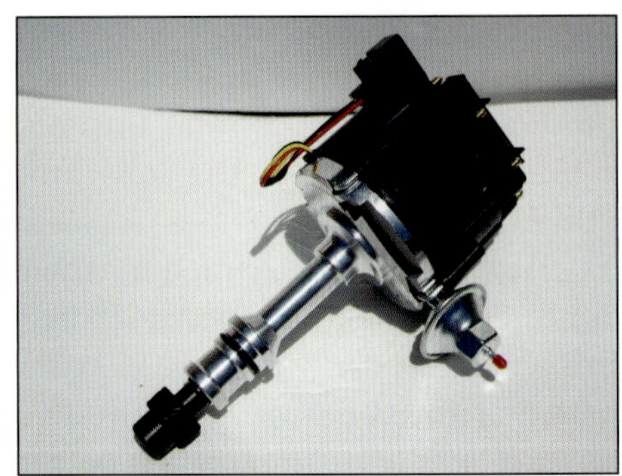

HEI distributors debuted on 1975 Oldsmobiles. They represented a huge improvement over the points ignition systems of the day and are still a great choice for performance builds today.

Whether or not you convert to electronic ignition, you can generally gain power by optimizing the distributor's advance curve. Within certain limits, the more ignition advance that can be achieved at a particular RPM without preignition (pinging), the better the engine will perform. Optimizing the timing will often improve fuel economy, and there's generally no downside if done with care.

During wide-open-throttle performance, the ignition advance is determined by the initial advance and the mechanical (sometimes called "centrifugal") advance. Initial advance is what you check at tune-up time with a timing light.

The factory specification is usually somewhere between 5 and 12 degrees BTDC. You can usually increase the initial advance to 14 to 18 degrees without issues. However, if you notice that the engine is harder to crank or it idles poorly when you increase initial timing, dial back the initial timing a degree or two until the issues go away.

Mechanical advance adds timing as engine RPM increases, adding in the neighborhood of 20 degrees BTDC, depending on the application. Adding initial advance to mechanical advance gives you total advance, which should not exceed about 36 to 38 degrees BTDC.

Another consideration is the RPM where total advance is achieved. Most stock distributors hold out total advance until about 3,500 rpm. In most cases, the distributor can be set up to achieve total advance at about 2,500 rpm, which will improve mid-range performance.

Optimizing the ignition curve can be done using a "dial-back" timing light that allows you to observe all aspects of the distributor's advance curve while the engine is running. A quality dial-back timing light is a great investment for performance tuning as well as conventional tuning and troubleshooting.

If you're running a radical street engine or race engine, you can benefit from a multiple-spark ignition system that delivers a stronger spark. It has the additional benefit of the timed spark being delivered in multiple pulses, which helps to overcome ignition issues arising from high-overlap camshafts.

Dial-type timing lights allow you to check the advance curve of the ignition system. They are more expensive than standard-type timing lights, but if you need to buy a timing light anyhow, consider spending a little extra to get this helpful added feature.

As a general rule, engines with camshafts that have a duration of 240 degrees at 0.050 inch or more will benefit from a multiple-spark system. It's a common misconception that a multiple spark system will cause an engine to run better at higher RPM. This is not necessarily the case. In fact, many of the popular ignition systems do not deliver multiple sparks at high RPM.

The primary advantage of a multiple-spark system is that it allows better performance at lower RPM. Long-duration camshafts bleed off cylinder pressure at low RPM, and the air/fuel mixture can mix with the outgoing exhaust gases. This makes complete combustion more difficult and increases the possibility of misfire.

A multiple-spark system will allow the engine to run more efficiently at idle and low RPM, which will help keep the spark plugs from getting carbon fouled and might help to smooth out the idle a bit.

Another ignition system upgrade that is necessary at higher performance levels is a high-output ignition coil. The factory HEI system used on 1975-and-later engines provided a huge improvement over points-type ignition systems. Those of us who began servicing these systems in the late 1970s were shocked to discover how significant the improvement was! What is not well understood is that increases in engine RPM cause coil output to be reduced.

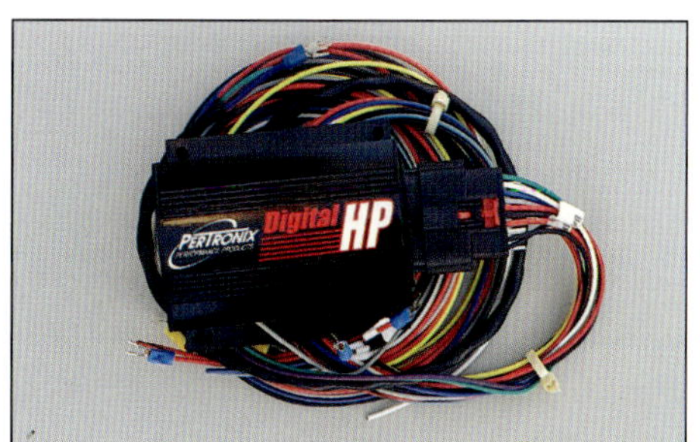

On engines with high-overlap camshafts, an ignition box with multispark capability will keep the engine running more efficiently at idle and low RPM. Shown here is the Pertronix Digital HP, which is one of the latest entries into the market, competing with companies such as MSD and Mallory.

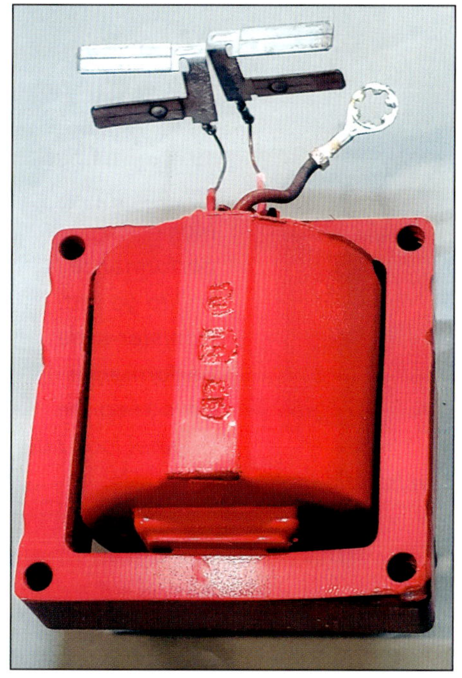

High-performance ignition coils are available that fit directly into the HEI distributor cap. A coil upgrade is recommended for any engine that will see over 5,500 rpm. Adapters for remote coils are available that allow the HEI distributor to run with an external coil.

Up to 5,500 rpm or so, the standard HEI coil can deliver a strong spark for full combustion. As RPM increases, that output is reduced. If your engine will see over 5,500 rpm, select a coil that's up to the job. The better coils will deliver a strong spark through 10,000 rpm. They are pricey but worth every penny for high-RPM engines.

If you choose an electronic ignition system upgrade kit for your 1974-or-earlier vehicle, get a high-performance coil to go with it. Canister-style performance coils keep the original look but can handle higher RPM levels.

For street-driven vehicles, you'll almost certainly want a dual-plane intake manifold. Dual-plane intakes provide great low- and mid-range performance. This Edelbrock Performer provides excellent power through about 5,500 rpm. Note the mounting flange at the bottom center. This allows you to retain your original EGR valve.

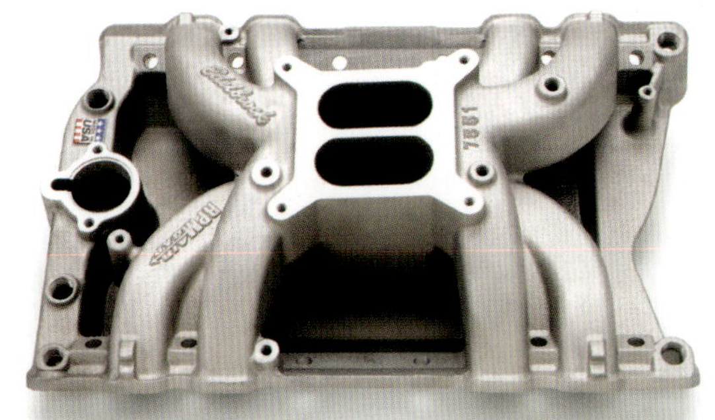

Edelbrock's Performer RPM dual-plane Air Gap manifold is available for big-block Oldsmobiles. See the gap between the intake runners and the bottom of the manifold? This keeps hot oil off the runners, creating a cooler (and therefore denser) intake charge. The larger runners on this manifold extend the top of the RPM range to about 6,500.

Intake Manifolds

Contrary to what some might think, Oldsmobile did not intend to make its intake manifolds heavy and restrictive. The designs reflected a compromise of requirements, and high performance was not at the top of the list. Primary considerations were for reliability and smooth engine operation under all conditions, including extremes in temperature.

Cast iron is a heavy material, but it is dimensionally stable (does not warp easily) and has excellent heat retention capability. This allows the factory heat riser system to bring up manifold temperature quickly on a -20 degree winter morning. But today's Oldsmobile enthusiasts aren't so interested in cold-weather starting performance or perfect drivability under all conditions. Performance is what's at the top of the list, and compromises be damned!

Today, there is a greater selection of Oldsmobile aftermarket intake manifolds than ever before. The design of modern intake manifolds takes advantage of decades of experience gained in racing. Modern computer modeling has taken intake manifold design to an even higher level. The materials and machining capabilities available today could have only been dreamed of when Oldsmobile engines were originally designed.

The point here is that factory intake manifolds are mostly obsolete from a performance standpoint. Unless the main goal is to keep a factory muscle car all original, we recommend that serious performance builds include an aftermarket aluminum intake manifold that was designed for the performance level you intend.

Careful selection of an intake manifold is essential to achieving maximum performance, fuel economy, and drivability. Selecting the most appropriate manifold for the application will show gains in all these areas. An additional benefit of aftermarket performance intake manifolds is that they are made from aluminum, which will save weight over the cast-iron manifold that was used on virtually all Oldsmobile engines.

As with cylinder heads, Edelbrock is the standard for Oldsmobile intake manifolds, providing a full line to suit all types of engine builds. There are great manifolds produced by established brands such as Weiand, Offenhauser, and Holley. ProComp and Speedmaster have inexpensive manifolds with up-to-date designs. These lower-priced options can be very appealing to those on a budget.

Dual-plane Manifolds

For street performance, get a "dual-plane" intake manifold. The shared runner design of the dual-plane manifold maintains higher intake velocity at lower RPM. A well-matched dual-plane intake will improve power across the RPM range while maintaining good fuel economy and drivability.

When we talk about low- and mid-RPM performance, we talk about runner volume and the velocity of the intake gases. Runners are the tunnels in the intake manifold that run from the plenum area under the carburetor to each intake port in the cylinder head. Most dual-plane intakes designed for street performance use runners that are moderately sized and maintain high velocity in the runners.

Higher velocity benefits low- and mid-RPM performance. Why? Well, engineers could bore you to death with discussions of fluid dynamics, but to put it simply, flowing gases have inertia, and the greater the velocity, the greater the inertial force that is available to fill a cylinder when the intake valve opens.

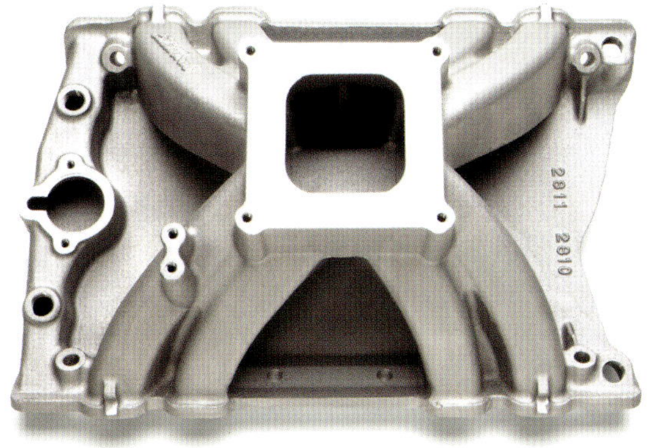

Single-plane intakes should be reserved for engines that will regularly see high RPM. The only real advantage to a single-plane manifold is a slight improvement in airflow at high RPM. This Edelbrock Victor manifold is available for both small-block and big-block Oldsmobiles. The RPM range for this manifold is listed as 4,500 to 7,500 rpm. You're not likely to see that in normal street driving! This is a race manifold.

Single-plane Manifolds

Single-plane manifolds are best suited to racing and maximum-performance street applications. These manifolds require higher airflow to achieve maximum efficiency. Compared with a dual-plane manifold, a single-plane manifold will not perform as well at the low- and mid-RPM ranges.

With intake manifolds, like most other performance parts, bigger is not always better. If the manifold is too big (meaning the interior volume is too much for the application), the power goals will not be achieved, and the engine will run poorly in the low- and mid-RPM ranges.

Many manifolds are available for Oldsmobile engines, and they are all designed to deliver performance in certain ranges and with complimenting performance upgrades elsewhere on the engine. Contact parts manufacturers and other Oldsmobile performance enthusiasts to select the right manifold for your engine.

Tunnel Ram Manifolds

Tunnel ram intake manifolds are excellent eye candy and will attract lots of attention at cruise nights. But do they add any power to your engine? Well, actually, yes! In fact, for a radical street engine or a drag engine, the tunnel ram is probably the setup that will provide the most power short of turbocharged and supercharged systems.

The main disadvantages are obvious. Not many people want to remove their hood or cut a hole in it. And having the induction system exposed to the elements is probably not a good thing either. Engine starting might be more difficult due to the long distance between the carburetor and the cylinder head. But if you like the look, want ultimate naturally aspirated performance, store the car in a garage, and don't drive it in the rain, this might be the setup for you.

Fitting an Intake Manifold

Moving from the theoretical to the practical, not every intake manifold will physically fit under every hood or have all the provisions in regard to accessory brackets, vacuum ports, and emissions components.

One of the biggest considerations when selecting an intake manifold for street use is hood clearance. Manifolds

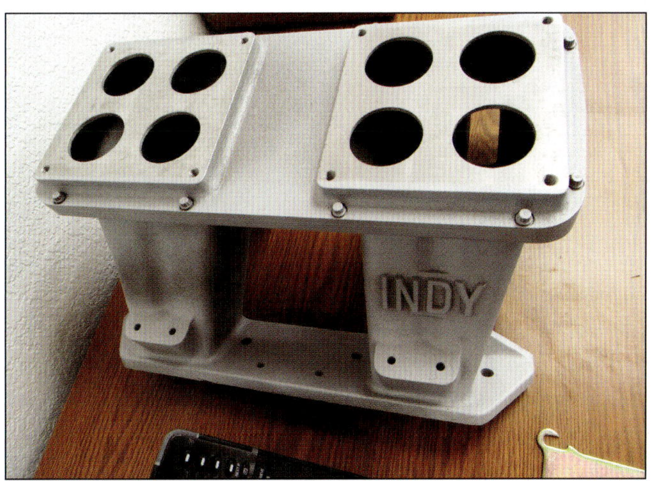

Tunnel rams look really, really cool and produce more power than single-plane or dual-plane manifold types. Since they have the complexity of multiple carburetors and are exposed to the elements, they really aren't practical for most of us.

High-flow air cleaners can offer better performance, but they can also improve hood clearance versus a stock air cleaner.

designed for maximum performance will often not fit under the hood of an Oldsmobile car without modification. Most enthusiasts will want to maintain the original flat hood on their car, so some intake choices will be eliminated out of the gate.

Intake manifold manufacturers list the critical dimensions of their intake manifolds on their websites. Compare their dimensions to the dimensions on the current manifold and check the clearance available with the current air cleaner in place.

Carburetor Flanges

If you run the stock-type Quadrajet carburetor on your engine, you will need a manifold to match its unique "spread-bore" design. Most manifolds are designed with four equally sized holes for the throttle plates (known as "square bore"). While adapters are available to fit a Quadrajet onto a square-bore manifold, they will increase the effective height of the manifold and potentially cause issues with hood clearance.

Emissions Devices

In the late 1960s, an ever-increasing trend toward more vacuum-controlled devices began, as well as thermostatic devices, primarily for emissions control systems. These devices frequently tapped into intake manifold vacuum and the hot coolant flowing through the crossover passages in the intake manifold. Many performance intake manifolds do not have provisions for all of the factory devices. Make sure your intake manifold supports all of the systems you need to maintain.

If using a Quadrajet carburetor, be sure that the manifold you select accommodates the "spread-bore" mounting flange. A Quadrajet cannot be put on a square-bore manifold without an adapter. Many modern manifold designs have a compromise design that accepts both square-bore and spread-bore. Check with the manufacturer before purchasing a manifold.

Carburetors

If you're planning performance upgrades for an engine that was originally equipped with a 2-barrel carburetor, upgrade to a 4-barrel carburetor and intake manifold. The additional two "barrels" of a 4-barrel carburetor open only under hard acceleration and provide additional airflow, which allows the engine to generate more horsepower at higher RPM.

The most common carburetors in the aftermarket are based on proven designs that were originally offered by the major auto manufacturers. Different methods are used to open the secondary barrels on the various designs, providing either better fuel economy or faster throttle response. High-performance and racing carburetors provide a range of optional features that improve the ability to tune for performance and drivability on race engines that are notoriously finicky.

Holley

Holley carburetors are by far the most popular carburetor designs used on high-performance and racing engines. The primary advantage of the Holley designs is that they are in widespread use and are therefore well understood in the world of high performance. Tuning parts and expertise are easily available.

Holley-type carburetors are available in a myriad of airflow ranges (measured in cubic feet per minute, or CFM) and configurations. For high-performance and racing engines, select the precise set of features you desire, including specialty features not available on some other carburetor designs. Holley carburetors range in price from about $300

Holley carburetors with vacuum-controlled secondary throttles will usually deliver better fuel economy than double pumpers. The popular universal variants include an electric choke for easy installation.

If you have an original 4-barrel carburetor on your Oldsmobile engine, it will almost certainly be a Quadrajet. Quadrajets are good for mild- to moderate-performance engines.

to more than $1,500. Higher-priced carburetors flow more air and have more features that allow the carburetor to be more precisely tuned to the application.

One potential disadvantage to using a Holley-type carburetor is that they have a square-bore design, where almost all Oldsmobile factory intake manifolds used a spread-bore design that will accept only a Quadrajet-type carburetor. Although adapter plates are available, it's usually best to use a Quadrajet carburetor on a stock intake manifold. Many aftermarket intake manifolds have a standard-bore design, so a Holley or an AFB/AVS carburetor is usually preferred.

The most common Holley designs use vacuum secondaries. Vacuum-secondary carburetors are available in a variety of flow ratings with 600 cfm being the most popular. A vacuum diaphragm delays the opening of the secondary throttle plates under hard acceleration, which prevents engine bog. Using springs of varying tension above the vacuum diaphragm, adjust the rate of opening of the secondary throttle valves to tune them precisely to a particular engine/vehicle combination.

Keep in mind that carburetor tuning varies by vehicle weight and other factors. Vacuum-secondary carburetors are well suited to street use and will achieve similar fuel economy as the Quadrajet type. Inexpensive and versatile, the vacuum-secondary designs are a great choice for mildly modified street cars where fuel economy is a consideration. These carburetors usually have choke valves, and aftermarket versions will usually use an electric choke that is easy to hook up.

Holley's mechanical-secondary designs (commonly referred to as double pumpers) are best suited to racing and high-level street-performance applications. They are available in ratings up to 950 cfm. While vacuum-secondary carburetors open the secondaries slowly to prevent engine bog, mechanical-secondary carburetors open all four barrels simultaneously.

The bog is overcome by squirting extra fuel into the secondaries while the throttles are opened. The name "double pumper" relates to the second accelerator pump required to achieve this function.

Many mechanical-secondary carburetors have an idle mixture screw at each of the four throttle plates, which allows better idle tuning range for engines with high-overlap camshafts. Double pumpers often have a manual choke or no choke at all by design. The Holley HP series of carburetors are an example of a carburetor without a choke. They are designed primarily for race use. HP carburetors are rich in race tuning features. Those features, of course, come at a higher price.

The Holley Dominator (model 4500) is the ultimate performance model and is available in ratings of 1,050 to 1,400 cfm. These are not street-friendly carburetors. They are to be used on only the highest-performance racing engines. Because of their characteristic enlarged throttle body, they can only be used on intake manifolds that have been manufactured specifically for Dominators. Unless you're planning to build a race engine with horsepower near the four digits, a Dominator is not needed.

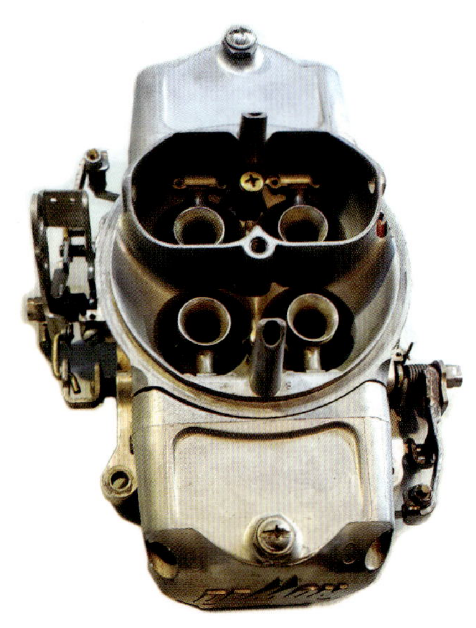

Double pumpers mechanically open the secondaries through a progressive linkage. To compensate for the sudden drop in vacuum when you punch the pedal, a second accelerator pump is needed. The advantage of a double pumper is that there is no delay in the opening of the secondary barrels. The disadvantage is that you'll use more fuel if you have a heavy foot. Shown here is Demon's version of the double pumper, the Mighty Demon.

Demon

A design similar to the Holley designs is the Demon style. Demon carburetors are available in very similar designs and CFM ratings and have the same features available as standard Holley carburetors (Demon Carburetion is owned by the Holley Performance Group).

While Demons have a more modern appearance, they operate similarly and use most of the same replacement parts as standard Holleys. In fact, Holley rebuild kits can be used for Demon carburetors. Still, many racers and performance enthusiasts shy away from Demon carburetors because tuning is different than with Holley carburetors. For example, Demon carburetors tend to use larger jets to flow the same amount of fuel. Demon carburetors are similarly priced as Holleys and have loyal fans (including the author!).

Quadrajet

Quadrajet carburetors came as original equipment on GM cars from the 1960s through the 1980s. While not as popular in performance circles as other designs, they can support the fuel-system requirements of all but the most powerful racing engines. Since they were designed for street use on passenger cars, they are fuel efficient and work exceptionally well in daily driven street cars.

The secondary barrels use an adjustable air valve that prevents bogging under hard acceleration. The air valve does not respond to throttle input as quickly as a Holley double-pumper design, but it is as responsive as a Holley vacuum-secondary design when adjusted properly. The main advantage (or disadvantage) of the Quadrajet is that it is a spread-bore design.

To use a Quadrajet carburetor, an intake manifold is needed that is specifically designed for the Quadrajet. Another option is to use an adapter plate under the carburetor to adapt it to a standard-bore flange. If you plan to use a stock Oldsmobile intake manifold, the Quadrajet is often the preferred design.

AVS/AFB

Commonly available aftermarket carburetors are based on designs originally marketed by Carter and installed on many Chrysler Corporation vehicles in the 1960s and 1970s. Today, Edelbrock manufactures the AVS design, and tuning parts are widely available.

The AVS design uses an air valve that functions similarly to the Quadrajet. Unlike the Quadrajet, the AVS has a square-bore throttle body, meaning it can be installed on most aftermarket intake manifolds. AVS carburetors use electric chokes and are easy to install.

They are popular on street-performance engines and commonly available in 500- and 800-cfm ratings. These carburetors are known for their simplicity and durability. They provide good fuel economy and are

The original Carter AVS and AFB designs have been improved upon by Edelbrock and are being manufactured in the United States. They come with an electric choke and are a great option for a street car.

relatively inexpensive.

Demon offers carburetors that are loosely based on the AVS design. Marketed as the Street Demon, these carburetors incorporate modern design features and are available in 625- and 750-cfm ratings. Since the Street Demon is a significant departure from the AVS design, parts interchange and availability could be an issue.

Carburetor Sizing

Select a carburetor that will just meet the airflow requirements of your engine. A carburetor that is too big for the application is not likely to add any power, even in the high-RPM range. In fact, an oversized carburetor will probably lead to poor performance in the low- and mid-RPM ranges.

There is little to gain and much to lose when your carburetor is oversized to the engine build. Carburetor manufacturers can provide recommendations as to the best carburetor CFM rating for your engine. They have charts and calculators online that are specific to their carburetor designs.

Want your Oldsmobile to start and run as flawlessly as a new car? If so, EFI is your best choice. Aftermarket EFI systems use an oxygen sensor and have a feedback control loop to maintain the optimum air/fuel ratio (AFR). The AFR updates are continuous, immediately responding to changes in operating conditions. Idle speed and mixture never require adjustment, and you don't have to rely on a finicky choke at cold start.

Electronic Fuel Injection

Whether electronic fuel injection (EFI) will make more power versus a properly sized and tuned carburetor is debatable. The main argument for choosing fuel injection is that it can provide improved drivability (particularly when the engine is cold) and also improve fuel economy.

If you're not experienced with carburetor adjustments and tuning, an EFI system with "self-tuning" capabilities can be an attractive option. Tuning changes with EFI don't require mechanical disassembly as with a carburetor, and it can be done in real time while driving. Additionally, many EFI systems can automatically compensate for changing weather conditions and altitude.

Although prices have come down significantly for retrofit EFI systems, they are still significantly pricier than the average carburetor. They also require installation of a high-pressure electric fuel pump.

Here's a general recommendation: If you're familiar with carburetor tuning and mainly drive your car at the racetrack and/or the occasional drive around town on nice days, a carburetor might be a logical choice. But if the car is driven every day or on long cruises, it will benefit from the improvement in fuel economy and drivability that fuel injection can provide.

As with carburetors, it's important to select an EFI system that's matched to the expected performance level of the engine. Many of the less-expensive systems are limited as to the airflow they will support. A low-end system might not meet the needs of a hot street engine.

How Does It Run?

After you've rebuilt the engine and carried out the performance modifications, you'll be eager to see if the engine performs as you expected. Don't be discouraged if the initial performance is not spectacular. Most performance builds require tuning to achieve their full potential.

It's common to "find" an additional 50 hp just through basic tuning that includes optimizing the air/fuel ratio and ignition timing curve. This is best done on a chassis dynamometer and with the aid of a tuning expert. Get recommendations from other performance enthusiasts in your area to find a good tuner. The cost of the services may seem high, but they're often the best bang for the buck in the engine build.

Specifications

Torque Specifications (All Engines)	
Part	**Torque (ft-lbs)**
Air cleaner to carburetor stud	5
Carburetor to intake manifold bolts	15
Choke tube and plate to intake manifold bolts	15
Connecting rod nuts	42
Crankshaft bearing cap bolts (455 ci)	120
Crankshaft bearing cap bolts No. 1, 2, 3 & 4 (all except 451 ci)	80
Crankshaft bearing No. 5 (all except 451 ci)	120
Cylinder head bolts (7/16-inch bolts)	85
Cylinder head bolts (1/2-inch bolts) Note: 1/2-inch bolts were used on 1977-and-later 350 engines and all 403 engines	130
Distributor clamp to cylinder block bolt	17
EGR valve to intake manifold	25
Engine mount to cylinder block bolts	75
Engine mount to frame mount	50
Exhaust manifold to cylinder head bolts	35
Fan-driven pulley to hub bolts	20
Fan-driven pulley to balancer bolts	20
Drive plate to crankshaft (automatic)	60
Flywheel to crankshaft (manual)	90
Front cover to cylinder block (Toronado only)	50
Front cover to cylinder block bolts, 3/8 inch (except Toronado)	35

Torque Specifications (All Engines)	
Part	**Torque (ft-lbs)**
Fuel pump eccentric to camshaft bolt	65
Fuel pump to block bolt and nut	25
Harmonic balancer crankshaft bolt (minimum)	180
Ignition coil to intake manifold	15
Intake manifold (cast iron) to cylinder head bolts	40
Intake manifold (aluminum) to cylinder head bolts	35
Oil deflector to bearing cap (Toronado)	35
Oil filter adapter to cylinder block bolts	35
Oil filter element to base	20
Oil pan bolts	10
Oil pan drain plug	30
Oil pump cover to pump bolts	9
Oil pump to bearing cap bolts	35
Rocker arm pivot bolt to head	25
Starter brace to cylinder block bolts	25
Starter brace to starter motor bolt	15
Starter brace to starter motor stud	8
Starter motor to cylinder block bolts	35
Timing gear to camshaft	65
Valve cover bolts	8
Water outlet to manifold bolts	20
Water pump to engine block bolts	25

260 and 307 Engines		
	260 ci	**307 ci**
Cylinder Block		
Engine type	90-degree V-type	90-degree V-type
Number of cylinders	8	8
Bore and stroke	3.500 x 3.385	3.800 x 3.385
Piston displacement	260 ci	307 ci
Compression ratio	8.0:1	8.5:1
Firing order	1-8-4-3-6-5-7-2	1-8-4-3-6-5-7-2
Bore out of round	0.001 inch	0.001 inch
Bore taper (top)	+0.0003 inch	+0.0003 inch
	-0.0007 inch	-0.0007 inch
Bore taper (bottom)	+0.0007 inch	+0.0007 inch
	-0.0003 inch	-0.0003 inch
Crankshaft		
Main bearing journal diameter	2.4985–2.4995 inch (No. 2, 3, 4, 5)	2.4985–2.4995 inch (No. 2, 3, 4, 5)
	2.4988–2.4998 inch (No. 1)	2.4988–2.4998 inch (No. 1)
Connecting rod bearing journal	2.1248–2.1238 inch	2.1248–2.1238 inch
End clearance	0.0035–0.0135 inch	0.0035–0.0135 inch
Main Bearings		
Bearing clearance:		
–No. 1, 2, 3, and 4	0.0005–0.0021 inch	0.0005–0.0021 inch
–No. 5	0.0015–0.0031 inch	0.0015–0.0031 inch
Bearing Shell Width:		
–No. 1, 2, and 4	0.970–0.980 inch	0.970–0.980 inch
–No. 3	1.193–1.195 inch	1.193–1.195 inch
–No. 5	1.624 inch	1.624 inch
Connecting Rods		
Vertical bearing clearance	0.0004–0.0033 inch	0.0004–0.0033 inch
Big end side clearance	0.006–0.020 inch	0.006–0.020 inch
Pistons		
Nominal outside diameter	3.500 inch	3.800 inch
Clearance in bore	0.00075–0.00175 inch	0.00075–0.00175 inch
Weight less pin and rings (all)	482 ±2 g	569 ±2 g
Skirt taper	0.0003–0.0017 inch larger at bottom	0.0003–0.0017 inch larger at bottom
Number of compression rings per piston	2	2
Number of oil rings per piston	1	1
Ring width (2 compression)	0.0780–0.0770 inch	0.0780–0.0770 inch
Ring width (1 oil)	0.1881–0.1891 inch	0.1881–0.1891 inch

260 and 307 Engines		
	260 ci	**307 ci**
Piston Pins		
Diameter	0.9803–0.9807 inch	0.9803–0.9807 inch
Pin to piston clearance	0.0003–0.0005 inch	0.0003–0.0005 inch
Pin to rod fit	0.0008–0.0018 inch press fit	0.0008–0.0018 inch press fit
Valve Lifter		
Leakdown rate:		
–Used	6 seconds (minimum)	6 seconds (minimum)
–New	12–87 seconds	12–87 seconds
Overall length	2.000 inch	2.000 inch
Body diameter	0.8422–0.8427 inch	0.8422–0.8427 inch
Clearance in boss	0.0005–0.0020 inch	0.0005–0.0020 inch
Camshaft		
Bearing journal diameters:		
–No. 1	2.0365–2.0357 inch	2.0365–2.0357 inch
–No. 2	2.0165–2.0157 inch	2.0165–2.0157 inch
–No. 3	1.9965–1.9957 inch	1.9965–1.9957 inch
–No. 4	1.9765–1.9757 inch	1.9765–1.9757 inch
–No. 5	1.9565–1.9557 inch	1.9565–1.9557 inch
Journal clearance in bearing (all)	0.0020–0.0058 inch	0.0020–0.0058 inch
End clearance	0.011–0.077 inch	0.011–0.077 inch
Pushrod Length		
	8.265 inch	8.265 inch
Valves		
Valve lash	Hydraulic	Hydraulic
Intake head diameter	1.517–1.527 inch	1.745–1.755 inch
Stem diameter	0.3425–0.3432 inch	0.3425–0.3432 inch
Valve angle	44 degrees	44 degrees
Valve seat angle	45 degrees	45 degrees
Valve seat width	0.037–0.075 inch	0.037–0.075 inch
Overall length	4.667 inch	4.667 inch
Clearance in guide	0.0010–0.0027 inch	0.0010–0.0027 inch
Exhaust head diameter	1.295–1.305 inch	1.497–1.507 inch
Stem diameter	0.3420–0.3427 inch	0.3420–0.3427 inch
Valve angle	30 degrees	30 degrees
Valve seat angle	31 degrees	31 degrees
Valve seat width	0.050–0.090 inch	0.050–0.090 inch
Overall length	4.675 inch	4.675 inch
Clearance in guide	0.0015–0.0032 inch	0.0015–0.0032 inch
Valve Springs		
Free length	1.96 inch	1.96 inch

260 and 307 Engines		
	260 ci	**307 ci**
Load	76–84 pounds at 1.670 inch	76–84 pounds at 1.620 inch
	180–194 pounds at 1.270 inch	180–194 pounds at 1.270 inch
Flywheel		
Number of teeth on starter gear	166	166
Number of teeth on starter pinion	9	9
Lubrication System		
Crankcase capacity drain and refill	4 quarts	4 quarts
Crankcase drain and refill with filter change	5 quarts	5 quarts
Oil pressure at RPM	35 psi at 1,500–3,000	35 psi at 1,500–3,000
Oil pump pressure relief valve in bore clearance	0.0025–0.0050 inch	0.0025–0.0050 inch
Gear end clearance	0.0025–0.0065 inch	0.0025–0.0065 inch

330 Engines	
Cylinder Block	
Engine type	90-degree V-type
Number of cylinders	8
Bore and stroke	3.9385 x 3.385 inch
Piston displacement	330 ci
Compression ratio	2 barrel, 8.5:1; 4 barrel, 10.25:1
Firing order	1-8-4-3-6-5-7-2
Main bearing bore (ID)	2.687–2.688 inch
Crankshaft	
Main bearing journal diameter	2.4995–2.4985 inch
Main bearing journal width (with fillets):	
–No. 1	1.185 inch
–No. 2 and 4	1.156–1.166 inch
–No. 3	1.199–1.201 inch
–No. 5	1.872 inch
Connecting rod bearing journal	2.1248–2.1238 inch
Connecting rod bearing width (with fillets)	1.877–1.880 inch
Overall crankshaft length	26.470 inch
Oil hole diameter	0.201–0.209 inch
End clearance	0.004–0.008 inch
Main Bearings	
Bearing Clearance:	
–No. 1, 2, 3, and 4	0.0015–0.0031 inch
–No. 5	0.0015–0.0031 inch

330 Engines	
Bearing Shell Width:	
–No. 1, 2, and 4	0.970–0.980 inch
–No. 3	1.193–1.195 inch
–No. 5	1.624 inch
Connecting Rods	
Center to center length	5.998–6.002 inch
Connecting rod bore diameter	2.2495–2.2500 inch
Pin bore	0.9791–0.9795 inch
Vertical bearing clearance	0.0015–0.0030 inch
Big end side clearance	0.002–0.013 inch
Pistons	
Nominal outside diameter	3.9375 inch
Overall length	3.620 inch
Top of piston to center of pin	1.615 inch
Clearance at thrust surface (selective)	0.00075–0.00125 inch
Weight less pin and rings	20.67 ounces
Skirt taper	0.0000–0.0010 inch larger at bottom
Ring width (top compression)	0.0803 inch
Ring width (second compression)	0.0803 inch
Ring width (1 oil)	0.1886 inch
Piston Pins	
Diameter	0.9803–0.9807 inch
Overall length	3.116–3.136 inch
Pin to piston clearance	0.0003–0.0005 inch
Pin to rod clearance	0.0008–0.0016 inch press fit
Piston Rings	
Number of compression rings per piston	2
Width of compression rings	0.0775–0.0780 inch
Compression ring gap clearance	0.010–0.020 inch
Compression ring clearance in groove:	
–Upper	0.0018–0.0033 inch
–Lower	0.0018–0.0038 inch
Number of oil rings per piston	1
Oil ring gap clearance	0.015–0.055 inch
Oil ring clearance in groove	0.0001–0.0051 inch
Camshaft	
Bearing journal diameters:	
–No. 1	2.0365–2.0373 inch
–No. 2	2.0165–2.0173 inch
–No. 3	1.9965–1.9973 inch
–No. 4	1.9765–1.9773 inch

330 Engines	
–No. 5	1.9565–1.9573 inch
Main bearing journal width (including chamfers):	
–No. 1	0.810 inch
–No. 2, 3, and 4	0.768 inch
–No. 5	0.775 inch
Journal clearance in bearing (all)	0.0012–0.0050 inch
End clearance	0.011–0.077 inch
Pushrod Length	
	8.265 inches
Valve – Intake	
Head diameter	1.886–1.870 inch
Stem diameter	0.3425–0.3432 inch
Valve angle	44 degrees
Valve seat angle	45 degrees
Valve seat width	0.037–0.075 inch
Overall length	4.740 inch
Clearance in guide	0.0010–0.0027 inch
Lash	Hydraulic
Valve – Exhaust	
Head diameter	1.557–1.567 inch
Stem diameter	0.3420–0.3427 inch
Valve angle	44 degrees
Valve seat angle	45 degrees
Valve seat width	0.037–0.075 inch
Overall length	4.728 inch
Clearance in guide	0.0015–0.0032 inch
Lash	Hydraulic
Valve Springs	
Length	1.96 inch
Wire diameter	0.192 inch
Inside spring diameter	1.065–1.041 inch
Load	76–84 pounds at 1.670 inch, 180–194 pounds at 1.270 inch
Valve Lifters	
Body diameter	0.8422–0.8427 inch
Overall length	2.000 inch
Clearance in boss	0.0005–0.0020 inch
Camshaft Sprockets	
Pitch	0.500 inch
Number of teeth	36

330 Engines	
Crankshaft Sprockets	
Pitch	0.500 inch
Number of teeth	18
Timing Chain	
Width	0.740–0.750 inch
Number of links	48
Type	Linkbelt
Pitch	0.500 inch
Flywheel	
Number of teeth on starter gear	166
Number of teeth on starter pinion	9
Lubrication System	
Crankcase capacity drain and refill	4 quarts
Crankcase drain and refill with filter change	5 quarts
Oil pressure at RPM	35 psi at 1,500–3,000
Pump pressure relief valve in bore clearance	0.0025–0.0050 inch
Pump gear end clearance	0.0025–0.0065 inch

350 and 455 Engines		
	350 ci	**455 ci**
Cylinder Block		
Engine type	90-degree V-type	90-degree V-type
Number of cylinders	8	8
Bore and stroke	4.057 x 3.385 inch	4.126 x 4.250 inch
Piston displacement	350 ci	455 ci
Compression ratio	8.5:1	8.5:1
Firing order	1-8-4-3-6-5-7-2	1-8-4-3-6-5-7-2
Main bearing bore (ID)	2.687–2.688 inch	3.188–3.189 inch
Crankshaft		
Main bearing journal diameter:		3.0003–2.9993 inch (all)
–No. 1	2.4998–2.4988 inch	
–No. 2, 3, 4, and 5	2.4995–2.4985 inch	
Width – main bearing journal (with fillets):		
–No. 1	1.185 inch	1.185 inch
–No. 2 and 4	1.156–1.166 inch	1.156–1.166 inch
–No. 3	1.199–1.201 inch	1.199–1.201 inch
–No. 5	1.882 inch	1.882 inch
Connecting rod bearing journal diameter	2.1248–2.1238 inch	2.4998–2.4988 inch

350 and 455 Engines		
	350 ci	**455 ci**
Connecting rod bearing width (with fillets)	1.877–1.887 inch	1.877–1.887 inch
Overall crankshaft length	26.470 inch	26.470 inch
Oil hole diameter	0.201–0.223 inch	0.201–0.223 inch
End clearance	0.004–0.008 inch	0.004–0.008 inch
Main Bearings		
Bearing clearance:		
–No. 1, 2, 3, and 4	0.0005–0.0021 inch	0.0005–0.0021 inch
–No. 5	0.0015–0.0031 inch	0.0020–0.0034 inch
Bearing shell width:		
–No. 1, 2, and 4	0.970–0.980 inch	0.970–0.980 inch
–No. 3	1.193–1.195 inch	1.193–1.195 inch
–No. 5	1.624 inch	1.624 inch
Connecting Rods		
Center to center length	5.998–6.002 inch	6.733–6.737 inch
Connecting rod bore diameter	2.2495–2.2500 inch	2.6243–2.6250 inch
Pin bore	0.9789–0.9795 inch	0.9789–0.9795 inch
Vertical bearing clearance	0.0004–0.0033 inch	0.0004–0.0033 inch
Big end side clearance	0.002–0.013 inch	0.002–0.013 inch
Pistons		
Nominal outside diameter	4.057 inch	4.1245 inch
Overall length	3.620 inch	3.490 inch
Top of piston to center of pin	1.613–1.617 inch	1.738–1.742 inch
Clearance at thrust surface (selective)	0.001–0.002 inch	0.001–0.002 inch
Weight less pin and rings	22.60 ounce	24.057 ounce
Skirt taper	0.0005–0.0015 inch larger at bottom	0.0005–0.0015 inch larger at bottom
Ring width (2 compression)	0.0798–0.0808 inch	0.0798–0.0808 inch
Ring width (1 oil)	0.1881–0.1891 inch	0.1881–0.1891 inch
Piston Pins		
Diameter	0.9803–0.9807 inch	0.9803–0.9807 inch
Overall length	2.980 inch	2.980 inch
Pin to piston clearance	0.0003–0.0005 inch loose fit	0.0003–0.0005 inch loose fit
Pin to rod fit	0.0008–0.0018 inch press fit	0.0008–0.0018 inch press fit
Piston Rings		
Number of compression rings per piston	2	2
Width of compression rings	0.0770–0.0780 inch	0.0770–0.0780 inch
Compression ring gap clearance	0.010–0.023 inch	0.010–0.023 inch
Compression ring clearance in groove:		
–Upper	0.0020–0.0040 inch	0.0020–0.0040 inch
–Lower	0.0020–0.0040 inch	0.0020–0.0040 inch

350 and 455 Engines		
	350 ci	**455 ci**
Number of oil rings per piston	1	1
Oil ring gap clearance	0.015–0.055 inch	0.015–0.055 inch
Camshaft		
Bearing journal diameters:		
–No. 1	2.0365–2.0357 inch	2.0365–2.0357 inch
–No. 2	2.0165–2.0157 inch	2.0165–2.0157 inch
–No. 3	1.9965–1.9957 inch	1.9965–1.9957 inch
–No. 4	1.9765–1.9757 inch	1.9765–1.9757 inch
–No. 5	1.9565–1.9557 inch	1.9565–1.9557 inch
Width (including chamfers):		
–No. 1	0.810 inch	0.810 inch
–No. 2, 3, and 4	0.761 inch	0.761 inch
–No. 5	0.788 inch	0.788 inch
Journal clearance in bearing (all)	0.0020–0.0058 inch	0.0020–0.0058 inch
End clearance	0.011–0.077 inch	0.011–0.077 inch
Pushrod Length		
	8.265 inch	9.570 inch
Valve - Intake		
Lash	Hydraulic	Hydraulic
Head diameter	1.880–1.870 inch	2.000–1.990 inch
Stem diameter	0.3425–0.3432 inch	0.3425–0.3432 inch
Valve angle	44 degrees	44 degrees
Valve seat angle	45 degrees	45 degrees
Valve seat width	0.037–0.075 inch	0.037–0.075 inch
Overall length	4.667 inch	4.667 inch
Clearance in guide	0.0010–0.0027 inch	0.0010–0.0027 inch
Valve - Exhaust		
Lash	Hydraulic	Hydraulic
Head diameter	1.627–1.617 inch	1.627–1.617 inch
Stem diameter	0.3420–0.3427 inch	0.3420–0.3427 inch
Valve angle	30 degrees	30 degrees
Valve seat angle	31 degrees	31 degrees
Valve seat width	0.050–0.090 inch	0.050–0.090 inch
Overall length	4.675 inch	4.675 inch
Clearance in guide	0.0015–0.0032 inch	0.0015–0.0032 inch
Valve Springs		
Length	1.96 inch	1.96 inch

350 and 455 Engines		
	350 ci	**455 ci**
Wire diameter	0.192 inch	0.192 inch
Inside spring diameter	1.065–1.041 inch	1.065–1.041 inch
Load	76–84 pounds at 1.670 inch	76–84 pounds at 1.620 inch
	180–194 pounds at 1.270 inch	180–194 pounds at 1.270 inch
Valve Lifters		
Body diameter	0.8422–0.8427 inch	0.8422–0.8427 inch
Overall length	2.000 inch	2.000 inch
Clearance in boss	0.0005–0.0020 inch	0.0005–0.0020 inch
Camshaft Sprockets		
Width of sprocket	0.400–0.410 inch	0.520–0.530 inch
Pitch	0.500 inch	0.500 inch
Crankshaft Sprockets		
Width of sprocket	0.400–0.410 inch	0.520–0.530 inch
Overall width of gear	1.001–0.991 inch	1.001–0.991 inch
Pitch	0.500 inch	0.500 inch
Number of teeth	18	18
Timing Chain		
Number of links	48	48
Pitch	0.500 inch	0.500 inch
Flywheel		
Number of teeth on starter gear	166	166
Number of teeth on starter pinion	9	9
Lubrication System		
Crankcase capacity drain and refill:		
–Toronado	5 quarts	5 quarts
–All except Toronado	4 quarts	4 quarts
Crankcase drain and refill with filter change:		
–Toronado	6 quarts	6 quarts
–All except Toronado	5 quarts	5 quarts
Oil pump		
Pressure relief valve in bore clearance	0.0025–0.0050 inch	0.0025–0.0050 inch
Gear end clearance	0.0025–0.0065 inch	0.0025–0.0065 inch

1965–1967 400 and all 425 engines		
	Early 400 ci	**425 ci**
Cylinder Block		
Engine type	90-degree V-type	90-degree V-type
Number of cylinders	8	8
Bore and stroke	4.000 x 3.975 inch	4.125 x 3.975 inch
Piston displacement	400 ci	425 ci
Compression ratio	10.5:1	Variable
Firing order	1-8-4-3-6-5-7-2	1-8-4-3-6-5-7-2
Main bearing bore (ID)	3.188–3.189 inch	3.188–3.189 inch
Crankshaft		
Main bearing journal diameter	3.0003–2.9993 inch	3.0003–2.9993 inch
Width – main bearing journal (with fillets):		
–No. 1	1.185 inch	1.185 inch
–No. 2 and 4	1.156–1.166 inch	1.156–1.166 inch
–No. 3	1.199–1.201 inch	1.199–1.201 inch
–No. 5	1.872 inch	1.872 inch
Connecting rod bearing journal	2.5003–2.4988 inch	2.5003–2.4988 inch
Connecting rod bearing width (with fillets)	1.877–1.880 inch	1.877–1.880 inch
Overall crankshaft length	26.470 inch	26.470 inch
Oil hole diameter	0.201–0.209 inch	0.201–0.209 inch
End clearance	0.004–0.008 inch	0.004–0.008 inch
Main Bearings		
Bearing clearance:		
–No. 1, 2, 3, and 4	0.0015–0.0031 inch	0.0015–0.0031 inch
–No. 5	0.0020–0.0034 inch	0.0020–0.0034 inch
Bearing shell width:		
–No. 1, 2, and 4	0.970–0.980 inch	0.970–0.980 inch
–No. 3	1.193–1.195 inch	1.193–1.195 inch
–No. 5	1.624 inch	1.624 inch
Connecting Rods		
Center to center length	6.996–7.000 inch	6.996–7.000 inch
Connecting rod bore diameter	2.6243–2.6250 inch	2.6243–2.6250 inch
Pin bore	0.9791–0.9795 inch	0.9791–0.9795 inch
Vertical bearing clearance	0.0008–0.0018 inch	0.0008–0.0018 inch
Big end side clearance	0.002–0.013 inch	0.002–0.013 inch
On nominal outside diameter	4.000 inch	4.125 inch
Overall length	3.620 inch	3.620 inch
Top of piston to center of pin	1.615 inch	1.615 inch
Clearance at thrust surface (selective)	0.00075–0.00125 inch	0.00075–0.00125 inch

1965–1967 400 and all 425 engines		
	Early 400 ci	**425 ci**
Weight less pin and rings	23.46 ounce	23.46 ounces
Skirt taper	0.0000–0.0010 inch larger at bottom	0.0000–0.0010 inch larger at bottom
Ring width (2 compression)	0.0803 inch	0.0803 inch
Ring width (1 oil)	0.1886 inch	0.1886 inch
Piston Pins		
Diameter	0.9803–0.9807 inch	0.9803–0.9807 inch
Overall length	3.116–3.136 inch	3.116–3.136 inch
Piston-to-pin clearance	0.0003–0.0005 inch	0.0003–0.0005 inch
Pin-to-rod fit	0.0008–0.0016 inch press fit	0.0008–0.0018 inch press fit
Piston Rings		
Number of compression rings per piston	2	2
Width of compression rings	0.0775–0.0780 inch	0.0775–0.0780 inch
Compression ring gap clearance	0.013–0.023 inch	0.013–0.023 inch
Compression ring clearance in groove	0.0018–0.0033 inch	0.0018–0.0033 inch
Number of oil rings per piston	1	1
Oil ring gap clearance	0.015–0.055 inch	0.015–0.055 inch
Oil ring clearance in groove	0.0021–0.0081 inch	0.0021–0.0081 inch
Camshaft		
Bearing journal diameters:		
–No. 1	2.0365–2.0373 inch	2.0365–2.0373 inch
–No. 2	2.0165–2.0173 inch	2.0165–2.0173 inch
–No. 3	1.9965–1.9973 inch	1.9965–1.9973 inch
–No. 4	1.9765–1.9773 inch	1.9765–1.9773 inch
–No. 5	1.9565–1.9573 inch	1.9565–1.9573 inch
Width (including chamfers):		
–No. 1	0.810 inch	0.810 inch
–No. 2, 3, and 4	0.768 inch	0.768 inch
–No. 5	0.775 inch	0.775 inch
Journal clearance in bearing (all)	0.0012–0.0050 inch	0.0012–0.0050 inch
End clearance	0.011–0.077 inch	0.011–0.077 inch
Pushrod Length		
	9.625 inch	9.625 inch
Valve - Intake		
Head diameter	2.067–2.077 inch	2.000–1.990 inch
Stem diameter	0.3425–0.3432 inch	0.3425–0.3432 inch
Valve angle	30 degrees	44 degrees
Valve seat angle	30 degrees	45 degrees
Valve seat width	0.030–0.045 inch	0.030 inch
Overall length (measured from tip to middle of valve seat):		

1965–1967 400 and all 425 engines		
	Early 400 ci	**425 ci**
–All except Starfire	4.593 inch	4.557 inch
–Starfire	N/A	4.587 inch
Clearance in guide	0.001–0.003 inch	0.001–0.003 inch
Lash	Hydraulic	Hydraulic
Valve - Exhaust		
Head diameter	1.629–1.619 inch	1.629–1.619 inch
Stem diameter	0.3420–0.3427 inch	0.3420–0.3427 inch
Valve seat angle	45 degrees	45 degrees
Valve seat width	0.037–0.075 inch	0.037–0.075 inch
Overall length:		
–All except Starfire	4.593 inch	4.557 inch
–Starfire	N/A	4.587 inch
Clearance in guide	0.001–0.003 inch	0.001–0.003 inch
Lash	Hydraulic	Hydraulic
Valve Springs		
Length	1.96 inch	1.96 inch
Wire diameter	0.192 inch	0.192 inch
Inside spring diameter	1.065–1.041 inch	1.065–1.041 inch
Load	76–84 pounds at 1.670 inch	76–84 pounds at 1.620 inch
	180–194 pounds at 1.270 inch	180–194 pounds at 1.270 inch
Valve Lifters		
Body diameter	0.9210–0.9215 inch	0.9210–0.9215 inch
Overall length	2.125 inch	2.125 inch
Clearance in boss	0.0005–0.0020 inch	0.0005–0.0020 inch
Pushrod Length		
	9.644 inch	9.622 inch
Camshaft Sprockets		
Width of sprocket	0.521–0.529 inch	0.529–0.521 inch
Pitch	0.500 inch	0.500 inch
Number of teeth	36	36
Crankshaft Sprockets		
Width of sprocket	0.520–0.530 inch	0.520–0.530 inch
Overall width of gear	1.001–0.993 inch	1.001–0.993 inch
Pitch	0.500 inch	0.500 inch
Number of teeth	18	18
Timing Chain		
Width	Morse 0.875 inch, Linkbelt 0.844 inch	Morse 0.875 inch, Linkbelt 0.844 inch
Number of links	48	48
Pitch	0.500 inch	0.500 inch

1965–1967 400 and all 425 engines		
	Early 400 ci	**425 ci**
Flywheel		
Number of teeth on starter gear	166	166
Number of teeth on starter pinion	9	9
Lubrication System		
Crankcase capacity drain and refill Toronado	5 quarts	5 quarts
All except Toronado	4 quarts	4 quarts
Crankcase drain and refill with filter change Toronado	6 quarts	6 quarts
All except Toronado	5 quarts	5 quarts
Oil Pump pressure relief valve in bore clearance	0.0025–0.0050 inch	0.0025–0.0050 inch
Gear end clearance	0.0025–0.0065 inch	0.0025–0.0065 inch

1968 and 1969 400 and All 403 Engines		
	400	**403**
Cylinder Block		
Engine type	90-degree V-type	90-degree V-type
Number of cylinders	8	8
Bore and stroke	3.870 x 4.250 inch	4.351 x 3.385 inch
Piston displacement	400 ci	403 ci
Compression ratio	10.5:1	8.5:1
Firing order	1-8-4-3-6-5-7-2	1-8-4-3-6-5-7-2
Main bearing bore (ID)	3.188–3.189 inch	2.687–2.688 inch
Crankshaft		
Main bearing journal diameter:		
–No. 2, 3, 4, 5	3.0003–2.9993 inch	2.4985–2.4995 inch
–No. 1	3.0003–2.9993 inch	2.4988–2.4998 inch
Width – main bearing journal (with fillets)		
–No. 1	1.185 inch	1.185 inch
–No. 2 and 4	1.156–1.166 inch	1.156–1.166 inch
–No. 3	1.199–1.201 inch	1.1985–1.2015 inch
–No. 5	1.882 inch	1.882 inch
Connecting rod bearing journal	2.4988–2.4998 inch	2.1238–2.1248 inch
Connecting rod bearing width (with fillets)	1.877–1.880 inch	1.877–1.887 inch
Overall crankshaft length	26.470 inch	26.470 inch
Oil hole diameter	0.201–0.209 inch	0.250 inch
End clearance	0.004–0.008 inch	0.0035–0.0135 inch

1968 and 1969 400 and All 403 Engines		
	400	**403**
Main Bearings		
Bearing clearance:		
–No. 1, 2, 3, and 4	0.0005–0.0021 inch	0.0005–0.0021 inch
–No. 5	0.0020–0.0034 inch	0.0015–0.0031 inch
Bearing shell width:		
–No. 1, 2, and 4	0.970–0.980 inch	0.970–0.980 inch
–No. 3	1.193–1.195 inch	1.193–1.195 inch
–No. 5	1.624 inch	1.624 inch
Connecting Rods		
Center to center length	6.733–6.737 inch	5.998–6.002 inch
Connecting rod bore diameter	2.6243–2.6250 inch	2.2495–2.2500 inch
Pin bore	0.9789–0.9795 inch	0.9789–0.9795 inch
Vertical bearing clearance	0.0004–0.0033 inch	0.0004–0.0033 inch
Big end side clearance	0.002–0.013 inch	0.002–0.013 inch
Pistons		
Nominal outside diameter	3.870 inch	4.351 inch
Overall length	3.490 inch	3.620 inch
Top of piston to center of pin	1.738–1.742 inch	1.613–1.617 inch
Clearance at thrust surface (selective)	0.00075–0.00125 inch	0.001–0.002 inch
Weight less pin and rings	21.094 ounces	700 ± 2 g
Skirt taper	Larger at bottom, 0.0000–0.0010 inch	Larger at bottom 0.0003–0.0017 inch
Ring width (2 compression)	0.0798–0.0808 inch	0.0798–0.0808 inch
Ring width (1 oil)	0.1881–0.1891 inch	0.1881–0.1891 inch
Piston Pins		
Diameter	0.9803–0.9807 inch	0.9803–0.9807 inch
Overall length	2.980 inch	
Pin-to-piston clearance	0.0003–0.0005 inch loose fit	0.0003–0.0005 inch loose fit
Pin-to-rod fit	0.0008–0.0016 inch press fit	0.0008–0.0018 inch press fit
Piston Rings		
Number of compression rings per piston	2	2
Width of compression rings	0.0770–0.0780 inch	0.0770–0.0780 inch
Compression ring gap clearance	0.010–0.020 inch	0.010–0.023 inch
Compression ring clearance in groove:		
–Upper	0.002–0.004 inch	0.0020–0.0040 inch
–Lower	0.002–0.004 inch	0.0020–0.0040 inch
Number of oil rings per piston	1	1
Oil ring gap clearance	0.015–0.055 inch	0.015–0.055 inch
Oil ring clearance in groove	0.001–0.010 inch	0.001–0.010 inch

1968 and 1969 400 and All 403 Engines		
	400	**403**
Camshaft		
Bearing journal diameters:		
–No. 1	2.0365–2.0357 inch	2.0365–2.0357 inch
–No. 2	2.0165–2.0157 inch	2.0165–2.0157 inch
–No. 3	1.9965–1.9957 inch	1.9965–1.9957 inch
–No. 4	1.9765–1.9757 inch	1.9765–1.9757 inch
–No. 5	1.9565–1.9557 inch	1.9565–1.9557 inch
Width (including chamfers):		
–No. 1	0.810 inch	0.810 inch
–No. 2, 3, and 4	0.761 inch	0.741 inch
–No. 5	0.788 inch	0.788 inch
Journal clearance in bearing (all)	0.0020–0.0058 inch	0.0020–0.0058 inch
End clearance	0.011–0.077 inch	0.011–0.077 inch
Pushrod Length		
	9.556 inch	8.265 inch
Valve – Intake		
Head diameter	2.077–2.067 inch, 4-barrel; 1.990–2.000 inch, 2-barrel	2.000–1.990 inch
Stem diameter	0.3425–0.3432 inch	0.3425–0.3432 inch
Valve angle	30 degrees, 4-barrel; 46 degrees, 2-barrel	44 degrees
Valve seat angle	30 degrees, 4-barrel; 45 degrees, 2-barrel	45 degrees
Valve seat width	0.030–0.045 inch	0.037–0.075 inch
Overall length	4.703 inch	4.667 inch
Clearance in guide	0.0010–0.0027 inch	0.0010–0.0027 inch
Lash	Hydraulic	Hydraulic
Valve – Exhaust		
Head diameter	1.629–1.619 inch	1.497–1.507 inch
Stem diameter	0.3420–0.3427 inch	0.3420–0.3427 inch
Valve angle	46 degrees	30 degrees
Valve seat angle	45 degrees	31 degrees
Valve seat width	0.037–0.075 inch	0.050–0.090 inch
Overall length	4.695 inch	4.675 inch
Clearance in guide	0.0015–0.0032 inch	0.0015–0.0032 inch
Lash	Hydraulic	Hydraulic
Valve Springs		
Length	1.96 inch	1.96 inch
Wire diameter	0.192 inch	0.192 inch
Inside spring diameter	1.065–1.041 inch	1.065–1.041 inch

1968 and 1969 400 and All 403 Engines		
	400	**403**
Load	76–84 pounds at 1.670 inch, 180–194 pounds at 1.270 inch	76–84 pounds at 1.620 inch, 180–194 pounds at 1.270 inch
Valve Lifters		
Body diameter	0.8422–0.8427 inch	0.8422–0.8427 inch
Overall length	2.000 inch	2.000 inch
Clearance in boss	0.0005–0.0020 inch	0.0005–0.0020 inch
Camshaft Sprockets		
Width of sprocket	0.521–0.529 inch	0.400–0.420 inch
Pitch	0.500 inch	0.500 inch
Number of teeth	36	36
Crankshaft Sprockets		
Width of sprocket	0.520–0.530 inch	0.400–0.410 inch
Overall width of gear	1.001–0.991 inch	1.001–0.991 inch
Pitch	0.500 inch	0.500 inch
Number of teeth	18	18
Timing Chain		
Width	Morse 0.827 inch, Linkbelt 0.844 inch	Morse 0.627 inch, Linkbelt 0.720–0.750 inch
Number of links	48	48
Pitch	0.500 inch	0.500 inch
Flywheel		
Number of teeth on starter gear	166	166
Number of teeth on starter pinion	9	9
Lubrication System		
Crankcase capacity drain and refill Toronado	5 quarts	5 quarts
All except Toronado	4 quarts	4 quarts
Crankcase drain and refill with filter change Toronado	6 quarts	6 quarts
All except Toronado	5 quarts	5 quarts
Oil Pump		
Pressure relief valve in bore clearance	0.0025–0.0050 inch	0.0025–0.0050 inch
Gear end clearance	0.0025–0.0065 inch	0.0025–0.0065 inch

Source Guide

Accel Performance Ignition
1801 Russelville Rd.
Bowling Green, KY 42101
866-464-6553
holley.com/brands/accel

American Racing Headers (ARH)
880 Grand Blvd.
Deer Park, NY 11729
631-608-1986
americanracingheaders.com

ATK Performance Engines
1102 W. Carrier Pkwy.
Grand Prairie, TX 75050
866-721-2315
atkvege.com

Brothers Automotive Products
2019 E. Spruce Circle, Ste. A
Olathe, KS, 66062
913-764-0403
oldsparts.com

BTR Performance
1517 Mt. Read Blvd., Area B
Rochester, NY 14606
585-303-7560
btrperformance.com

Cloyes Gear & Products
7800 Ball Rd.
Fort Smith, AR 72908
479-646-1662
cloyes.com

CNC Motorsports
118 Front St.
Brookings, SD 57006
800-341-1528
cnc-motorsports.com

COMP Cams
3406 Democrat Rd.
Memphis, TN 38118
800-365-9145
compcams.com

Crane Cams
8649 Hacks Cross Rd.
Olive Branch, MS 38654
866-388-5120
cranecams.com

Demon Carburetion
1801 Russelville Rd.
Bowling Green, KY 42101
866-464-6553
holley.com/brands/demon

Dick Miller Racing
214 Sunrise Dr.
Scence Hill, KY 42553
662-233-2301
dickmillerracing.com

Doug's Headers
440 E. Arrow Hwy.
San Dimas, CA 91773
909-599-5955
pertronixbrands.com/pages/dougs-headers

Eagle Specialty Products
8530 Aaron Lane
Southaven, MS 38671
662-796-7373
eaglerod.com

Edelbrock Performance
2700 California St.
Torrance, CA 90503
310-781-2222
edelbrock.com

Enginekits.com
931 19th St.
Bakersfield, CA 93301
661-861-0167
enginekits.com

Erson Cams
7301 Global Dr.
Louisville, KY 40258
800-641-7920
pbm-erson.com

Flowtech Exhaust
1801 Russelville Rd.
Bowling Green, KY 42101
866-464-6553
holley.com/brands/flowtech

Fusick Automotive Products
21 Thompson Rd.
East Windsor, CT 06088
860-623-1589
fusick.com

Hedman Hedders
12438 Putnam St.
Whittier, CA 90602
562-921-0404
hedman.com

Holley Performance Products
1801 Russelville Rd.
Bowling Green, KY 42101
270-781-9741
holley.com

Hooker Headers
1801 Russelville Rd.
Bowling Green, KY 42101
866-464-6553
holley.com/brands/hooker

Howards Cams and Engine Parts
280 W. 35th Ave.
Oshkosh, WI 54902
920-233-5228
howardscams.com

Iskendarian (Isky) Racing Cams
16020 South Broadway
Gardena, CA 90248
310-217-9232
iskycams.com

Jasper Engines
P.O Box 650
Jasper, IN 47547-0650
800-827-7455
jasperengines.com

Jegs Performance
751 E. 11th Ave.
Columbus, OH 43211
614-294-5151
jegs.com

Jet Hot Coatings
2611 LaVista Dr.
Burlington, NC 27215
800-432-3379
jet-hot.com

Lunati Performance Parts
8649 Hacks Cross Rd.
Olive Branch, MS 38654
662-892-1500
lunatipower.com

Melling Engine Parts
2620 Saradan Dr.
Jackson, MI 49204
517-787-8172
melling.com

Mondello Performance Products
1103 Paso Robles St.
Paso Robles, CA 93446
877-322-4489
mondelloperformance.com

Moroso Performance
80 Carter Dr.
Guilford, CT 06437
203-458-0542
moroso.com

MSD Ignition
1490 Henry Brennan Dr.
El Paso, TX 79936
951-857-5200
msdignition.com

Northern Auto Parts
801 Lewis Blvd.
Sioux City, IA 51105
800-831-0884
northernautoparts.com

Offenhauser
5300 Alhambra Ave.
Los Angeles, CA 90032
323-225-1307
offenhauser.co

Olds Performance Products
4 Executive Blvd., Ste. 100
Suffern, NY 10901
800-382-1320
oldsperformanceproducts.com

Olds Rocket Parts
1926 Beechwood Dr.
Paso Robles, CA 93446
805-975-8601
oldsrocketparts.com

Original Parts Group
1770 Saturn Way
Seal Beach, CA 90740
800-243-8355
opgi.com

PerTronix Performance Products
440 E. Arrow Hwy.
San Dimas, CA 91773
909-547-9058
pertronix.com

Powertrain Products Inc.
520 Thompson Creek Rd.
Stevensville, MD 21666
888-842-0023
powertrainproducts.net

Rock Auto Parts
6418 Normandy Lane, Ste. 100
Madison, WI 53719
608-661-1376
rockauto.com

Rocket Racing Performance
8207A Big Bend Rd.
Waterford, WI 53185
262-706-3277
rocketracingperformance.com

Sanderson Headers
517 Railroad Ave.
South San Francisco, CA 94080
650-583-6617
sandersonheaders.com

Speedmaster
1101 W. Rialto Ave.
Rialto, CA 92376
310-361-0020
speedmaster79.com

Speedway Motors
340 Victory Lane
Lincoln, NE 68528
800-979-0122
speedwaymotors.com

Summit Racing
1200 Southeast Ave.
Tallmadge, Ohio 44278
800-230-3030
summitracing.com

Weiand
1801 Russelville Rd.
Bowling Green, KY 42101
866-464-6553
holley.com/brands/weiand

Wenzler Engineering
2710 E. Sharon Dr.
Oak Creek, WI 53154
414-764-4586
wenzlerengineering.com

Year One
1001 Cherry Dr., Unit 1
Braselton, GA 30517
800-932-7663
yearone.com